SOCIAL STUDIES
LIBRARY
45 WELLINGTON SQUARE,
OXFORD.

WITHDRAWN

SOCIAL STUDIES
LIBRARY
SOCIAL STUDIES FACULTY CENTRE
OXFORD. OX1 2RL

WITHDRAWN

D1477111

On Military Ideology

Studies presented at Varna
International Sociological Association
Conference 1970. Part II

Contributions to studies on military sociology
Vol. 3

On Military Ideology

Edited by
MORRIS JANOWITZ
and
JACQUES VAN DOORN

1971
Rotterdam University Press

33225

Copyright © 1971 by Universitaire Pers Rotterdam
No part of this book may be reproduced in any form, by print, photoprint, microfilm
or any other means without written permission from the publisher.
Printed in Belgium

ISBN 90 237 6215 0

Preface

J. VAN DOORN

At the Seventh World Congress of Sociology at Varna, September, 1970, over one hundred sociologists participated in the four-day sessions of the Research Committee on Armed Forces and Society. The papers presented supplied the basis for two volumes of selected proceedings: this book, Volume II, entitled *On Military Ideology*, and the companion book, Volume I, *On Military Intervention.*

These efforts were the outgrowth of a number of years of international collaboration in the study of militarism and the military profession. One of the first efforts at international exploration of the comparative sociology of military institutions took place at a Conference on Armed Forces and Society in Western Europe in London, July 1964. The Conference was sponsored jointly by the Committee on Political Sociology of the International Sociological Association and the Inter-University Seminar on Armed Forces and Society, located at that time at the University of Chicago. Morris Janowitz served as chairman of the conference. It brought together, for the first time, scholars from the United States and Western Europe and resulted in the publication of a special issue of the subject by *The European Journal of Sociology* (Archives européennes de Sociologie, Tome VI, 1965, Numéro 2).

Subsequently, at the Sixth World Congress of Sociology, which was held in Evian, France in September, 1966, a special working group was organized by the International Sociological Association on 'The Professional Military Man and Militarism.' For the first time some seventy scholars from Western Europe, Eastern Europe, including the USSR, the Middle East, The Far East and South America convened to evaluate the current state of sociology of military institutions, war, revolution and international peace keeping and arms control. The result of this conference was the publication of a volume edited by Jacques van Doorn, *Armed Forces and Society: Sociological Essays* (Mouton, The Hague, 1968). At Evian, a separate working group on Armed Forces and Society of the International Sociological Association was organized. The Steering Committee members included Ludwig von Friedeburg, Federal Republic of Germany, John Jackson, Great Britain, Morris Janowitz, chairman, United States, Jacques van Doorn, The Netherlands, and Jerzy J. Wiatr, Poland. In 1970, at Varna, this group was designated as a Research Committee by the Council of the International Sociological Association.

A special International World Congress meeting of the group was held in September 1967 in London. Although the actual number of participants was smaller than in Evian, the world coverage by twenty-four papers was much broader. The resulting volume edited by Jacques van Doorn was entitled *Military Profession and Military Regimes* (Mouton, The Hague,

1968). The Steering Committee was reorganized in anticipation of the Varna Congress and included Bengt Abrahamsson, Rapporteur General, Sweden, Dario Canton, Argentina, Jacques van Doorn, Holland, Morris Janowitz, Chairman, United States, John A. Jackson, Great Britain, Ali Mazrui, Uganda, David Solomon, Canada, Jerzy Wiatr, Poland, and P. Zhilin, USSR.

In 'International Perspectives on Militarism,' *The American Sociologist*, February, 1968, there is a report on the issues and debate presented at the London Conference.

The proceedings of the Research Committee on Armed Forces and Society at Varna made possible a more intensive analysis and debate on military professionalism and on the role of ideology in the military establishment. At the Varna Conference the themes of the work of the Research Committee for the Eighth World Congress to be held in Montreal, September, 1974, were selected: (a) 'The Social and Civil Position of Military Personnel' and (b) 'Military Regimes and Group Violence.' Special emphasis will also be placed on questions of political legitimacy and military institutions.

The Executive Committee was enlarged and consists of Morris Janowitz, Chairman, United States; Jacques van Doorn, First Vice-Chairman, The Netherlands; Dario Canton, Vice-Chairman, Argentina; V. K. Konopliev, Vice-Chairman, USSR; J. J. Wiatr, Vice-Chairman, Poland. Members of the Executive Committee are Bengt Abrahamsson, Sweden; Akinsola Akiwowo, Nigeria; Hans-Adolf Jacobsen, Federal Republic of Germany; Manfred Kossok, Democratic Republic of Germany; Ali Mazrui, Uganda; Charles C. Moskos, Jr., United States.

While the funding of these international sessions was mainly underwritten by the participants, the resources of the Inter-University Seminar on Armed Forces and Society supported by the Russell Sage Foundation, New York, made possible the essential planning and secretarial activities.

The editors are grateful to those who cooperated by contributing their papers to this book. They are particularly indebted to Ger Teitler for his unfailing help in preparing the volumes.

University of Chicago
Netherlands School of Economics
May, 1971

Contents

Introduction

Ideology and the Military

J. VAN DOORN

1. IDEOLOGY, LATENT AND MANIFEST

We are inclined to assume that military man, being fundamentally and traditionally suspicious of political matters, tends to reject strongly any commitment in ideological disputes. As a man of action, interested first and foremost in hard facts which can help him to stand firm amidst the harsh reality of violence and war, he will be proud to call himself a 'realist', safe from the pretensions and pitfalls of political ideas and ideals.

Not only the individual military, but his institution as well, has the reputation of staying outside the political and ideological sphere. 'Neutral', 'instrumental' and 'professional' are the concepts used to characterize the functioning of modern armed forces. Even the military of the new nations, who clearly play an active role in the political establishment of their countries, are said to display a technocratic rather than an ideological orientation.[1]

In contrast to this, research in the field of military sociology shows a marked interest in ideological issues. These studies are focused in part on the relation between the political order and the military, dealing with subjects like the inherent conservatism of the officer corps or the more general disposition to intervene in politics. Another trend stresses the phenomenon of politicization by totalitarian systems, which is sometimes built into the armed forces as a program for political indoctrination.

The articles collected in this volume illustrate this dilemma. Though confining their attention to internal problems of military institutions, most of the authors identify some sort of ideological influence or commitment in their special field of interest. Abrahamsson and Van Doorn go so far as to bring together a wide variety of ideological components, the first author in summarizing the various expressions of military 'conservatism', the second in analyzing the patterns of justification developed in a situation of strong political pressure and need for military action.

A familiar problem, but one which is nevertheless fascinating because of the sharp contrast it presents with pre-war German history, is posed by Von Bredow, who describes the systematic attempts on the part of the Federal German government 'to make the *Bundeswehr* safe for democracy', while at the same time gradually committing itself to a full-fledged policy of anti-communist indoctrination of the troops.

At first sight, the other contributions seem to be less directly connected with the issue of ideology in their emphasis on the nature and functions of military professionalism. But they in fact introduce a similar problem in another form, that is, the defence of the military identity against so-called non-military tendencies like the introduction or the sheer existence of other professions (engineers: Harries-Jenkins; physicians: Indisow) or the struggle against control by political authorities (Moskos).

A special subject which is also of importance in relation to our problem is the changing pattern of the profession in periods of revolution (Scott; Graczyk) or rapid social change, with its urge to adapt itself to the new situation (Hansen; Coulombe). In all such cases, highly diversified as they are in many respects, military professionalism proves to be open to various and obviously ideologically distorted interpretations.

Even Grundy and Shank, in debunking 'the myth of the politicised ex-serviceman', point to the problem of ideology and the military by showing how fear of political consciousness among colonial ex-soldiers activated a demobilization policy devised to integrate the returning veterans into their local communities as soon as possible, that is, to suppress the assumed rise of national movements among ex-servicemen. Besides the desired effect of political control what seems to have been striven after here was the additional control of undesired consequences.

In searching for common ground, however, it is not nearly enough to indicate loose similarities or to apply *ad hoc* classifications. First of all a systematic analysis of the concept of ideology has to be undertaken, plus an adequate specification of the various aspects of military performance. Given some theoretical notions it will be more fruitful to take a second look at the contributions with a view to making distinctions without neglecting the general insights gained by the use of a coherent framework.

The first difficulty is that the phenomena we call ideological are often very diversified. Creeds, doctrines, beliefs and values are frequently related in some way to ideology, for all evaluations of social reality suffer from the selectivity and distortion which are so highly characteristic of ideological beliefs. The only way to avoid vagueness and confusion is to narrow down the definition of ideology to the ideas which suffer from deformed perception as a consequence of the defence of vested interests. 'Vested interests' means in this context all kinds of advantages that are endowed with some measure of legitimacy and protection by the *status quo* at any given time.[2]

The desire to defend those interests can be the source of many other attributes of ideology, for example the selectivity of perception, the need for rationalization and justification in the psychological sense, and the emergence of ideological definitions of reality from a general situation of uncertainty.

A second problem in defining ideology is the emphasis usually placed on its systematic and coherent nature. Such coherence is in fact exceptional rather than normal. Well-integrated ideologies generally exist only in the sphere of institutional political life, and even there in a more or less latent form, becoming manifest only in reaction to a major challenge. Many ideas about social reality are ideologically 'coloured' but do not grow into a comprehensive system of rationalizations. For this to happen, special agents like an intelligentsia or a group of theorists in the field of action are required. This condition can only be fulfilled if the relevant social system has reached a certain level of intellectual ripeness and refinement.

Most armies, even modern armies, lack this potency. Their leaders and staff officers are selected not so much by criteria of intellectual creativity as by standards of resoluteness and energy, by the ability to make decisions under circumstances of exceptional danger. This is why the military seem to lend themselves to contrasting political and ideological interpretations, for they are quite happy to be freed from the obligation to formulate the ultimate legitimacy of their mission.

So it is safe to conclude that armed forces normally tend to draw on existing political doctrines if they are in need of institutional self-justification. But even this need is not usually felt: being a legitimate state apparatus the military are generally accepted without having to make any effort to justify themselves.

Only very exceptional circumstances sometimes bring about the development of an autonomous military ideology, as exemplified by the French doctrine of *guerre révolutionnaire*, including a theory on both counter-revolutionary and psychological warfare.[3] The emergence of this doctrine can only be understood against the background of a range of accumulating factors in the history of the French army in the pre- and post-war periods. The military felt themselves humiliated beyond endurance, while at the same time they had sufficient reason to believe that the French politicians lacked a clear appreciation of events in the international scene and did not support the military efforts in Indo-China and Algeria. This situation, combined with the presence of some brilliant military theorists, offered an unprecedented opportunity to develop a new and fully military interpretation of political affairs to be used as an alternative *idéologie nationale*. General Chassin, a leading strategist and military author, wrote in 1956:

What can the Western nations do to avoid the accomplishment of Mao's plan for world conquest? We must oppose a struggle based on subversion with the same weapons, oppose faith with faith, propaganda with propaganda, and an insidious and powerful ideology with a superior one capable of winning the hearts of men.[4]

As stated above, coherent and explicitly worked out ideologies are exceptional. It is much more common for the ideological distortion of perception resulting from threat, conflict or frustration to serve the need for solidarity, and justify action which has aroused criticism. These conditions are typical of the military and their missions, especially at the present time when unpopular and even utterly rejected wars are being waged and anti-militarism is on the increase.

Ideological viewpoints function here in the fields of public relations and civil-military relations. Efforts to gain a grip on public opinion and on the national budget can be successful only if the military are able to formulate goals and outlooks with a strong appeal to the nation. Elements of the latent corporate ideology of the armed forces – nationalism, law and order – are mobilized in the service of vested military interests and future claims.

Ideological arguments are brought forward with much more emphasis in conflicts lacking massive or in any case solid support from the politicians and the public at large than in situations where the nation is united behind the military mission. Comparison of Vietnam and World War II provides a clear illustration of the difference.

It is of crucial significance that political and corporate ideologies among the military primarily reflect the problems of the military establishment and part of the officer corps. Research has shown the limited influence exercised by ideological notions on the morale of the rank and file, both in the barracks and in combat.[5]

Nevertheless there is a relation between combat motivation and some sort of social and political consciousness labelled 'latent ideology' by Moskos.[6] In seeking the ideological components of military behavior it will be most fruitful to distinguish this type of justification. We propose to term it 'operational ideology', since the latency of the ideas is not an implicit aspect.

In the following pages of this article we shall focus our attention on the political, the corporate and the operational ideologies of the military. The concluding section will be devoted to the social location of these notions in an attempt to construct a relation between the various types of thinking and their basis in the social structure.

2. THREE TYPES OF IDEOLOGY

Political ideology. As already stated, political doctrines, particularly the more comprehensive and detailed ones, originate not in military circles but in political movements and leaders. These doctrines reflect broad social conflicts and define the social order from a selective viewpoint.

It is possible that some ideologies, especially those of a right-wing character, attract the attention and support of the career soldiers. In earlier and recent studies Abrahamsson has pointed out that the majority of Swedish officers sympathize with conservative parties, as Janowitz has also shown in his study of the American elite.[7]

A question of quite a different order is the extent to which the forces as a social institution are prepared to accept and to become involved in a given political doctrine. Empirical evidence shows this to be a most exceptional development. Even in times of political revolution the armed forces experience the penetration of political ideas inside their institution as a policy of coercive indoctrination and political control. Elsewhere in this volume Graczyk confirms a more generally valid observation that even communist armies tend ultimately to accept the introduction of selection and recruitment criteria other than class affiliations and political preferences.[8]

Scott's analysis of the process of professionalization of the French officer corps during the French revolution shows the marked relevance of processes of selective recruitment as against ideological indoctrination as a means of political control of the armed forces. It was not the revolutionary élan but the self-selection of the military personnel which made the greatest contribution to the reconstruction of the officer corps as a reliable and efficient instrument of the new regime.

The acceptance of a political belief system by the armed forces does not guarantee its proper functioning. The postwar German idea of the 'citizen in uniform', for instance has gradually been transformed into an instrument to strengthen military morale:

Here political education does not so much aim at integrating the military norms and values into the society by making the soldier pledge to it, but rather by integrating the soldier into the armed forces.[9]

This instance of displacement of goals is not uncommon in organizations expected to work in accordance with the values of the society at large which can be used for special internal controls as well. The goals will then be subverted, with the means of external integration serving as instruments for internal integration. Expressing it in sociological terms, the political ideology is transformed into a part of the corporate ideological system.

Of much greater importance than party preference is the philosophical attitude of the military man, defined by Huntington as 'the man of Hobbes':

Human nature is universal and unchanging. Men in all places and at all times are basically the same. The military view of man is thus decidedly pessimistic.
... Success in any activity requires the subordination of the will of the individual to the will of the group. Tradition, *esprit*, unity, community – these rate high in the military value system. [10]

It is clear from this characteristic that conservative ideologies are basically similar to the military ethic. Psychologically, we might speak of a 'conservative syndrome' as Abrahamsson does, like McClosky and others who stress the relation between authoritarianism and militarism. It would seem safer, however, not to oversimplify the relation between personal and social system variables, and to restrict ourselves to the less sweeping conclusion that the military system of values may function as a latent ideology which becomes manifest in response to challenge and is thereupon moulded into the political pattern of the historical period in question.

Corporate ideology. This type of ideological valuation is generally a product of the military system itself. It does not present a view of society as a whole, but of the armed forces and their social function and position. So military corporate ideology is in part similar to industrial ideology, as described by Bendix in his elaborate study of

the ideologies of management which seek to justify the subordination of large masses of men to the discipline of factory work and to the authority of employers. [11]

Here the interrelation between ideas and actions is much stronger and more direct than is the case with purely political ideologies. The justification tends to reflect the particular problems which have to be solved in the large-scale organization of manpower needed to achieve success under highly unfavorable work conditions. It can be seen from these problems that hierarchy and discipline, centralization and calculation are among the cornerstones of military organization and are consequently key concepts of corporate ideology.

The ideological deformation becomes clearly visible once those values find appropriate vehicles for their expression in ritual and symbolism. The often vehement defence of these functionally obsolete customs seem to reflect the ideological bases justifying an organizational structure that has lost part of its *raison d'être*.

 Corporate ideologies are likely to flourish and spread under circumstances of external criticism and crisis. The armed forces then assume the role of 'nationbuilder' or in any case of 'school of the nation'; the military virtues are transformed into societal values; the military organization model seems applicable to other types of collective effort; the military way of doing things is presented as the best way. Despite their moral and technical inadequacy they are in a favourable position to take the lead in the struggle for national integrity against external and internal enemies and to identify themselves in a unique way with the 'national interest'.[12] The corporate ideology is in this way gradually transformed into a political doctrine.

Operational ideology. The political and corporate varieties of ideology have their particular significance in peacetime situations. Yet it is precisely the commission of violence and the consequences of this in terms of danger, guilt and uncertainty which seem to be the most fertile soil for a distorted perception of reality and an ideological justification of action.

If this is correct, the evidence seems to indicate that the various systems of justification of violence have to date attracted very little attention. Perhaps the production of violence by armed forces is too patently the outcome of the system as such to give rise to the question of ideological justification. Of course there is war propaganda and psychological warfare on an enormous scale, but these activities are too obviously manipulated for the concept of ideology to be used in the proper sense.

It would be much more productive to analyse the different types of violence and war in order to isolate the ideological distortion of the relevant doctrines. This is what Janowitz has done in tracing the social, political and historical backgrounds of the opposing doctrines of the 'absolutists' and 'pragmatists' among the American strategists. One of his most striking conclusions is the influence of wartime experiences on strategic conceptions of the future.[13]

Sometimes even the personal and career experiences of military leaders shape doctrines in that they function as a rationale for the pursuit of personal glory. Intense personal loyalties resulting from shared wartime experiences generalize the way in which the strategy will be interpreted.

Of the variety of personal networks that existed in the military establishment during World War II, alliances centering around George C. Marshall and Douglas MacArthur and their followers were the most dramatic, and in the end could be linked most clearly to differences between pragmatic and absolute conceptions of warfare, respectively.[14]

Other types of operational ideologies develop around guerrilla and counter-guerrilla warfare and in relation to the international police functions of United Nations Forces. In these fields, however, military doctrines are much more insecure and tend to keep the claims of missions like these at a distance. Moskos' article about the U.N. Force in Cyprus demonstrates the well-known criticism voiced by the military: 'We are soldiers, not policemen'.[15]

The ideological overtones of military doctrines and statements are in fact strengthened by outside criticism. As long as wars are successful it is not too difficult to gain public support, but as soon as serious setbacks and failures begin to create uncertainty, public opinion demands a satisfactory explanation. When this happens ideological justification is often the only way out. The growing resentment is combated with the help of face-saving comments on the situation and by stressing the unavoidable temporary measures needed to bring things under control.

Sometimes criticism is directed specifically against the means of violence employed. Unable to create opposition in terms of political aims, the mass media devote their attention to incidents like atrocities committed by the troops.

Comparing the treatment of such incidents, which serve as symbols of an unpopular war, a sharp increase in the number of critical comments on the military methods is to be observed in the later phases of the conflict. My Lai has become a political issue as a consequence of the growing uneasiness about the war as such; the same thing happened in France when conclusive victories in Algeria proved to be unattainable and in the Netherlands when the last blow against the Indonesian Republic did not end the war as the military and political authorities had predicted.[16]

The army, institutionally and psychologically involved in the outcome of the struggle, then tries to justify its ruthless actions by referring the critics to the impossibility of keeping clean hands in a dirty war and by indicating that orders come from the top. Though such military tactics are nothing new in themselves, such attempts to justify them constitute a new element:

The French bore a heavy burden in Algeria for past sins committed in a time when simple massacre was held to be an efficacious means of pacification…. Patterns of atrocity were already well fixed in Algeria before they were rationalized in practice or defended by theory.[17]

A fascinating subject is to be found in the various tensions between different types of ideology. Contradiction may exist between traditional corporate ideology (honor) and the operational code, justified in terms of military success (torture); between political indoctrination and professional autonomy; between the traditional corporate way of handling men and the introduction of technical weapons systems, causing a 'crise de modernisme dans l'armée'.[18]

Conflicts like these do not always concern the armed forces as a whole, but are felt more especially in some parts of the system. As a general rule, military ideological conceptions flourish at certain organizational levels and within special units and groups.

3. THE STRUCTURAL LOCATION OF IDEOLOGY

Vertical diversification. Up to this point the armed forces have been considered to act as a unified whole. This, however, is an oversimplification of reality. Like most other large-scale organizations, military institutions seek to overcome the built-in tensions between stability and flexibility by internal segmentation. Sociologists and management theorists can find common ground by indicating the allocation of several functions to distinct subsystems of the organization.

In accordance with Parsons, Thompson has suggested that formal organizations can be divided into three more or less separate levels of responsibility and control:[19]

a. the institutional level, linking the total system with the larger environment which is the source of its ‚meaning', thus legitimating its existence as a social institution;
b. the technical level, where the problems are focussed in terms of effective performance of the technical function;
c. the managerial level, which serves as a mediating subsystem between the institutional top and the technical base of the organization.

It is not difficult to see that these abstract distinctions are useful in the analysis of the armed forces, dividing as they do the system in three levels, here labelled the political (Thompson: institutional), the professional (Thompson: managerial) and the technical subsystem.

The latter is located in the lower echelons, or the combat units – to speak in army terms – i.c. wherever soldiers, sailors, marines or pilots are actually facing the enemy. At their level, discipline and drill, the planned handling of arms and detailed training in the use of arms are normal, reducing the individual to a cog in the organizational machine.

The second level, which comprises most officers, is characterized by a mixture of professional and bureaucratic elements in terms of both responsability and control. The field officer, in particular, serves as the linking pin between the technical level, where violence is committed and the political level, where the action is planned and directed.

As the managerial or professional upper level there is a strong belief that military action can be fully predicted and controlled. The upper ranks however are continually confronted with a high degree of uncertainty, resulting in peace-time from international tensions, budget fluctuations and technical developments, in war from the ever-changing strategic situation. At the top of the armed forces, in a diffuse region of political and military responsibility, the legitimacy of the military institution itself has to be defined and protected.

In peace-time, and especially during the training period, military organizations can rely on coercion as the dominant mechanism of control at the lowest level. The lowest participants are part of the organizational machine. When the army goes into battle, however, the closed technical subsystem is disrupted by confrontation with a highly unpredictable factor, viz. the enemy forces and their operations. Uncertainty necessitates the introduction of normative sanctions; responsibility and initiative move down the line.[20]

At the same time the combat situation isolates the soldier from the higher echelons and their political and professional definitions of reality. He is out of touch with the operation of the ideological superstructure. As a German soldier in World War II said: 'Nazism begins ten miles behind the front line'.[21]

Even the conventional corporate norms lose their validity. In his excellent study on trench warfare in World War I Ashworth demonstrates that the formal norm of 'offensiveness' broke down at times under the weight of 'the live and let live principle' which was

an informal and collective agreement between frontline soldiers of opposing armies to inhibit offensive activity to a level mutually defined as tolerable. This understanding was tacit and covert.[22]

A similar mechanism is employed when commanders justify their actions in terms of their primary responsibility to ensure the safety of their men. Moskos, observing this attitude in Cyprus, points out that this is one of the causes of strain between civilian authorities, eager to avoid political 'incidents', and military officers. It can be viewed as simply one reaction of the military when he has to cope with dangerous and uncertain situations. There will then emerge a separate interpretation of reality, not determined by high-level aims but by low-level daily experiences, becoming the base of collective justification moving upwards after some time.

In the case of guerilla warfare, the degree of uncertainty becomes extremely high. The formation of a large number of small, relatively autonomous and mobile combat-units relegates responsibility to the level of the junior commanders, thus transforming battle into a 'platoon commander's' or 'sergeant's war'. The barrier between the professional and technical levels is in fact broken down or in any case lowered.

The distinction between the professional or managerial level and the political subsystem at the top is at the same time gradually eroded. Political decisions move down to the lower level, while at the same time the officers penetrate into the political sphere where the legitimacy and the ultimate aims of the war are discussed. New ambitions emerge, like the claim put forward by the officer corps they are the agency uniquely fitted to define the political aims of the war. Military intervention in politics now becomes a formidable danger.[23]

Thus the type of war directly influences the dislocation of responsibility and autonomy inside the armed forces, and can consequently stimulate the process of downward politicization. The ideological justification, usually restricted to the upper ranks, proceeds to spread throughout the ranks, at the very least making the rank and file accessible to ideological interpretations of the situation.

Horizontal diversification. As stated above, political ideologies are mostly introduced into the armed forces from above. To get a firm grip on the military it is even necessary to build up a second hierarchy along the existing chain of command as demonstrated by communist and fascist regimes. To the extent that ideological activities emerge inside the armed forces, they seem to be located primarily in intelligence services, where information and skill in political and propagandistic matters is concentrated. It cannot be altogether coincidental that the resistance in the German army against Hitler had its roots in the section of the *Abwehr* of the combined forces command (OKW), while the French-Algerian rebellion against the government had its origin in the *5es Bureaux,*

between 1957 and the settlers' insurrection of January, 1960, almost entirely free of control from Paris. They could develop their own methods of psychological action and psychological warfare, they were also able to assume a growing share in the formulation of the ideology and the political program these methods were to advance. From a subordinate agency of the government and the armed forces, *action psychologique* changed into a policy-making body whose members showed increasing readiness to interpret and even adapt policy to suit their view of the operational requirements in Algeria.[24]

Lang pointed out the fact that in both cases the putsches derived their main support from officers in the ground forces, that part of the military that was more likely than the air and naval forces to come into contact with the population of the occupied territories and to share the task of military administration.[25]

This observation could perhaps be generalized in the sense that those parts of the forces, that are exposed to the environment experience a greater measure of uncertainty and tend to adopt elements of social and political ideology, while the more closed formations stick to their traditional corporate ideology, i.e., their latent rightist political attitude.

Hansen's study on military careerism in the Chilean officer corps gives some support to this hypothesis. He suggests that officers with civilian orientations are ready to adapt the armed forces to social change and have predominantly leftist sentiments, whereas the isolationists hold rightist views. There is some similarity in the article by Harries-Jenkins in that he introduces a distinction between ascriptive professionals in the British Air Force who are trained within the organization in predominantly military skills, and achievement professionals trained outside the armed forces. Members of the first category find their reference groups and standards within the forces, those of the second group are more oriented toward the criteria and norms of civilian society. Indisow, discussing the integration of military physicians, indicates a similar situation. We find here the tensions between military and non-military roles, which are evidently connected with distinct valuations.

These problems are particularly relevant for the military corporate ideology. There is also a tendency to a differentiation in orientation between the combat-commander complex and the technical-managerial complex. It is an open question whether it will be possible to integrate both types of orientation, which also include a difference in ideological outlook. At this moment the traditional uniform self-concept of the soldier has become diffuse and ambiguous.[26]

The actual operation of the military in combat compounds the dilemma. Even if the modern professional soldier fully accepts the reality of thermonuclear weapons and their impact on strategy and politics, he is at the same time confronted with quite different types of violence, including counter-guerrilla warfare. Here a new operational ideology is emerging: the ideology of the elite troops with their emphasis on *esprit de corps* as a partial substitute for serving the national cause. Inside the military institution 'special forces' have come into existence exhibiting a special attitude toward war and politics, as a result of their limited social perspective and their resistance to the traditional officer corps. A new operational code leads to a new corporate ideology and ultimately to a latent political idea with fascist undertones glorifying strength, sacrifice and violence for their own sake.

4. CONCLUDING REMARKS

Armed forces are expected to act as an instrument in the hands of the policy-makers. Paradoxically, this instrumentality is defended with the argument that only the politician is competent to decide matters bearing on peace and war, that is, the most dubious and delicate decisions requiring to be taken. Those for whom violence is a profession are given no part to play here.

Actually, this sharp division of labor is unrealistic. In all political systems the military and political elites are interlinked, socially and morally. They often share the same outlook and values, and they defend the same social order against external and internal threats.

Yet this does not mean that the military holds the same ideological opinions as his civilian counterpart do. As a man of action he is inclined to suspect the world of words and ideas; as a professional soldier he will defend his profession and the interests of his institution; and confronted with the enemy he will try to justify his use of violence, so uncommon in civilian society.

One could hypothesize that in the future the justification of military action will draw much more attention from the armed forces. The rising tide of pacifism, the visibility of military performance, including acts of brutality, as well as the increasing cost of arms will inevitably oblige the military to rationalize his role in the political scene. Gradually he will discover the power of public opinion and the best means of controlling it. Finally he will learn that justification by incidence is not enough and that coherent ideological systems are needed. At that moment the military ideologist will have come into being.

NOTES

1. Morris JANOWITZ, *The Military in the Political Development of New Nations* (Chicago: The University of Chicago Press, 1964), pp. 63 ff.
   William F. GUTTERIDGE, 'Education of Military Leadership in Emergent States', in: James S. COLEMAN, ed., *Education and Political Development* (Princeton, N. J.: Princeton University Press, 1965), pp. 461 ff.
2. Harry M. JOHNSON, 'Ideology: Ideology and the Social System', in: David L. SILLS, ed., *International Encyclopedia of the Social Sciences* (The Macmillan Company & The Free Press, 1968), Vol. 7, p. 80.
3. Peter PARET, *French Revolutionary Warfare from Indochina to Algeria. The Analysis of a Political and Military Doctrine* (New York, Washington, London: Frederick A. Praeger, 1964).
4. George A. KELLY, 'The French Army Re-enters Politics 1940-1955', in: *Political Science Quarterly*, Vol. LXXVI, 1961, p. 385.
5. One might even say that this hypothesis has become one of the cornerstones of American military sociology since the classic analysis by Shils and Janowitz in 1948. Edward A. SHILS and Morris JANOWITZ, 'Cohesion and Disintegration in the Wehrmacht in World War II', in: *The Public Opinion Quarterly*, Volume XII, 1948, pp. 280–315.
6. Charles C. MOSKOS Jr., *The American Enlisted Man. The Rank and File in Today's Military* (New York: Russell Sage Foundation, 1970), pp. 146 ff.
7. Bengt ABRAHAMSSON, 'The Ideology of an Elite: Conservatism and National Insecurity: Some Notes on the Swedish Military', in: Jacques VAN DOORN, ed., *Armed Forces and Society* (The Hague and Paris: Mouton, 1968) pp. 76 ff.; see also his contribution in the present volume. Morris JANOWITZ, *The Professional Soldier* (The Free Press of Glencoe, Illinois, 1960), Chapter 12.
8. Jacques VAN DOORN, 'Political Change and the Control of the Military: Some General Remarks', in: Jacques VAN DOORN, ed., *Military Profession and Military Regimes* (The Hague and Paris: Mouton, 1969), pp. 17–25.
9. Cf. Wilfried VON BREDOW's article in this volume, p. 97.
10. Samuel P. HUNTINGTON, *The Soldier and the State* (Cambridge, Mass.: Harvard University Press, 1957), p. 63.
11. Reinhard BENDIX, *Work and Authority in Industry: Ideologies of Management in the Course of Industrialization* (New York: John Wiley & Sons; London: Chapman & Hall, 1956) p. xix.
12. S. E. FINER, *The Man on Horseback: The Role of the Military in Politics* (London and Dunmow: Pall Mall Press, 1962) Chapters 4–6.
13. JANOWITZ, *op. cit.*, chapters 13 and 14.
14. JANOWITZ, *op. cit.*, p. 294.
15. MOSKOS' contribution to this volume. See also David N. SOLOMON, 'The Soldierly Self and the Peace-keeping Role: Canadian Officers in Peace-keeping Forces', in: Jacques VAN DOORN, ed., *Military Profession and Military Regimes* (The Hague and Paris: Mouton, 1969) pp. 65 ff.
16. George A. KELLY, *Lost Soldiers: The French Army and Empire in Crisis 1947-1962* (Cambridge, Mass.: The MIT Press, 1965), pp. 196 ff.; see for Indonesia the article by Jacques VAN DOORN in the present volume.
17. KELLY, *op. cit.*, pp. 199 ff.
18. Jean PLANCHAIS, 'Crise de modernisme dans l'armée', in: *Revue Française de Sociologie*, Vol. II, April-June 1961, pp. 118–123.

19. James D. THOMPSON, *Organizations in Action* (New York etc.: McGraw-Hill Book Co., 1967), pp. 10 ff.
20. Amitai ETZIONI, *A Comparative Analysis of Complex Organizations* (New York: The Free Press of Glencoe, 1961), pp. 56 ff.
21. SHILS and JANOWITZ, *op. cit.*, p. 303.
22. A. E. ASHWORTH, 'The Sociology of French Warfare 1914-1918', in: *The British Journal of Sociology*, Vol. XIX, 1968, p. 411.
23. KELLY, The French Army, *op. cit.*, p. 386; see also the article by Robert KROES on the Dutch case in: Morris JANOWITZ and Jacques VAN DOORN, eds., *On Military Intervention* (Rotterdam: Rotterdam University Press, 1971).
24. PARET, *op. cit.*, pp. 76 f.; Kurt LANG, 'The Military Putsch in a Developed Political Culture: Confrontations of Military and Civil Power in Germany and France', in: Jacques VAN DOORN, ed., *Armed Forces and Society* (The Hague and Paris: Mouton, 1968), pp. 202–228.
25. LANG, *op. cit.*, pp. 213 ff.; John Steward AMBLER, *Soldiers against the State: The French Army in Politics* (New York: Doubleday and Co., 1968), pp. 367 ff.
26. Raoul GIRARDET, ed., *La crise militaire française 1945–1962* (Paris: Armand Colin, 1964), pp. 221 ff.; Philip ABRAMS, 'The Late Profession of Arms: Ambiguous Goals and Deteriorating Means in Britain', in: *Archives Européennes de Sociologie*, Vol. VI, 1965, pp. 238–261.

A Historical Case

The French Revolution and
the Professionalization
of the French Officer Corps, 1789-1793

S. F. SCOTT

SAMUEL F. SCOTT is an Assistant Professor of History at Wayne State University in Detroit, Michigan, USA. He was a Research Associate at the Institute of Human Sciences at Boston College in 1966. He is the author of a number of articles in French and American journals on the French army in the late eighteenth century and is currently working on a book on the role of the regular army during the French revolution.

In the first four years of the French Revolution the officer corps of the line, or regular, army experienced a rapid and radical transformation that was without precedent. Standards for admission to, and advancement in, the officer corps were drastically altered. More than ever before in the past, the explicit and dominant purpose of the officer corps became military efficiency. Between mid-1789 and early 1793 the personnel in every officer rank were almost completely changed. The very concept of a military career was essentially revised. This whole process can be best described as professionalization.

The process of professionalization is a phenomenon which is both quite complex and difficult to define satisfactorily. In one sense, professional armies are at least as old as the nation-state; certainly the military reforms implemented during the reign of Louis XIV made the French army more professional than its predecessors. On the other hand, the army of the Revolution would have difficulty in meeting the professional standards of late nineteenth or early twentieth century armies. To this extent, the changes brought about by the Revolution in the army, and particularly in the officer corps, represent a stage in a long and continuing process. Nevertheless, the transformation which occurred in the French officer corps between 1789 and 1793 merits special attention because it represents a fundamental break with the past and the initiation of a new set of principles which governed the future development of the officer corps, not only in France but throughout Europe.

The term professionalization, as used in this study, refers to certain structural characteristics which developed in the officer corps during this crucial period. These characteristics were new standards for commissions and promotions, a new emphasis on the purpose of the officer corps, new composition and a new definition of a military career. Each of these characteristics, which were closely related to one another, can be described as professional; and together they constitute professionalization.

The new standards for a commission and promotion were professional standards. Before 1789 social status and wealth were the primary means of entering and advancing in the officer corps. Early in the Revolution new criteria, based on the principle of careers open to talent, were established. Talent, or ability, was measured by professional criteria of education (determined at first by examination and later simply by literacy) and experience, or length of service.

The aim of the officer corps, although not in itself new, became more purely professional than ever before in the past. Military efficiency had always been the aim of armies; but other considerations, notably social and financial, had been allowed to interfere with it. The government of the Revolution, faced with a hostile Europe, made efficiency the one explicit and paramount goal which it required of its officers. This, in turn, made the officers concentrate on this professional aim to the exclusion of other considerations.

The establishment of professional standards and goals necessarily affected the composition of the officer corps. Their effects were compounded by the fact that by early 1793, approximately three-fourths of the pre-revolutionary officers had left the French army in reaction to the political and social policies of the new regime. This exodus, combined with the pressure of war, necessitated an almost complete renewal of the personnel of the officer corps. The new officers and those recently appointed to new positions and grades conformed to the new professional requirements. By 1793 the officer corps was composed almost exclusively of men whose adult life had been spent entirely in the army. In short, these officers were what are most commonly and accurately described as professional soldiers.

The professional character of the new standards, goals and composition of the officer corps necessitated a change in attitude toward a military career. In the Old Regime the performance of military duties was regarded by most officers as a service, not a full-time occupation. The inadequate pay which officers received made it difficult for them to support themselves without income from outside sources. The Revolution not only required a more complete dedication to military duties, but also provided a sufficient salary which permitted such concentration of energies. In this way, military service was transformed into a professional career.

These characteristics of the French officer corps – new standards, aim, composition and attitude toward career – were distinct from one another only in a logical sense. In reality they were intimately related to each other, and formed different aspects of the professionalization of the officer corps in the French Revolution. It is the purpose of this study to describe and analyse this process of professionalization in the early years of the Revolution.

This investigation will concern itself only with the line army during the period 1789 to 1793. The largely ceremonial units of Royal Household troops, which were disbanded in 1791, are not included. The levies of the National Guard called up in 1791 and 1792 are also excluded. These levies were composed of citizen-soldiers summoned to duty for one campaign; and they existed as entirely distinct units with their own uniforms, a higher pay scale, special methods of advancement (primarily election) and their own organization, until February 1793. Late in this month a decision of the National Convention decreed the amalgamation of these 'national volunteers' and the line army.

Partially for this reason, February 1793 was chosen as the terminal date in this study. More importantly, by early 1793 the principles of professionalization (as described above) had become firmly established and the process itself was well advanced. In the fifteen months immediately following this, however, a series of major crises upset and set back this process. Military defeats in the spring of 1793 and widespread civil war in the latter half of the same year put enormous pressures on the French government. The government's response included a mass mobilization (by the spring of 1794 France had approximately a million men under arms) and a series of social, economic, political and judicial measures known as the Terror. Under these circumstances, political reliability and loyalty superseded all other criteria. In the army this policy took the form of a temporary rejection of purely professional standards, e.g. the principle of election replaced proven ability as the basis for promotion in the officer corps.

Such a program was a temporary phenomenon. With the overthrow of Robespierre and the end of the Terror in July 1794, more professional criteria were once again enforced in the French army. This was, however, simply a reversion to the principles of professionalism which had been evidenced by 1793 and which were to remain essential to the army from the Revolution until the present, despite corruptions of, distortions in, and temporary rejections of these standards.

One of the basic problems in any historical study such as this is the application of sociological concepts and techniques to the historical data available. The rather restricted (but hopefully acceptable) definition of professionalization used in this study is but one example of this problem.[1] The surviving documentation simply does not always conform to the types of questions a researcher might choose to pose. The only alternatives in such a case are to modify and adapt the methodology to the sources and to reorganize the sources so that they might better conform to the methodology. The results, although perhaps not fully satisfactory, seem preferable to abandoning the investigation altogether.

There is one distinct advantage in an analysis of the French officer corps in the late eighteenth century. Of all the institutions of Western European society during this period, the military was likely to be the most bureaucratized. In particular, one is more likely to find reasonably ordered and complete records, or files, for the army than for almost any

7

other social institution, except on a local level. This does not mean, of course, that eighteenth century military records are as comprehensive or as well preserved as those of a twentieth, or even nineteenth, century army. Nonetheless, such sources of information are generally more useful than those of other national institutions.[2]

This study will begin with a general description of the French officer corps in the decades immediately preceding the Revolution, in the last years of the Old Regime. During this period one of the major problems facing French society as a whole was reflected in the officer corps, namely the difficulty of modernizing state institutions within the traditional social framework. The monarchy failed to provide an adequate solution to this problem. The modernization that did take place simply antagonized the traditional elite, the nobility, without satisfying the supporters of modernization. This failure succeeded only in focusing the discontent of all groups on the monarchy by 1789.

With the outbreak of the Revolution, there began a new phase in the development of the French officer corps. Because of a combination of legislation, widescale resignations by existing officers, and the advent of war, the officer corps was drastically changed. As a result of the new standards, aims, personnel and attitudes previously described, the officer corps became highly professional.

The primary focus of this study will be on the composition of the officer corps in early 1793, in order to evaluate the character and extent of professionalization among the various officer ranks. This examination has provided the basis for most of the conclusions about the professional character of the French officer corps as it emerged from the Revolution.

THE OFFICER CORPS OF THE OLD REGIME

Throughout the eighteenth century the French nobility dominated the officer corps of the Royal Army. This is not to say that the nobles monopolized all the officer ranks; at various times and in various circumstances a large number of non-nobles served as officers in the French army. The nobility did, however, always maintain control over a substantial majority of the officer positions, especially among the highest grades. Even beyond this, it was the nobility which set the standards and the tone for the entire officer corps, regardless of the role which commoners might play in this group. An officer of common origins was always something less than a complete officer, no matter what his skills, no matter what position he held.

One result of this noble dominance was that officers did not have a military career, in the modern sense of the term. Officers, according to the nobles' image, performed a service which had been the traditional social function of the noble estate for centuries, that of the warrior who protects civil society. This service did not constitute a full-time occupation; rather, it was often mixed with other activities (supervising estates, family business, social obligations, etc.) which had no relation to military functions. Furthermore, this service was interrupted by frequent leaves, especially in peacetime, and long winter quarters in which as much time as possible was spent away from the troops.[1] There were, of course, some individuals and certain groups, notably the 'officers of fortune' about whom more will be said later, who did indeed devote their full time to military duties. Such officers were, however, unusual and were in fact treated as peculiar members of the officer corps in the eighteenth century.

Another striking difference between the officer corps of the Old Regime and the officer corps which emerged from the Revolution is in the matter of finances. Far from providing a livelihood, a military career could, for those who desired to advance to the highest grades, represent a considerable expenditure. The only ranks that were venal were captain and colonel; and the purchase of these grades conferred the command of a company or a regiment. The price of such charges varied considerably according to the prestige of the unit and the market for it. A company could cost between 6 000 and 14 000 *livres*; an infantry regiment could be priced from 25 000 to 75 000 *livres* and a cavalry regiment from 22 500 to 120 000 *livres*.[2] The other officer grades were ostensibly non-venal; however, colonels frequently allotted these positions for financial considerations and so partially recouped their own expenditures. In addition, when promotions were extremely restricted, the officers of a regiment would sometimes form a *concordat*, i.e. all would contribute to a fund which was given to a senior officer in return for his premature retirement which would then provide some room for advancement within the regiment.[3] Promotion, then, could be an expensive proposition and the only alternative, influence at court, entailed at least a comparable expenditure. Obviously, in such a system wealth very often superseded talent.

Besides the cost of a commission and the expenses required for promotion, the style of life expected of eighteenth century French officers, especially superior officers, created a considerable financial burden. In addition to purchasing and maintaining all their clothing and equipment, superior officers were expected to keep a large entourage, set a good table and entertain lavishly.[4] Although much less was required of them, even

9

subaltern officers frequently were hard pressed to meet their expenses without independent income. The Chevalier de Mautort, a member of the *petite noblesse* of the provinces and a captain in the regiment of Austrasie Infantry in the 1770's and 1780's, is typical of this group in his frequent concern over his expenses for food, lodging, travel, etc.[5] Cavalry officers, who had to maintain horses and valets in addition to their other expenses, were even more pressed. Finally, this investment could be entirely lost in the event of demobilization. After each war of the eighteenth century there was a drastic reduction in the French military establishment; many units created in the war were disbanded altogether and their officers found themselves without employment.[6] For the poor provincial nobility this could be a disastrous financial blow.

In spite of all this, the French nobility continued to seek employment in the officer corps throughout the eighteenth century. Indeed, often the government's problem was not finding officers but finding sufficient officer positions for the nobility. After the massive demobilization following the Seven Years War many young nobles joined regiments as *volontaires* and served in these regiments, receiving neither pay nor lodging, until a vacancy among the junior officers should occur which they might fill.[7] Not only was nobility a criterion for becoming an officer but, it appears, military service was an essential element of nobility.[8]

This desire, or perhaps one should say obligation, which so many nobles felt to perform military service did not, however, assure the French monarchy of an efficient officer corps. The financial demands of high command made wealth a more important requirement than ability. The result was that colonels, who would later advance to general officer rank, were usually young men from the court aristocracy or very wealthy bourgeois who, although they could afford the expenses of the superior grades, often had little taste and even less talent for the military duties these positions required. The grades of lieutenant colonel and maor were usually filled by provincial nobles, and less often by commoners, who had long service but whose ambitions for further advancement were consistently frustrated by lack of financial resources. Captains and lieutenants were most frequently from the same class of the poorer nobility who could, after many years of service, hope to become lieutenant colonels or majors; or they were adolescents just embarking on a military career in which their wealth or influence would bring them rapid promotions.[9]

The venality of military offices was probably the most important obstacle to a complete monopolization of the officer corps by the nobility in the eighteenth century. The group most frustrated by this state of affairs was the provincial nobility who through the century advocated advancement by talent *exclusively for the nobility*, a sort of pre-modern professionalism limited by considerations of caste.[10]

The frequent wars in which France participated in the eighteenth century also prevented a noble monopoly of the officer corps. With the expansion of the army in time of war there was often an insufficient number of nobles to fill the officer positions, particularly the venal charges, and the government of necessity had to turn to the bourgeoisie.[11] The result was an influx of non-noble officers often wealthy enough to secure advancement for themselves, to the increased resentment of the poorer nobility. This incursion of commoners into the French officer corps probably reached a peak during the Seven Years War (1756-63) when perhaps as many as one-third of the infantry officers were of common origins.[12] Technical branches where a specialized education was essential, such as the Artillery and Engineers, remained a haven for well trained bourgeois officers until shortly before the Revolution.

Those non-noble officers who did manage to gain commissions and advancement in the infantry and cavalry could never be secure in their positions, however. It was difficult for the 'caste-conscious' nobles to accept commoners as their equals, and even more difficult when non-nobles served as superior officers. Officers of common origin could never be sure that they would not be arbitrarily treated or even dismissed by a noble superior or at the behest of their noble subordinates. Despite their records, non-noble officers had little recourse against such treatment.[13]

There was a special group of non-noble officers in the Royal Army whose situation was entirely peculiar; these were the *officiers de fortune*. These were men who by their unusual ability (or exceptional good luck) had risen from the ranks and were commissioned as officers, usually after a decade or two of service. Normally there were five or six such officers per regiment. Of all the officers, they had the closest contact with the troops, being in daily supervision of their activities. In the eyes of their superiors, as well as in function, they were little more than ranking non-commissioned officers.[14] Only in the most exceptional cases could these 'officers of fortune' rise to the rank of major or, still more unusually, lieutenant colonel; and even these promotions were prohibited in the last years of the Old Regime.

Thus, despite the frustrations of provincial nobles, the French aristocracy not only maintained a numerical superiority in the officer corps, but also exercised a psychological dominance and set the standards for all officers. Many noble officers found in the military an opportunity to indulge in activities of a now archaic warrior past. Duels were common in the boredom of garrison life, despite regulations against dueling. Often too, noble officers disregarded civil laws and arrogantly mistreated peasants, townspeople and even government officials. The same audacity on the battlefield contributed to a high incidence of casualties in combat.[15] Such bravery was, however, a poor substitute for military education and training. In spite of the increasingly technical and sophisticated character of eighteenth century warfare, few noble officers received any military education except in their regiments.

Even in garrison few officers applied themselves to the improvement of their military skills. In peacetime most officers absented themselves as frequently as possible from their regiments, leaving the lieutenant colonels, majors and officers of fortune to supervise the troops.[16] An ordinance of 25 March 1776 required lieutenant generals to spend at least four months per year on active service and six months service per year was required from *maréchaux de camp* (brigadier generals), colonels and lieutenant colonels. Such requirements were considered Draconian by the officers affected.[17] By the late eighteenth century even captains and lieutenants had little contact with their troops in peacetime and directly commanded them only on those rare occasions when manoeuvres were held. In the infantry and cavalry drill and instruction were handled almost exclusively by sergeants and corporals.[18] Officers even travelled separately from the troops whenever possible. Again, the Chevalier de Mautort offers a striking example: upon disembarking in France in 1786 after five years of campaigning in India, he immediately left his regiment so that he could travel alone in comfort.[19] Such a concept of military duty on the part of noble officers surely contributed to the alienation between officers and troops.

During the eighteenth century the royal government accepted the principle that there was a relationship between nobility and service as an officer, but official policy regarding the precise relationship was ambivalent. In November 1750 an edict conferred nobility on all non-noble general officers and also on officers who held the Cross of Saint-Louis and whose fathers and grand-fathers had performed military service. The edict noted: 'The King hopes that the nobility which owes its first origins to the glory of arms, will view with pleasure the communication of its privileges, considered the most flattering recompense, to those who have followed in their footsteps.'[20] As a result of this edict, from 1750 until the Revolution about two hundred officers were enobled.[21]

The more common policy, particularly in the latter half of the century, was to confer offices on nobles, rather than have the offices confer nobility. In order to furnish the provincial nobles with some needed military

12

education, the Comte d'Argenson in 1751 founded the École Militaire in Paris. This was open to boys between eight and eleven years of age who could furnish proof of four generations of nobility and who were impoverished (*sans biens*).[22] The edict of 28 March 1776 created twelve provincial military schools which demanded the same qualifications. The École Militaire at Paris was disestablished in 1787, but the provincial schools lasted until the Revolution. The results of these attempts to educate the poor nobility to its military role were very disappointing. One major difficulty was that wealthy nobles and even bourgeois usurped the places reserved for the sons of impoverished aristocrats. One author estimates that in 1787 one half of the students in the provincial schools were commoners.[23] The results never justified the expenses and for most officers their only military education, if they ever received one, came through active service.

After mid-century the French nobility as a whole attempted to regroup its forces and increase its waning influence. In the army this resurgence took the form of attempts to completely monopolize officer positions. In 1759 Belle-Isle, the Minister of War, demanded of all officer candidates a certificate of nobility signed by four gentlemen and reviewed by the intendant of the province where the candidate resided. This considerably restricted the inroads of commoners; but the ingenuity, wealth and influence of some non-nobles allowed them to evade these requirements.[24] In this attempt to close the officer corps to commoners, the 'nobility of the robe,' whose nobility originally derived from administrative and judicial service and who now provided a large number of army officers, united their efforts to those of the older 'nobility of the sword'.[25]

In spite of this growing unity of the nobility in their willingness to present a common front against the aspirations of non-nobles, other fissures among the nobles were widening. This, too, was reflected in the army. A regulation of 17 April 1760 made a distinction between those nobles who had been presented at court and the rest of the nobility. The highest military grades were reserved for the *noblesse présentée* and a noble could not pass the grade of colonel if he were not a member of this group.[26] This measure did little more than formalize the existing situation but its very formalization undoubtedly made it more intolerable to the provincial nobility.

Thus as the last quarter century of its existence commenced, the officer corps of the Royal Army was badly divided. The noble officers can be grouped into three major categories. First, there were the court nobles who would buy a prestigious company or regiment, usually of cavalry, and then quickly advance to the higher grades. The second group was composed of provincial nobles with an income of 10 000 to 15 000 *livres* who would normally enter the cavalry and advance to higher grades within this branch. The third, and by far the most numerous, group was composed of nobles with an income of 600 to 1 200 *livres*, or even less, who would serve in the infantry and make their limited advancement on the strength of their own merits.[27] This last group, primarily minor nobles of the sword, was bitterly dissatisfied with its inability to make a good career in the army. In a letter to the Minister of War, Marshal de Ségur, in November 1786, the Baron de Besenval estimated that the chances of most nobles to attain command of a regiment were less than one in one hundred. Yet, Besenval notes, the frenzy (*fureur*) of the French nobility for military service remained amazing.[28] In the same vein, a document of 1778 states that the nobility felt it essential that the government preserve 'a number of officer positions large enough so that every gentleman, upon reaching a suitable age, could be assured of finding employment'.[29]

In these circumstances the provincial nobles especially resented the few wealthy bourgeois who still bought high military positions solely as a means of social advancement.[30] Again, one is impressed by the professional character of this resentment felt against outside intruders who had no true dedication to military service. However, this attitude is strongly colored by an almost medieval sense of caste or estate. Most commoners came to view the army as an institution where their ambitions for advancement were doomed because of the increasing noble control over it. Only a very few commoners could expect to become officers of fortune, and these were condemned to the lowest officer grades and to treatment as inferiors by the noble officers.

From the end of the Seven Years War to the outbreak of the Revolution, the French army went through a period of almost continual ferment and reform, as extensive as any in its previous history. Although it was no longer a warrior society, the French army did not become a military society and break completely with feudal organization until after the Seven Years War.[31] After France's humiliating defeat in this war, civil and military officials embarked on a program of what can readily be called modernization.

Choiseul, whose ministry lasted from 1761 to his disgrace in 1770, began this reform era and inaugurated the most drastic changes. Choiseul's reforms, beginning with the ordinance of 10 December 1762, affected many levels and aspects of military life, but it is only those measures which affected the officer corps which concern us here. Prior to the ordinance of December 1762, the number of units in the army

14

fluctuated according to the demands of war or peace. Choiseul set the number of units and planned merely to increase the number of men in them during wartime. This change was clearly in the direction of greater efficiency, since it was much easier to induct men into established units than to create new units; but as a result of this measure, a large number of officers were retired, sometimes after long service, on meager pensions. Their opposition was considerable and bitter.[32]

Probably the most significant reform was the transfer of recruitment from the competence of captains and colonels to that of royal agents. Henceforth, the soldiers took an oath of loyalty directly to the king. This was a major step toward centralized control of the military by the state and vastly increased the administrative control and the problems of the government which then had to provide directly for almost all the needs of its military personnel. This regulation, however, greatly weakened what remaining solidarity there may have been between captains and the men in their companies whom they often personally recruited.[33]

Another reform in the direction of greater royal control gave the king the right to select the lieutenant colonel and major of a regiment from any regiment in the Royal Army, rather than, as previously, from only that regiment in which the vacancy existed. This too, a modernizing measure, aroused much hostility from officers since it often gave outsiders preference over the regiment's own officers. Indeed, this remained an important issue until the Revolution. In 1773 thirty-three officers of the regiment of Royal-Comtois Infantry were punished by a court-martial for their opposition to a lieutenant colonel and a major from outside the regiment. This opposition to centralized control festered, and even after the Revolution began there were complaints to the National Assembly about the tyrannical policy of the king toward the officers of the Royal-Comtois.[34]

The 1760's and 1770's saw other reforms in the interests of greater efficiency and standardization, but these affected the officer corps less directly than the reforms of Choiseul. The concept of the division as a self-sufficient unit was developed. Literacy was required of non-commissioned officers. Military uniforms were standardized. Gribeauval created lighter artillery pieces of standard parts and calibers and emphasized the importance of drill for maximum efficiency from an artillery crew. Numerous theoreticians, most notably Guibert, developed new concepts of strategy and tactics.

In 1775 Saint-Germain became Minister of War and continued these reforms to develop a more professional and efficient military, while at the same time increasing the control of the government over the army.

A number of the changes which he made before his dismissal in 1777 had an important impact upon the officer corps. He reduced the number of infantry companies per battalion from seventeen (of twenty-five men each) to six, thus decreasing the excessively high proportion of officers to men. This measure turned most of the small nobility against Saint-Germain because the opportunities for promotions to captain were correspondingly reduced.[35] Toward the same end, increased efficiency, Saint-Germain reduced the strength of the Royal Household troops by disbanding the Musketeers and *Grenadiers à cheval* and reducing the number of Gendarmes and Light Horse. This, in turn, infuriated the great nobles whose sons traditionally began their military service in these units of great prestige but little military value.[36]

To end a long-standing abuse and to complete Choiseul's work of giving the king control over all ranks of the army, Saint-Germain in 1776 suppressed venality of military offices. Henceforth, on the day that a company or regiment lost its commander due to death, resignation or transfer, the price of that unit would be reduced by one quarter. Thus, by the fourth turnover, all offices would be free and the government would be completely unrestricted in its appointments. This measure, of course, was implemented only over a period of years. However, by February 1790 when the National Assembly abolished venality, it had already almost completely disappeared in the infantry and was in effect in only sixteen regiments of cavalry.[37] This reform resulted in alienating not only some of the upper aristocracy, but also some of the wealthy bourgeoisie who were frustrated by what they believed to be legislation in favor of the nobility.

The most obdurate opposition to Saint-Germain's reforms, and that which was primarily responsible for his fall, came from the noble officers who saw in modernization a serious threat to their traditional control of the military. Their role in society, which heretofore had been theirs by birthright, could, if such a trend continued, become dependent on the acquisition of certain skills or on their usefulness to the government. The Old Regime was caught in a dilemma: whether to reorganize the military establishment along strictly rational lines or to maintain the nobility's traditional role of military leadership. The response was typically ambivalent, modernization of the organizational framework but maintenance of archaic social patterns within this framework. The results were that the nobles were discontented at what they felt was the loss of certain prerogatives, while non-nobles were made all the more aware of the irrational inequity of their situation.

The last years of the Old Regime were marked by the most successful

16

stage of the aristocratic movement to monopolize the officer corps. The commoners who had been able to attain commissions, often by falsifying certificates of nobility, became the more resented as they became fewer.[38] Noble agitation culminated in an ordinance of 22 May 1781, passed during the ministry of Ségur, despite his opposition. This ordinance required that henceforth four quarters, or generations, of nobility were necessary to become an officer; this to be verified by the court genealogist, Chérin, in cases of doubt. This regulation came quickly to be applied throughout the Royal Army. The only major exception was the officers of fortune, who could still rise from the ranks. Their professional commitment, their function as a liaison with the ranks, and their apparent acceptance of a subordinate role made them acceptable to the nobles. But lest these commoners threaten aristocratic hegemony, an ordinance of 1788 prohibited officers of fortune from rising above the rank of lieutenant.[39]

Under continuing pressure for military reform, Louis XVI, on 9 October 1787, convoked a Council of War composed of the leading generals and military theorists of France. This council was responsible for a number of important organizational and administrative changes which were promulgated in 1788. New, more flexible tactics were introduced. The line regiments were grouped into brigades and divisions to facilitate military operations. Improved pay scales were initiated. More of the Royal Household troops were disbanded. Attached officers and 'officers of replacement', who were carried on regimental roles but did not in fact serve, were eliminated. Once again, the army was reformed in a more rational, bureaucratic direction.

On the other hand, the same unwillingness to make more than organizational changes, or perhaps merely a blindness to the problems, led to a perpetuation of the serious inequities which existed in the military structure. The court aristocracy saw in the further reduction of the Royal Household troops another attack on its privileges. The provincial nobility felt betrayed since the distinction between nobles presented at court and others (as well as the monopoly of high rank which accompanied this) was maintained. Commoners were frustrated by the maintenance of the ordinance of 1781 which all but excluded them from the officer corps.

On the eve, therefore, of a major revolutionary upheaval in which the reaction of the armed forces would be crucial, the French officer corps was badly disaffected and the government was apparently unable to resolve the difficulties. The court aristocracy, secure in its dominance of the highest officer grades, preferred to concentrate its attention on what it felt to be encroachments on its prerogatives by the monarchy and was willing to join in an attack on the government in order to gain concessions. With the first stirrings of revolution from below, however, it was to quickly rally to the monarchy in their common peril.

The provincial nobility, which dominated the middle and lower officer grades, in its demands for promotion according to ability and not through court influence, did exhibit a distinct form of professionalism. In many cases these demands were sincerely in the interest of improving the French military establishment. However, almost none of these nobles envisioned opening opportunities beyond their caste, regardless of what military talents some commoners might have. Furthermore, it is unlikely that some of these nobles would have been satisfied unless they all became lieutenant generals after brief military service, a situation hardly conducive to military efficiency. Many members of this group would not make a decision against serving the Revolution until it had destroyed the social system which had produced them. Finally, a significant minority of these provincial nobles would make their peace with the new regime which offered them an opportunity for military advancement and service to the fatherland that would have been unthinkable under the Old Regime.

Likewise, the officers of fortune, who constituted about one-tenth of the total officer corps and almost all the officers of common origins by 1789,[40] generally embraced the Revolution which provided them with honors and promotions. Indeed, this group came to form the core about which the army of the Revolution was reconstructed. A few would even reach general officer rank under the Revolution and Napoleon. The same men were ineligible to rise above the rank of lieutenant under the Old Regime!

THE REVOLUTION AND THE OFFICER CORPS

At the outbreak of the Revolution the one common sentiment among the officers of the Royal Army was discontent, a discontent which focused on the government. A quarter of a century of reform had improved the efficiency of the military institution but had exacerbated relations among its personnel. The various social groups within the officer corps had been alienated by the reforms and entertained mutually contradictory expectations for the future. The monarchy, in order to thoroughly modernize the army, would have had to ignore considerations of caste and privilege. Yet these were the very principles upon which French society of the eighteenth century was based. To ignore them would have meant revolution from above, and Louis XVI was incapable of this. Their maintenance, however, was a fundamental cause of the revolution from below.

18

The political developments of the Revolution were the agencies of change within the officer corps. The changes in governmental institutions and policies were reflected by changes in military personnel and principles. Drastic reform of the officer corps was not the result of some well prepared plan of the revolutionaries; but it inevitably accompanied the fundamental political and social changes brought about by the Revolution. Just as these changes came about gradually in the period from 1789 to 1792, so too the officer corps was radically altered in composition and in standards by stages, over a period of time. By 1793 this had resulted in a new officer corps, fundamentally different from that of the Old Regime. Significantly, the military organization, strategic and tactical theory, weapons and equipment developed in the last decades of the Old Regime were essentially maintained throughout the Revolution and into the Napoleonic era.

The alienation of the officer corps from the government was evidenced before the revolutionary events of mid-1789. When the *parlement* of Rennes defied the royal authority and attempted to assert Breton autonomy in May and June 1788, troops were sent to maintain order and enforce the government's will. Many of the officers, although they performed their duties, expressed sympathy with the local officials and assured them that they did not intend to become involved in this political quarrel.[1] A similar disturbance occurred at the same time in Grenoble. Here the troops sent to repress disorders which had broken out in defence of the local *parlement* were attacked by crowds. One of the officers commanding these troops, Lieutenant Colonel de Boissieux, although himself wounded by the rioters, forbade his men to fire on the crowd.[2] Similar expressions of sympathy by noble officers for the opponents of 'royal despotism' occurred elsewhere in France, e.g. at Toulouse, in Béarn. In March 1789 at Besançon the military commandant, the Marquis de Langeron, said that the army was to be used against enemies of the state and not against citizens; and he refused to employ his troops to suppress rioters.[3] Thus, noble officers set an example of unreliability and disobedience which was later to be followed by the soldiers under their command.

Discontent within the officer corps was more explicitly indicated in the *cahiers de doléances*, the lists of grievances drawn up in preparation for the meeting of the Estates General, scheduled for the spring of 1789. Preliminary assemblies organized according to estate (Clergy, Nobility, Commons) met and drew up their *cahiers*. A dominant influence in the assemblies of the Second Estate was the noble officers. Indeed, when the final selection of deputies to be sent to the meeting at Versailles was completed, well over one half of the representatives of the nobility were officers, again indicative of the correlation between nobility and military service.[4] Typical of the attitudes of many of the nobility was the *cahier* of the Second Estate of Artois: 'No one should be able to enter the service as a cadet or officer who is not noble.' But, on the other hand, 'Nobles ought to admit among themselves the most perfect equality'[5]. A number of noble *cahiers* and the *cahiers* of the commoners of the Third Estate demanded more completely rational criteria, notably full equality of opportunity for advancement into and within the officer corps for all classes.[6] Amidst these conflicting demands the Estates General met and the Revolution began in 1789.

From its opening The Estates General gave evidence of the deadlock between the forces of reform and the government's reluctance to make any significant changes. Even when the intransigence of the bourgeois deputies of the Third Estate forced the king to make some concessions, Louis XVI still tried to preserve the privileges of the nobility. In his declaration of 23 June 1789 the king stated that he would preserve the institution of the army exactly as it was. The officer corps would remain a noble monopoly.[7] In order to insure that such decisions were obeyed and in preparation for the dismissal of the Estates General, Louis XVI summoned troops, some twenty thousand of them, to the Paris-Versailles area in late June and early July.

By July the French nobility, especially the upper aristocracy, had begun to see the commoners as their greatest enemy and the monarchy as the defender of their special status. Quarrels over reductions in the Royal Household were forgotten and the superior officers rallied to the crown in the face of the serious danger. By now, however, the soldiers were displaying the same lack of discipline and disobedience as their officers had in the previous year. The troops summoned to the Paris area could not, for the most part, be relied upon to repress the growing spirit of rebellion. When the people of Paris began to arm themselves, a movement which culminated in the attack on the Bastille on 14 July, all hopes for a successful counteroffensive by the monarchy were gone.[8] The recently arrived troops were sent back to their garrisons without their dubious loyalty being tested.

Immediately began a slow purge of the officer corps, carried out by the voluntary resignation and emigration of the noble officers themselves. This process took place gradually and began right after the fall of the Bastille when the king's brother, the Comte d'Artois, and a handful of court nobles emigrated. Most noble officers had no difficulty in accepting the oath of loyalty to 'the Nation, the Law and the King' which was

20

required by the National Assembly on 11 August 1789.[9] The provincial nobility in particular now expected military reforms, including the end of the monopoly of high commands by the court aristocracy. At the same time, however, a few nobles were alarmed by what they regarded as bourgeois pretensions to military commands.[10]

The alarm and premonition felt by some nobles in mid-1789 increased and spread in the following months as revolutionary activity and legislation made further attacks on the Old Regime. Feudalism was abolished in August 1789. In early October the king and his court were forcibly removed from Versailles to turbulent Paris. More officers now emigrated and many others who stayed behind did so out of a sense of duty to the king. In November 1789 Church lands were secularized and in July 1790 the Catholic clergy were put under civil control. These measures injured the religious sensibilities of many noble officers.[11]

Even more seriously from a military point of view, discipline began to break down. In the latter half of 1789 instances of indiscipline among the troops occurred in Rennes, Auxonne, Strasbourg, Caen, Thionville, Lille and Nancy, all garrison towns.[12] Early 1790 saw a continuation of such behavior in Besançon, Hesdin, Perpignan, Gray and Marseille.[13] The attack on privilege being carried out in civil society was thus accurately reflected among the armed forces.

A decree passed by the National Assembly on 28 February 1790 abolished venality of military office, one of the eagerly sought goals of the noble officer corps. The same decree, however, opened all military ranks to commoners and so destroyed a cherished aim of noble officers. In June hereditary nobility was abolished. Emigration by noble officers increased in reaction to these changes and was accelerated by the growing insubordination of the troops.[14]

Although many of the officers from the provincial nobility resented the institutional changes brought about by the Revolution, they were probably more alienated by the deterioration of discipline and outright hostility which they experienced among their troops. The Revolution had abolished the most serious obstacles to advancement, venality and the court monopoly of the highest ranks. Furthermore, in spite of the opening of the officer corps to commoners, the nobles' self-esteem and traditional role as military leaders could assure them of a continued dominance in the army. Their soldiers' refusal to accept their authority, however, presented an insurmountable obstacle and, at the same time, threatened their entire system of social values.

Insubordination and even mutiny continued through 1790. At Lille in April soldiers garrisoned there rioted for nine days and ceased only on an order signed by Louis XVI. In May at Tarascon the men of the regiment of Lorraine Dragoons drove off their noble officers. From 20 April to 21 August the regiment of Royal Champagne Cavalry, stationed at Hesdin, refused to obey its officers.[15] These examples could be multiplied many times over for 1790 as discipline throughout the army disintegrated. Increased contact with the civilian populace contributed to this situation and the National Federation held in Paris on the first anniversary of the fall of the Bastille climaxed the growing movement of unity between civil and military societies. The large scale mutiny of three regiments at Nancy came six weeks after this celebration, in late August 1790. The suppression of this rebellion cost the lives of scores of soldiers and hundreds of wounded. Although discipline was temporarily restored the chasm between noble officers and their troops remained.

The National Assembly itself was appalled by the military disintegration and took measures to insure that, for the protection of the nation, order would be restored in the army. Deliberating associations within the regiments were forbidden. The ringleaders of the Nancy revolt were punished and two of the regiments involved were disbanded. In September 1790 troops were forbidden to join political clubs, an effort to depoliticize them and restore traditional discipline.

More positive steps were also taken by the government to assure it of a reliable and disciplined army. These reforms, at the same time, contributed to the professionalization of the officer corps. The abolition of venality and the opening of all ranks to all citizens in February 1790, both measures based on the principle of advancement by merit, had already initiated this process. In July 1790 substantial pay increases were voted for officers. Officers above the grade of lieutenant received the most substantial raises; colonels' salaries, for example, were increased from 4 000 to 6 000 *livres* per year and captains likewise received a raise of approximately 50%. Henceforth a military career would afford a livelihood without the necessity of 'outside' financial support.

In order to increase the efficiency of the officer corps the number of officers was markedly reduced. In 1788 before the suppression of attached officers and 'officers of replacement' there had been approximately 35 000 officers in the army, less than one-third of whom were on active duty. Over one thousand of these held general officer rank and another thousand were colonels.[16] In February 1790 the number of generals was reduced to ninety-four, of whom six could be marshals and thirty-four lieutenant generals. Subsequently the total number of officers was fixed at 9 406.

In the fall of 1790 legislation established new methods of advancement within the officer corps. Three-fourths of the sub-lieutenants were to be admitted solely by examinations. The remaining one fourth of the vacancies in this rank were to be filled by non-commissioned officers selected by their superior officers. Lieutenants and captains were to be appointed solely on the basis of longevity. Two-thirds of the lieutenant colonels and colonels were to be selected according to longevity and one-third of these appointments were to be made by the king. The king also had the right to select half of the brigadier and lieutenant generals; the other half were to be appointed according to length of service. Subsequent changes in promotion procedures put an even greater emphasis on experience and with the exception of the period 1793-94, when the democratic government made election the primary criterion for advancement, experience and competence henceforth became the accepted principles for promotion. Even under the restored Bourbon monarchy the military law of March 1818 maintained these norms.[17] Professional standards were rapidly replacing the ascribed status of nobility as criteria for service as an officer and for promotion within the officer corps.

These regulations were but one aspect of a more general rationalization of institutions which was being carried out by the National Assembly. Public administration, taxation, judicial proceedings, economic institutions (such as internal tolls, weights and measures, land tenure) were all being standardized according to different, more rational principles. In the military this general policy of rationalization was spurred on by the continued disintegration within the army.

New outbursts of insubordination in early 1791 further exacerbated relations between officers and men. The decree of the National Assembly on 29 April 1791, which once again allowed all military men to attend political clubs while off duty, helped to increase this rift. Some of these clubs and a number of the more radical newspapers were now calling for the wholesale dismissal of all noble officers on the grounds of their hostility to the new regime.[18] Undoubtedly the career ambitions of non-commissioned officers contributed to some of this agitation. A new decree of 24 June 1791 reserved half the vacant sub-lieutenancies for them, in place of the previous one quarter. The dismissal of noble officers would, obviously, greatly facilitate rapid advancement for NCO's and officers of fortune.[19] The Assembly was gravely concerned at the continuing insubordination and moderate deputies argued that a wholesale dismissal or resignation of officers would ruin the army since these men and their skills could not be replaced overnight.[20]

Pressures on noble officers to resign and emigrate increased greatly in 1791. Their superiors and comrades who had already emigrated intimidated and cajoled those still serving. The *émigrés* threatened officers still in the ranks with revocation of their commissions and offered bonuses to those who came to join them.[21] On 11 June 1791 the National Assembly required a reaffirmation of the oath of loyalty to the nation, the law and the king. This had to be taken individually and in writing, whereas the previous oath had been given collectively and orally.

The turning point of the military emigration was the failure of the flight of the king on 21 June. Louis XVI had attempted to seek refuge in the Austrian Netherlands. From there, with the military assistance of the Emperor, his brother-in-law, and of the *émigrés*, he hoped to return to crush the Revolution. The king himself had now given the example and emigration could no longer be construed as dereliction of duty. A new oath required of officers contained no mention of the king. This event initiated a massive wave of emigration by noble officers, including many of the provincial nobility. Comeau de Chary, a member of this class and a lieutenant of artillery, was typical of hundreds of his fellow officers in his decision that after this episode he could no longer serve the king by remaining in France. He emigrated in September 1791.[22] By August, approximately 1 500 officers had already refused to take the new oath.[23] Between September and December an additional 2 000 officers had emigrated and by the end of 1791 there were perhaps as many as six thousand French officers on foreign soil.[24]

The National Assembly was torn between the political danger of widespread disloyalty within the officer corps and the military danger of losing its experienced military leadership just as the threat of war with Austria was rapidly escalating. The Assembly sent commissioners to the army to receive the new oath of loyalty to the National Assembly and the Constitution (not yet promulgated). On 25 June 1791 the Assembly disbanded the old Royal Bodyguard and replaced it with a Constitutional Guard, as much to watch the king as to protect him. Civilian control over the army was increased by forbidding any police activity by the army except on the initiation of civil authorities. At the end of July the Assembly suppressed all orders of chivalry and all military decorations, except the Cross of Saint Louis. Furthermore, it forbade any use of a noble title, even if preceded by 'former.' At the same time, the Assembly pointed out to French officers that the only real honors were those which were awarded for virtues and talents; and to French soldiers it urged subordination to the law and obedience to their officers.[25]

Such efforts were, however, unsuccessful and relations between officers and men continued to deteriorate. In a perverse but understandable way, the emigration of so many officers had made the loyalty of those who remained more suspect. Even the acceptance of the new oath did not mitigate suspicions. The officers of fortune and NCO's resented those who took the oath and so continued to block their own promotions. In addition, it was suspected, not without some justification, that many of those noble officers who remained did so only to further the cause of royalism.[26] The lot of the noble officer was becoming intolerable. He not only had to accept his former social and military subordinates as his equals, but he also found that the few personal ties which had connected him to his men were destroyed beyond recovery. In late 1791, a few months before his emigration, Captain de Mautort visited some of the men with whom he had served for five years in India. Despite some lingering affection, the atmosphere was strained and after his visit Mautort concluded: '... it was no longer the same.'[27]

Indeed, it was not. Voluntarily and involuntarily the officer corps was being purged of the social group which had dominated it for centuries. The local political club at Saintes convinced the men of the 16th Infantry Regiment to disobey their officers' orders to return to their camp. At Blois the second battalion of the 58th Infantry, with the support of the local Jacobin club, chased off its officers. Similar episodes occurred in the 17th Infantry and 38th Infantry regiments, in the 13th Cavalry and 2nd Dragoons, as well as in a number of other units.[28]

On 16 October 1791 the Minister of War, Duportail, announced that there were 1 468 officer vacancies in the infantry, for which there had been 508 replacements; and 464 vacancies in the cavalry for which there had been 256 replacements. Between 15 September and 1 December 1791, 2 160 officers had resigned or emigrated. On 29 November the requirement of examinations for officer candidates was suspended, in an attempt to fill these gaps, since available educational facilities were totally inadequate for the training of the hundreds of new officers now required. From 27 April to 15 July 1792, 398 infantry officers and 144 cavalry officers more emigrated. Even the artillery, the most stable of the three major branches, lost over one hundred officers between 1 September 1791 and 15 July 1792.[29] Some regiments were almost without officers; and in April 1792 France went to war!

The declaration of war on Austria by France on 20 April 1792 presented the noble (or formerly noble) officers of the French army with a cruel choice: to remain in their functions and fight for France or to emigrate and fight for royalism. Many officers, as evidenced by the emigration figures between April and July, joined the foreign armies in an attempt to restore the authority of the king.[30] The invasion of the royal palace and the insults inflicted on Louis XVI by the Parisian populace on 20

25

June further helped to convince a number of officers to emigrate. The attack on the Tuileries and deposition of Louis XVI, which occurred on 10 August, motivated still more officers, including moderate or constitutional monarchists (such as General Lafayette and his staff), to leave France. Their number was, however, comparatively small for the simple reason that most of the officers not firmly committed to the new regime had already left the country, or at least military service.

By the end of 1792 the period of voluntary emigration was virtually over. Except for individual instances, the only major episode which resulted in further large-scale emigration was the treason of General Dumouriez. After the battle of Valmy on 20 September 1792 in which his army had played a crucial role, Dumouriez had commanded the French offensive into Belgium and the Netherlands in the winter of 1792-93. Defeated by the Austrians in March 1793 and alienated from the government at Paris, he had gone over to the enemy on 5 April taking with him his staff and a handful of troops. Dumouriez's treason entailed, directly or indirectly, the emigration of another, comparatively small, group of officers. On the other hand, this episode initiated a purge of the officer corps by the civil authorities. Between the spring of 1793 and the fall of Robespierre in July 1794, political loyalty and reliability outweighed all other criteria for military command. This period, which coincides with the Terror, was the most critical period of the Revolution, as France combatted both foreign invasion and civil war simultaneously. The emphasis upon political attitudes above other factors was a significant, but temporary, departure from the more impersonal standards which had been established by 1793 and which were to be implemented once again after 1794.

The changes made in the French officer corps by early 1793 had established the basic criteria and principles according to which this body was to develop in the future. Despite the departures from these principles, especially in times of national crisis, and despite the corruptions which inevitably occurred, the standards of the Old Regime would never be reestablished. Even when the French nobility attempted to reassert its dominance in the officer corps in the late nineteenth century, its path to a commission and promotion was by way of a professional education at Saint-Cyr, not simply by virtue of its social status.[31]

The Revolution accomplished in the army what the dynastic state was incapable of accomplishing: it created a professional officer corps. The hierarchical social system of the Old Regime had maintained the military preeminence of the nobility. The Revolution proclaimed the principle of equality of opportunity and opened military grades to all citizens. The limited financial powers of the monarchy had led to venality of office and inadequate pay for its officers. The new, representative government with the power to tax all citizens and institutions abolished venality and provided military officers with a sufficient income so that their time and energy could be fully devoted to their career. Under the Old Regime an ancient tradition of military service had been sufficient justification for any young noble to expect a commission in the army. The bourgeois representatives of the nation restricted the number of military officers to that which would provide efficient security and established new, more rational standards for service as an officer, most notably military experience.

This professionalization of the officer corps was a part of the general bureaucratization of French political and social institutions, so frequently associated with democratization and the growth of a capitalist economy.[32] As such, it was an integral part of the legislation of the National Assembly which established the new constitutional framework for politics and society. In addition to the desire to rationalize French institutions, another motivation for the professionalization of the officer corps was the danger of war, which increased continually from mid-1791 to its realization in the spring of 1792. In order to deal with this threat an expert and efficient officer corps, one based on professional standards, was required. Finally, the resignation and emigration of a substantial majority of the officers of the Royal Army had necessitated the admission of new, but competent men to the officer corps.

It is impossible to give exact figures on the number of officers who emigrated between 1789 and 1793. The very nature of the activity is such that secrecy was a desideratum. Furthermore, it is impossible in some cases to determine emigration. If an officer failed to report to a new command, did this constitute emigration; or was the cause a mix-up in orders, illness or perhaps even death? The record keeping, although reliable on the whole, could be inaccurate in individual instances, especially after the outbreak of the war. Donald Greer, who has made the most comprehensive study of emigration, has determined the social background of 78% of the *émigrés*. Of these, 7 513 were officers; and of this group, 75.5% were noble officers. Greer further points out that most of the nobles emigrated before 1793.[33] For lack of more precise data, we might, therefore, conclude that by early 1793 approximately seven thousand officers had emigrated and that the overwhelming majority of these were nobles.

Up to this point, this study has concentrated on legislation concerning the organization of the officer corps and general descriptions of its personnel. It is clear that the French aristocracy dominated the officer corps in the second half of the eighteenth century, and that this dominance increased in the years before the Revolution. Furthermore, during the last decades of the Old Regime an extensive modernization in the organization of the army was carried out; always, however, stopping short of fundamental change in the social structure of the officer corps. It is likewise clear that the Revolutionary government abolished the traditional criteria of a society based on privilege and established more rational, more impersonal standards for military officers. This was a policy required not only by new political and social principles, but also by the threat of war and the departure of most of the previous military leadership.

What has yet to be examined is the effect of these policies and developments. It was the intention of the new regime to modernize the officer corps by the application of professional criteria. By their resignation and emigration the old officers had rejected the new principles. This wholesale defection had both allowed and forced the introduction of a very large proportion of new men into the officer corps. It still remains to be seen how well these new officers conformed to the standards of the new government. In short, to what degree was the officer corps which emerged from the Revolution a truly professional institution?

THE NEW OFFICER CORPS

To determine the effects of the Revolution on the composition of the officer corps requires a somewhat comprehensive investigation of the personnel who were serving as officers by early 1793. The sources from which this information on the officer corps was derived deserve a brief explanation.[1]

The basic source of data on the infantry officers, through the rank of colonel, was a collection of reports to the National Convention in the early spring of 1793. Each regiment was required to provide the government with a report on the civil and military status of all the officers serving in it. Among the data demanded were date and place of birth, residence, civilian profession and a synopsis of the military career of each officer.[2] From this series was drawn information on 1 771 infantry officers (27 colonels, 58 lieutenant colonels, 564 captains and 1 122 lieutenants) in fifty regiments.

Unfortunately, the comparable series for cavalry regiments (*Série* xc) contained no such reports for the officers in this branch. Consequently, a different source of information was used for cavalry officers.[3] This series did not normally provide data on the civilian profession of the officers. However, those cavalry regiments serving with the Army of the West were required, in the summer of 1794, to send reports including this information to the government; and these reports are contained in this series. By extracting from these reports information on men who were serving as cavalry officers in early 1793, some information on the social background of cavalry officers was acquired. In all, complete or partial information on 366 cavalry officers (9 colonels, 20 lieutenant colonels, 96 captains and 241 lieutenants) in thirteen regiments was thus obtained.

Most difficult was acquiring data on the social or occupational backgrounds of artillery officers. There were a few officers for whom the reports prepared for the government in early 1793 were found.[4] For the remainder of the artillery officers studied, their names and units had to be gleaned from correspondence and then their individual dossiers checked for further information on their civilian backgrounds and military careers.[5] A total of 109 artillery officers in four regiments (1 colonel, 7 lieutenant colonels, 53 captains and 48 lieutenants), for whom full or partial data were available, were studied.

The total sample of regimental grade officers included 2 246 officers. The authorized officer strength of the ninety-eight line infantry regiments which existed in early 1793 was 5 880 or sixty officers per regiment.[6] However, an examination of the reports submitted to the National Convention in the spring of 1793 indicated that the average officer strength was about fifty per regiment. This means that slightly more than one-third of the line infantry officers serving in early 1793 were included in this study. Each cavalry regiment, on the other hand, apparently had two or three officers more than were authorized (a total of 1 972 in sixty-four regiments). The group of cavalry officers studied, therefore, amounted to slightly more than one-sixth of the total in early 1793. The artillery regiments seem to have had two or three officers less than their complement (736 officers authorized for eight regiments), so that the one hundred and nine officers in this study represent slightly more than one-seventh of the artillery officer corps in early 1793.

Data on general officers was much more readily accessible, thanks to the excellent two volume biographical dictionary of Georges Six.[7] As of the date selected for this sample, there were 195 men serving as general officers: 64 lieutenant generals, 118 brigadier generals or *maréchaux de camp* and 13 provisional brigadier generals (all but two of whom were confirmed in their grade by 15 May 1793). All of these have been included in this study.

Before the results of these investigations are presented, a few further notes are in order. The rank of major had been suppressed on 1 January 1791. On 21 February 1793 the title *chef de bataillon* (*chef d'escadron* in the cavalry) replaced the grade of lieutenant colonel, and *chef de brigade* replaced that of colonel. However, the old, more familiar titles will be used here. All lieutenants (sub-lieutenants, first and second lieutenants) have been, for the purposes of this study, grouped together as simply lieutenants. Likewise, captains, whether captains in second or captains commanding, have been treated as one group. This simplification, perhaps offensive to military specialists, can be justified on the grounds that all lieutenants or captains, whatever their precise rank, formed identifiable and cohesive echelons in the military hierarchy.

Two important groups of officers are not dealt with; the reason being that no adequate documentation on them could be discovered. The first of these groups was the officers of light infantry battalions, some four hundred officers in all. Also unrepresented are the officers of the general staffs, including Engineer officers, whose number is very difficult to estimate but may have reached five hundred.

Finally, in order to construct all of these samples, a precise date was necessary; otherwise the arrival of new officers, promotions, transfers and losses would have greatly complicated the data. The date that has been selected is 28 February 1793. By early 1793 the new military principles had become well established and the period of military emigration had almost completely ended. Furthermore, this period was a military turning point: in late February 300 000 more men were called up for military service and the National Convention decreed the amalgamation of the regular army and the volunteer units of the National Guard; in the next month began a series of military reverses which led to foreign invasion and the beginning of the Terror.

Officers of regimental grade, lieutenant through colonel, will be examined as one group, and general officers will be dealt with as another. The variables which will be investigated include: age, military experience and career patterns, geographic origins (including rural-urban distinctions) and social background.

As for the age of regimental officers in February 1793, there was, as might be expected, a strong correlation between age and rank. Only one infantry colonel out of twenty-seven was thirty years of age or younger. The majority of colonels in the infantry were between fifty and sixty years of age. Lieutenant colonels in the same branch were somewhat younger; one-tenth of them were thirty or younger and less than one half were over fifty. Because in early 1793 it was rather common for a lieutenant colonel to command a regiment, due to a shortage of colonels, these two grades might be considered together when dealing with regimental commanders.

The most even distribution of ages was found among infantry captains. A sizeable minority (14.2%) were thirty years old or younger. Captains in the next three age groups were rather evenly divided: 23.9% were between thirty-one and forty; 29.8% were between forty-one and fifty; and 26.2% were older than fifty. Of the infantry lieutenants, 36.3% were thirty or less; 61.6% were forty or younger; and less than 7% were over fifty.

This situation was in a number of ways quite different from the age distribution among infantry officers on the eve of the Revolution. The most notable difference was that the colonels of the pre-Revolutionary officer corps were much younger. They were young court nobles, most of whom were in their thirties. Lieutenant colonels in 1789, who were often the *de facto* regimental commanders, were approximately the same ages, their late forties and early fifties, as their counterparts of 1793. Pre-Revolutionary captains also fell roughly into the same age groups, between thirty-five and fifty-five, as the captains of 1793. The lieutenants of 1793, on the other hand, were considerably older than their noble predecessors of the Old Regime.[8]

As can readily be seen from these data, in the course of the Revolution the noble officers who held grades primarily through favor had generally disappeared. Gone were most of the colonels who had been appointed, through connections at court, before the age of thirty, with little experience or proof of ability. Gone too were most of the lieutenants still in their teens who started their military careers with a commission based on birth rather than talent. Whatever the problems connected with a criterion based on simple experience, this was still a more rational standard than ascribed social status.

Colonels and lieutenant colonels in the cavalry were comparable in age to their infantry comrades. More than one half of the officers in these two grades were older than fifty, and only about one-tenth of them were thirty or younger. Although there was about the same proportion of captains under thirty-one years of age in the cavalry as in the infantry, cavalry captains were generally older. Four-tenths of them were older than fifty and more than 70% were over forty years old. Cavalry lieutenants were much closer in age to their counterparts in the infantry. Slightly more than one-third of them were thirty or younger, and nearly two-thirds (62.2%) were forty or younger. There were, however, twice as many cavalry lieutenants over fifty as there were in the infantry.

Although the data on artillery officers is less conclusive, it does appear that artillery captains were more comparable in age to the cavalry captains than to those in the infantry. Artillery lieutenants also were generally older than those of the same rank in the other two branches. The fact that artillery officers tended to be older than men of the same rank in other branches is a reflection of the greater stability which existed among artillery personnel during the tumultuous period of 1789-93.[9] Much more technical skill was required of officers in this branch than in the other two major branches; and these specialists were apparently more devoted to their career than to the political regime. The infantry, the least specialized of all branches, underwent the greatest changes in personnel and this is reflected in the fact that infantry officers, especially junior officers, tended to be younger and, as we shall soon see, less experienced than men of the same rank in other branches.

The oldest captains and lieutenants in all branches seldom served with front line troops in combat zones. Usually they performed administrative duties behind the lines. Entirely typical of this kind of employment is Captain Carbonel of the 49th Infantry Regiment. Carbonel, an old soldier, sixty-five years of age with forty-six years service, commanded the regimental depot of his unit and concerned himself primarily with training replacements for the major part of the regiment which was at the front.[10]

By 1793 the field grade officers were, on the whole, more elderly than the officers of the same ranks in the Old Regime. Even most of the captains were middle-aged or older. Only among lieutenants was there a clear majority of comparatively young men. However, whatever disadvantages there may have been in having an older officer corps was more than compensated for by the extensive military experience of almost all the officers in the three branches.

Of all the colonels, none had less than ten years of service and 80% of them had served twenty-five years or more. Nearly two-thirds of the lieutenant colonels also had twenty-five years or more of experience, while less than one in twenty had served fewer than ten years in the army. Among captains, less than one-tenth had served fewer than ten years; and most of these were in the infantry, where the changes in the officer corps had been greatest. More than one half of all the captains had twenty-five years or more service. Even among the lieutenants, more than one quarter had served in the army for at least twenty-five years. On the other hand, more than one-fourth (28.9%) of the lieutenants had served less than ten years. In all, more than 80% of the infantry officers had served five years or more; approximately 85% of the cavalry officers had served an equal time; and nearly all (97%) of the artillery officers had five years or more of service. Almost all of the officers with under five years service were lieutenants.

32

Factors other than simple length of service must be considered in a discussion of military experience. With little variation according to branch, 70% of the regimental officers in 1793 had served some time in the ranks. There were, however, substantial differences according to rank. Of thirty-seven colonels in the three branches, only five had any enlisted service. Almost 40% of the lieutenant colonels had served at one time in the ranks. These were mostly 'officers of fortune' who had already been promoted to officers before the Revolution. On the other hand, more than 70% of the captains and lieutenants had prior service as enlisted men.

Generally, then, by 1793 the former NCO's of the regular army dominated the officer ranks below the grade of lieutenant colonel. A lieutenant colonelcy was as high as most of the ex-rankers had reached. Colonel was still a grade dominated by men whose only military service had been in the capacity of officers. However, since many lieutenant colonels were commanding regiments, there was still a sizeable minority of regimental commanders who had had experience in the ranks.

Although most of the men who were regimental officers by 1793 had received one, two or three promotions since 1789, meteoric rises were very unusual. None of the colonels in this study had been enlisted men in July 1789; almost all of them had been majors or captains at that date and a small number, less than one-tenth, had been lieutenants. Some few men who had been sergeants in 1789 had reached the rank of lieutenant colonel by 1793. More than one half of the lieutenant colonels of 1793 had been in the rank of captain before the Revolution; and approximately one-third of them had been lieutenants.

Nearly 45% of the captains of 1793 had been lieutenants in 1789 and an equal number had been sergeants at the same date. Approximately one-tenth of the captains serving in the line army in 1793 had held the same rank before the Revolution. A very small number, one out of one hundred, had risen from simple soldier to captain since 1789. A very large majority (85%) of the lieutenants of 1793 had been sergeants in 1789. Approximately 7.5% of the lieutenants of 1793 had been corporals before the Revolution; and one in twenty of them had served as an ordinary soldier.

Those rare soldiers who received very rapid promotions did so, almost undoubtedly, on the basis of merit. One example of this was Michel Ney. He enlisted in the regiment of the Hussars of Saxony (later the 4th Hussars) on 6 December 1788, one month before his twentieth birthday. He was promoted to corporal in January 1791 and to sergeant in February 1792; in April of the same year he became sergeant-major and in June adjudant and sub-lieutenant. By October 1792 Ney had become a full lieutenant.[11] His brilliant career ended before an Allied firing squad in 1815 after he had proven himself one of the most loyal of Napoleon's marshals. This admittedly extreme example should be taken as an indication that only the most exceptional soldiers experienced unusually rapid promotions. The expectations of most men, even if talented, were much more limited. However, the Revolution had at least opened the possibility of such a career.

One final aspect of military service remains to be discussed, that experience which above all others was valuable on the battlefield, combat experience. In this, the regimental officers of the line army showed an impressive record by early 1793. More than 40% of the infantry officers had participated in military campaigns prior to the Revolution and almost another 40% had seen combat in the campaign of 1792. Less than one-fifth of the line infantry officers of 1793 had no previous combat experience and almost all of these were young lieutenants. The proportion of officers with campaign experience was smaller in the cavalry, but still almost two-thirds (63%) of them had combat experience by 1793. Only one-fourth of the cavalry officers had served in campaigns prior to the Revolution, since these had been primarily overseas conflicts (e.g. in America, on Corsica) where mostly infantry units had been employed. Another 38% had experienced combat in the campaign of 1792. The proportion of artillery officers in 1793 with campaign experience was high, more than 80%; but since such information was indicated in only half the cases, this figure might be treated with some caution.

The general situation among regimental officers of the line army in 1793 was that the officers were men of long service and considerable campaign experience; they were, at least by these criteria, professional soldiers. Their age and length of service indicate that few of them, since reaching adulthood, had much experience with civilian occupations or had known a residence outside of military garrisons. Most of them had received rapid but limited promotions since the Revolution; more importantly, the majority, who had risen from the ranks, knew how restricted their chances for such promotion had been before the Revolution. Despite the fact that the highest grades were still controlled by officers from the old army, there were clear opportunities for junior officers to attain these grades. Although many officers, even among the captains and lieutenants, were in their forties and fifties, there was a substantial minority of young officers, and only two percent of the regimental officers were sixty years of age or older. The officers were battle-hardened veterans, younger probably than in any other army in Europe,[12] and certainly more familiar with the situation of the men under their command.

The officer corps of 1793 might well, then, be considered professional in a number of important ways. For their recent promotions and future career, these officers were dependent on the maintenance of rational standards based on experience and ability. Furthermore, for most of these officers, an important part of their life had been spent in military society and military affairs had become the focus of their lives. Under these circumstances, it might appear that an investigation of their civilian origins could contribute little which would be relevant to the professionalism of the officer corps. Hopefully, however, it can be shown that such an investigation will shed further light not only on the composition of the officer corps, but also on the process of its professionalization.

One very striking fact about the regional origins of regimental officers in 1793 is the high proportion of officers, especially of captains and lieutenants who were born in the frontier regions of the north and east (Flandre and Artois, Champagne, Lorraine, Alsace, and Franche-Comté). With approximately 17% of the total population of France these provinces produced almost 25% of the colonels and lieutenant colonels and over 38% of the captains and lieutenants whose birthplace has been identified. Since the proportion of junior officers from these frontier provinces is almost exactly identical with the percentage of enlisted men in 1789 who came from the same areas,[13] this further confirms previous evidence that most of the captains and lieutenants of 1793 had been promoted from the ranks. The higher percentage of superior officers from provinces in southern and western France (e.g. Languedoc, Bretagne and Poitou) reflects, on the other hand, the regional origins of the officer corps of the Old Regime, since a majority of the colonels and lieutenant colonels had already been officers before the Revolution.[14]

There was also a marked difference between superior and junior officers of foreign birth. There were almost three times as many foreigners among the colonels and lieutenant colonels as among the captains and lieutenants, at least in the infantry and cavalry. This too was a reflection of the changes brought about by the influx of ex-rankers into the lower echelons of the officer corps.[15] Even in the former Irish regiments of the Royal Army, which had maintained the most distinctively foreign character, this change was evident. For example, in the 87th (formerly Dillon) Infantry Regiment in 1793 the colonel, lieutenant colonel, adjutant major and all but one of the captains were foreign born. In contrast, five of the eight lieutenants and only one of the four sub-lieutenants were foreigners.[16] Foreign officers who did not emigrate were kept, but few foreigners were being admitted to French service as officers. The reorganization of the officer corps was tinged, not untypically, with nationalism.

When the regional origins of these officers were judged by domicile rather than by place of birth, the results were almost the same.[17] Moves from region of birth to an entirely different region were rare. When this occurred, however, it usually took the character of moving from a predominantly rural area to a more urbanized region, particularly to Paris and the Parisian area.

One of the most marked characteristics of the regimental officer corps was the urban background of so many of the officers. Toward the end of the eighteenth century the most common population figure which was used as a measure of 'urban' was two thousand or more inhabitants;[18] and this was also used as the standard for this study. According to this criterion, approximately 19% of the French population in 1789 lived in urban agglomerations.[19] Of the infantry officers whose birthplaces were identified as either rural or urban, approximately one half (50.2%) were from urban centers. The cavalry officers of regimental rank whose birthplace was specifically identified were 44.1% urban in background. Even in the artillery, which had the most rural composition of the three major branches, 42.1% of the officers were from urban areas.

When the domiciles of these officers were used as the measure of rural-urban origins, the results were even more remarkable.[20] Of the infantry officers whose domiciles were identified as urban or rural, three-fifths (60.6%) were from urban areas. Almost one half (48.4%) of the artillery officers made their homes in cities or towns of two thousand or more inhabitants. Approximately one quarter (24.9%) of the infantry officers lived in cities of 25 000 or more. One infantry officer in ten lived in Paris. One-eighth of the artillery officers had their residence in a city whose population exceeded 25 000 inhabitants. Such a population in eighteenth century France indicated a contemporary metropolis; indeed, there were only twenty-nine cities in the country which could boast of such a large population.

The regional origins of the regimental officers of 1793 were not only much more urban than that of the general population, they were also considerably more urban than those of the men under their command, of whom less than 31% came from urban centers.[21] This was due in part to the fact that people from urban areas rallied to the Revolution more completely than country people. More than two-thirds (67.5%) of the officers who had joined the army since 1789 came from cities. Another reason for the disproportionate number of officers from an urban background was that literacy was a prerequisite for officers and men from urban communities were more likely to possess this requirement.[22] In fact, literacy represents an important, but until now neglected, aspect of the professionalization of the officer corps. It can, however, be more adequately treated in the following section on the social background of the regimental officers of 1793.

The civilian occupation or social status of the officers was not always recorded, and frequently it was impossible to find any indication of this in the surviving records used for this study. Of the 2 246 regimental officers studied, the civilian professions of 1 602 were recorded; this represents about one-fifth of the officer strength of the line regiments in February 1793. However, the overwhelming majority of instances where such data were found was in the case of infantry officers; information on social background was found for only 106 cavalry officers and 35 artillery officers. Consequently, in the following discussion of social origins the regimental officers will be treated as one group, divided according to rank but not by branch. The infantry officers, thus, are overrepresented; but this is less of a distortion than it might at first appear since infantry officers constituted approximately 70% of the regimental officer corps. Differences and variations according to branch will be indicated as the evidence permits. Also, because of the similarities in their positions in the military hierarchy, as well as in their military careers, the officers will be treated as two basic groups, field grade and company grade officers. Differences in social origins also seem to justify such a division.

The overwhelming majority of field grade officers was from the highest social groups. Fully 40% of them were nobles and another 37% were from groups which represented the highest elements of non-noble society, i.e. military officers, government officials, members of the liberal professions, the business middle class and those called simply 'bourgeois.' Less than five percent of them derived from popular classes, e.g. artisans, wage earners, peasants.

Although of less lofty lineage, the social origins of the company grade officers were markedly higher than those of the enlisted men under their command.[23] Only one-third of these officers were from popular social groups, i.e. artisans and shopkeepers, apprentices, wage earners, peasants below the group of large farmers and those who gave their occupation as simply 'soldier'. Approximately 9% of the captains and lieutenants were nobles; and over 30% were from those groups which have been called 'notables', e.g. the liberal professions, bourgeois. One-eighth of them came from the intermediate social groups of merchants, manufacturers, master artisans, clerks and large farmers.

Approximately one-eighth of the officers who provided some information on their civilian background must be classified as of indeterminate social origins. This group is composed of officers whose civilian status was given as either 'without profession' or 'living with his parents'. The indication *'sans profession'* meant simply not having a trade, but the implications of this could vary greatly. Such a response could indicate an agricultural day laborer who had no trade; on the other hand, a wealthy bourgeois, or even a nobleman, who did not work at a trade could give the same response. Indeed, as the Revolution became more radical, an aristocrat might have been wise to respond in this way. There is no doubt that some nobles did precisely this.

Captain Alexandre-François-Léopold Wichard du Perron of the 94th Infantry, whose civil status was recorded as having no profession, was commissioned as a sub-lieutenant at the age of sixteen on 10 March 1785. Captain Jean-Bernard-Joseph Stipplin of the 77th Infantry gave his civil status simply as 'living with his father'. He became a sub-lieutenant on 7 August 1787 at the age of seventeen.[24] Almost certainly, in view of the dates of their commissions and the ages at which they received them, these two officers were young nobles. Sometimes the connection between having no trade and being a noble was made explicit. Lieutenant Colonel Gourcy of the 33rd Infantry indicated his previous civilian status as 'no profession, a poor count without land'.[25] It is impossible to determine, however, exactly how many officers who reported that they had no civilian profession were in fact nobles. Certainly there were many, perhaps most of the officers in this category.

For this reason and others that will be discussed shortly, the proportions of nobles given above must be considered minimum estimates and there is a strong possibility that these proportions were markedly higher. Many officers in responding to the inquiry of the Convention did not, perhaps out of political expediency, disclose their noble origins. Sometimes this was done by officers who described their civil status without reference to class or estate. For example, Charles-Gabriel Mallevault, a lieutenant in the 110th Infantry, who was commissioned on 9 August 1787 at the age of fifteen gave his civilian status as 'son of a proprietor' [i.e. of land]. Lieutenant Jean-Louis-Benjamin Lahaye of the same regiment who was commissioned on the same date at the age of nineteen, gave the same response about his civilian background.[26] Because of the date of their commissioning and their ages when they became officers, it is virtually certain that these two officers were nobles. Captain Viart of the 14th Cavalry gave his civilian occupation as 'student' and specifically denied that he was a noble. However, he admitted that his father had carried the title of squire (*écuyer*) and the register showed that he had been a page of the Queen, a position reserved exclusively to nobles.[27]

Therefore, it is clear that the proportion of noble officers in early 1793 could have been significantly higher than the figures given here, perhaps as high as 20% of all regimental officers. Nobles whose status was not indicated as such have possibly been included among students, military officers, large farmers and the group of indeterminate status. At the least, 40% of the field grade officers and a minimum of one-tenth of the subordinate officers were nobles in February 1793, a tacit admission by the government of the contributions of noble officers. The proportion of nobles among the cavalry officers seems to have been even higher than this.[28]

Despite the significant number of nobles who continued to serve as regimental officers, drastic changes had taken place within the officer corps. In 1789, except for the officers of fortune who constituted about 10% of the regimental officers, the number of non-noble officers had been negligible. By early 1793, commoners completely dominated the junior officer grades and shared the field grades with former nobles. Furthermore, the noble officers who still served were very different from the aristocratic officers of the Old Regime. Most of the young and inexperienced colonels from the greatest noble houses in France had gone into exile. Most of the cadets of noble families, who received their commissions while still adolescents, were gone with them. The noble officers who remained were hardened veterans who had spent most of their life in military service.[29] The nobles who had become colonels and lieutenant colonels by 1793 would, in all likelihood, have finished their careers as captains had it not been for the Revolution. Their continued service was at the same time a recognition of their military ability and an indication of their attachment to a military career.

The most remarkable contribution to the officer corps from non-noble groups came from men in the liberal professions (law, medicine, the arts and sciences), who comprised one-fifth of all regimental officers. This contribution was out of all proportion to the number of men in these professions in the general population. In addition, it is indicative that it was the professional middle class, rather than the bourgeoisie of business that formed the most direct support for the Revolution.[30] Particularly important among the members of the liberal professions were the students who, as a group, furnished more than one-eight of the regimental officers.

It must be pointed out, however, that these officers who had been students in civilian life were not young scholars who had rushed off to the colors to support the Revolution. The vast majority of regimental officers in 1793 who had been members of the liberal professions and students had long service in the army, usually as enlisted men, before the Revolution. They were not young idealists rallying to save the nation.

They were, rather, professional soldiers whose skills and experience enabled them to advance only after the Revolution had destroyed the feudal concept of, and requirements for, an officer.

The commercial bourgeoisie did not, perhaps typically, constitute a very numerous group in the officer corps (2.2%). Those who called themselves simply 'bourgeois' and lived on an income were more numerous among regimental officers (6.2%). Possibly their concept of 'living nobly' was satisfied by holding an officer's commission in the line army.

In view of their small number in both the population at large and in the ranks of the army,[31] a disproportionately large number of clerks had become officers since 1789; by 1793 they provided over 5% of regimental officers. Like the members of the liberal professions, most of these former clerks had been soldiers with long service before their promotion to officer. In the same way, they owed their opportunity for advancement to the Revolution.

Artisans and shopkeepers constituted one-sixth of the officer corps. This was considerably less than the percentage of men from such occupations in the ranks, where fully half of the soldiers and non-commissioned officers came from these groups. Generally, the officers who had previously been engaged in artisanal trades tended to be from more urban areas than their compatriots in the ranks.[32]

Peasants, who made up approximately 80% of the population of France in the late eighteenth century, were greatly underrepresented in the officer corps, as they were in the army as a whole.[33] The peasants who had become officers by 1793 came primarily from the more substantial peasantry, large farmers and plowmen (*laboureurs*). The lower classes of peasants (gardeners, winegrowers, agricultural laborers) provided only 2% of the regimental officers.

The same was true of the lowest classes of non-agricultural workers. Apprentices and wage earners (e.g. domestic servants, transportation workers) furnished a very small number of officers (1.2% of the total), compared to their numbers in the general population and in the ranks of the army itself. This was indicative of a more general truth about the officer corps of the line army: it was the higher non-noble classes of society who took over military commands following the voluntary and forced departures of nobles from these positions.

In other words, then, in the regimental officer corps the upper social classes of the Old Regime had been replaced, generally, by the upper classes of the Revolution. Although essentially correct, this statement conceals more than it reveals. Most importantly, the reason for such a change is not indicated. In the army of the Old Regime a man usually became an officer because such positions were naturally ascribed to an estate which had traditionally fulfilled these functions. Legislation, especially in the last half century of the Old Regime, had attempted merely to codify and detail what had been, or was thought to be, traditional custom and practice. No such legislation came out of the Revolution. The aim of the laws and decrees of the different Revolutionary governments was, essentially, to put in positions of military authority men who had proven that they were most competent to fill them, on the basis of their experience and ability.

In evaluating competence the new regime of the Revolution had relied primarily upon empirical standards; in fact, the most simple criterion, military experience, came to be the most widely applied. It was, however, the pressure of events, the wholesale resignation and emigration of the former officer corps, which forced the government to emphasize this standard. In the fall of 1790 the National Assembly had required examinations of candidates for three-fourths of the vacant sub-lieutenancies. In June 1791 the proportion of men admitted to commissions by examination was reduced to one-half. By November of the same year, in order to fill the hundreds of vacancies created by emigration, examinations were abolished altogether and military service became the essential criterion. The few military schools which had existed in France at the time of the Revolution were totally incapable of supplying the required number of officers, especially in so short a time. The government was obliged to gradually dispense with examinations, and the specialized education which they implied, and to depend more completely on the rational, but less bureaucratic, standard of experience.

The effects of this can be seen in the educational background of the regimental officers of 1793. Of the colonels in this sample, almost one-fifth (18.9%) had had either military schooling or cadet training; and approximately one quarter (24.7%) of the lieutenant colonels had such specialized preparation. On the other hand, only one-ninth (11.5%) of the captains and a mere 2% of the lieutenants had attended a military school or received cadet training; and these were mostly nobles whose only service had been as officers. The new regime had reluctantly (and temporarily) abandoned the requirement of a specialized, military education. It did not, however, at all ignore the importance of general education for its officers; it had, rather, reduced the educational requirement for officers to the most basic criterion, literacy.

In a period when the size of armies reached modern proportions, i.e. hundreds of thousands of men, but means of communications were still basically those of the past century, literacy was necessary for an efficient officer corps. Without officers who could read and write it would have been impossible to direct huge armies or coordinate their activities in the field. Yet in all of France during the period 1786-90 only 47% of the male population could sign their names, although this proportion reached 70% in parts of the North.[34] Of the 2 246 officers studied, only fourteen (four infantry captains and ten infantry lieutenants) were definitely illiterate.[35] In one regiment, the 104th Infantry, it was not until mid-1793 that the first officers who could not sign their names were appointed to the regiment.[36] There is every reason to believe that this was a typical case.

This high degree of literacy was due, in part, to the large proportion of officers who had previously been sergeants in the Royal Army and, as such, had been required to read and write since the ministry of Choiseul (1761-70). The requirement of literacy helps to explain the unusually high proportion of officers from urban areas, since literacy was much more common in the towns and cities. More to the point, the large number of regimental officers from upper and middle social groups was necessitated by the fact that it was precisely these groups that had the largest percentage of literates. The most striking example of this was the large number of officers who had been members of the liberal professions and clerks, occupations which assumed literacy. All of these factors were related to each other: literacy was highest among the upper social classes; these groups were found in large numbers only in the cities; men with this type of background, once inducted into the army, advanced most readily to the rank of sergeant since they fulfilled the basic requirement of literacy; and finally, once caste privileges were destroyed by the Revolution these men were best fit to replace the fleeing aristocrats.

The above pattern of advancement was not, of course, what happened in all cases. There were many officers from rural areas and from lower social classes. A significant minority of the officers had not come up through the ranks. There were even a few illiterates among the officers. Nevertheless, those officers who were from the urban middle class, who had reached the limit of advancement in 1789 after years of service and who had received unexpected promotions since the Revolution, lent a distinctive character to the regimental officer corps of the line army. These men and their fellow-officers from the lower nobility provided the French regiments with what was probably the most professional officer corps in Europe at the time.

There were striking similarities, as well as important differences, between the regimental officers of the French line army and the general officers who commanded them.[37] One distinctive characteristic of the group of general officers is, however, their professionalism. Like their subordinate officers, the generals of 1793 conformed to many standards which have come to be expected of professionals.

The general officers of early 1793 were older than the field grade officers of the same period, as one might expect. More than two-thirds (68.8%) of the lieutenant generals[38] were over fifty years old. On the other hand, approximately one-seventh (14.1%) of the lieutenant generals were forty years of age or younger. The youngest lieutenant general was the Duke of Chartres, the nephew of Louis XVI and future Louis-Philippe, King of the French; he was only nineteen years old in February 1793 and held his high rank on the basis of his family's position. It might be noted, however, that this young man had served admirably in the two greatest victories of the new French army, at Valmy and Jemappes in September and November 1792. Although slightly younger than their superiors, the brigadier generals of 1793[39] were older than the colonels and lieutenant colonels at the same period. Almost 40% of them were fifty years of age or younger. Only Grouchy, who was the brother-in-law of Condorcet and later became a marshal under Napoleon, was less than thirty years old.

The military experience of these generals was very impressive. Only four percent of all generals in 1793 had served less than fifteen years; and among those with less service than this were the Duke of Chartres, Santerre, a leader of the early Revolution in Paris, and Miaczynski, a Polish *émigré*. Almost four-fifths (79.1%) of the general officers of 1793 had twenty-five years or more of military service. Although they had served in the army somewhat less time than the lieutenant generals, the brigadier generals were also old military men, of whom less than one quarter (23.7%) had served for fewer than twenty-five years.

Of all the general officers, 42.1% had performed all or almost all of their military service in the infantry, 16.9% in the cavalry and 9.2% in the artillery. One-fourth (25.1%) of the generals had served in two or more branches; 4.1% were engineer officers; and one general had served most of his career in the Royal Navy. The branch background of four generals was uncertain. The only significant variation according to rank was that brigadier generals tended to be more specialized. While 29.7% of the lieutenant generals had served for some time in more than one branch, 22.9% of the brigadier generals had done so. Furthermore, a higher proportion of brigadier generals came from the most specialized branches, the engineers and the artillery, than did lieutenant generals (15.2% as against 9.4%). Since almost 90% of the brigadier generals had been promoted to this rank since mid-1789 and over half (57.8%) of the lieutenant generals had already been general officers before the Revolution, this higher degree of specialization is indicative of one more aspect of the general policy of professionalization implemented during the Revolution.

Only a few of the generals of 1793 had served previously in the ranks. Among the lieutenant generals, only two, Berruyer and Diettmann, had served in a grade below that of officer; and Diettmann's service as a soldier had been in the Gendarmes, a part of the Household troops with considerably more prestige than the line units. Service in the ranks was more common among the brigadier generals; a dozen, representing 9.2% of the total number, had served some period as enlisted men. Length of service in the ranks varied from one year to twenty-six years. Jacques Thouvenot had served as a soldier for a year in the regiment of Picardie Infantry in 1769-70; but it was his experience as a royal surveyor which earned him a commission and rapid promotion from 1787 on.[40] On the other hand, Joseph Gilot had come up laboriously through the ranks and had already served more than twenty-six years when he became a sub-lieutenant in 1776.[41] In fact, these two examples represent well the combination of skill and experience found among the general officers.

A majority of the sixty-four lieutenant generals had already achieved general officer rank by mid-1789; five of them were lieutenant generals and thirty-two were brigadier generals when the Revolution began. Thirteen officers who had been colonels and nine who had been lieutenant colonels in 1789 had been promoted to lieutenant general by the end of February 1793. Two officers had even risen from the rank of major to lieutenant general during this brief period. Three of the lieutenant generals of 1793 had not been in military service at the outbreak of the Revolution.

Some of the officers who were serving as brigadier generals in early 1793 had received extraordinary promotions since 1789. Of the one hundred and thirty-one brigadier generals of 1793, only fourteen had held the same rank in mid-1789. On the other hand, 17 colonels and 39 lieutenant colonels of 1789 had become brigadier generals by February 1793. Even more remarkable, twenty-four officers who were majors and twenty-three who were captains when the Revolution began had reached the rank of brigadier general in less than four years. One officer (Thouvenot, the royal surveyor mentioned above) had risen from lieutenant to general during the same period. Thirteen of the brigadier generals of 1793 were not on active duty in mid-1789, although all but one of them (Santerre, an obvious political appointee) had prior military service.

As among the regimental officers of 1793, only a minority of the general officers at the same date had received a special military education. Thirteen of the 64 lieutenant generals (20.3%) and thirty-one of the 131 brigadier generals (23.7%) had either attended a military school or received cadet training. Undoubtedly, specialized training was an asset in an officer's career; however, it had not yet been made a requirement. The pressure created by the emigration of the former officers and the foreign war prohibited the full establishment of this bureaucratic criterion.

Although the educational background of the generals of 1793 may have been, on the whole, inadequate, their military experience certainly compensated for part of this deficiency. At least three-fourths of the lieutenant generals and about two-thirds (65.6%) of the brigadier generals of 1793 had been in combat prior to the outbreak of the war in April 1792.[42] Furthermore, after the campaign of 1792 only about a dozen general officers had not yet served in combat.

Thus, by the character as well as the length of their service, most of the general officers of 1793, like their subordinates, could be classified as professional military men. Their experience had, naturally, come with age; yet, they were not excessively old. More than one third of them were fifty years of age or younger, and over 70% were sixty or less.[43] Especially among the brigadier generals, there were a large proportion of men (76.5%) who had received two or more promotions since 1789. More than one-fifth of the generals had received a specialized, military education. In 1789 general officer rank had been explicitly reserved to nobles who had the influence and wealth to be presented at court; by 1793 the career expectations of officers were limited primarily by experience and ability.

The regional origins of the generals in 1793 are in many ways similar to the regional origins of the colonels and lieutenant colonels of the same date. The same proportion, approximately one-fourth, of the generals came from the frontier provinces of the north and east as did the field grade officers. Officers of foreign birth constituted about 10% of both generals and regimental commanders. On the other hand, fewer generals came from certain provinces in the south and west (Languedoc, Guyenne and Poitou) than did the colonels and lieutenant colonels of 1793. Perhaps most striking is that more than twice as many generals came from the Parisian region, Ile-de-France, as did field grade officers (12.8% as against 5.7%); in fact, 10% of the generals of 1793 came from the city of Paris itself. This, in part, reflects the differences within the officer corps of the Old Regime. Many of the colonels and lieutenant colonels of 1793 were members of the provincial nobility who had been, in effect, barred from the highest regimental grades before the Revolution. In contrast, eighty-one (41.5%) of the generals of 1793 had held a rank of colonel or higher in 1789 and represented, in all probability, the aristocratic elite, the court nobility. These nobles seldom devoted their energies to their

45

estates, but rather gravitated to large cities, particularly Paris, where they found society, education and royal favor.

Of all the general officers whose place of birth has been determined, 58.6% came from urban centers, and more than one-fourth (26%) were born in cities whose population exceeded 25,000 inhabitants. No information on the domicile of the generals was available, but it is likely that an even higher proportion of generals had their residence in towns and cities. Although the proportion of generals from urban areas is comparable to that of the regimental officers, the social origins of the generals are quite distinctive.

There was, apparently, a greater homogeneity in the social background of the generals than among other echelons of the officer corps. Georges Six has calculated that of 202 generals serving on 1 January 1793, 139 (68.8%) were nobles;[44] and it is unlikely that this proportion changed significantly in the following two months. From the information provided in the same author's biographical dictionary, however, it is not possible to be very precise about the social origins of the generals serving on 28 February 1793. Of the 195 generals serving as of this date, the civilian status of only ninety-three is indicated; and of these, seventy-eight were nobles. Since noble status can be determined from information other than an explicit indication of civilian occupation (e.g. from titles, dates of commission, offices held, etc.), nobility is more readily, and more frequently, identified than any other social status. Therefore, the proportion of approximately 70% given by Six, who devoted his entire scholarly life to compiling data on the generals of the Revolution and Empire, is probably the most accurate estimation of the percentage of nobles among the generals of early 1793.

This substantial majority of nobles, however, can blur the diversity which existed among the general officers. Of the sixty-four lieutenant generals of 1793, fifty had held the rank of colonel or higher in 1789. Although it is not evident in every individual case, most of these officers were members of the court aristocracy. Of the 131 brigadier generals of 1793, only thirty-one had been colonels or brigadier generals before the Revolution. Thus, from the data available and what can be reconstructed, the following conclusions can be drawn. Approximately seven out of ten generals in 1793 were nobles; but this proportion was probably somewhat higher, perhaps 80%, among the lieutenant generals. Furthermore, the court aristocracy continued to dominate the rank of lieutenant general in early 1793. On the other hand, the predominant social group among brigadier generals was the provincial nobility; and these nobles, who had been lieutenant colonels, majors and captains in 1789, owed

46

their advancement to the new standards imposed by the Revolution.[45]

On the basis of the social origins of the generals of 1793, especially the lieutenant generals, it might appear that in these ranks social status still counted for more than professional ability. To assume this, however, would be to ignore the historical situation in which the professionalization of the officer corps took place. To promote a mass of company officers to regimental commands in less than four years is unusual but not unthinkable, since these officers continued to perform their functions in the same branch, or even the same regiment, although on a higher administrative level. To replace all general officers within less than four years and in the face of a major war would have been to court disaster. Indeed, a concern for military efficiency necessitated the maintenance of at least a core of officers with previous experience at the higher echelons. To adopt new social prejudices in place of the old would have been equally detrimental to military professionalization.

Furthermore, an exaggerated emphasis on the similar social background of general officers before and after the Revolution ignores the dramatic changes which had taken place. Of the more than two hundred marshals and lieutenant generals in the French army in mid-1789, only five remained in February 1793. Of the approximately eight hundred brigadier generals serving before the Revolution, forty-six were left only three years and eight months later.[46] There had been a large influx of provincial nobles into the general officer ranks; and their devotion to military service, whatever the motivation, can hardly be questioned. There was a sizeable minority of non-nobles who were serving as generals by 1793.[47] Finally, it is impossible to find fault with the military credentials of most of the nobles who were generals in 1793; almost all of them were officers who had long and distinguished service and who were, from all the evidence, dedicated to a military career. Despite different social origins and various career patterns, the term which would be almost universally applicable to the generals of 1793 is 'professional soldier'.

CONCLUSION

By 1793 the French officer corps had become a professional institution. Officers were evaluated according to new, impersonal standards whose exclusive aim was military efficiency. As a result, the officer corps was composed very largely of men whose lives had been spent in military service. Furthermore, the government provided a livelihood to officers so that full-time dedication to a military career was possible. All of these elements of professionalism, so closely related to each other, emerged from the historical circumstances of the French Revolution.

In the eighteenth century pressures for the rationalization of French institutions had been increasing. These came from such diversified sources as an ambitious foreign policy, the requirements of a modern state, the political and social criticism of Enlightenment writers and even what might be called popular opinion.[1] In the case of the army, the monarchy's response to such pressures had been a partial modernization which affected military organization but left the internal operation untouched. Such a policy, while antagonizing the opponents of reform, left the proponents of modernization dissatisfied. The success of the Revolution meant, among other things, a more thorough rationalization of French institutions.

In the army, rationalization took the form of the professionalization of the officer corps. Basic reforms in the officer corps began in February 1790 with the abolition of venality and the opening of all military grades to all citizens, regardless of their social status. In all likelihood, this process of professionalization would have advanced gradually over the course of many years, if new crises had not developed. However, before the new legislation could be broadly implemented, great difficulties arose. Most members of the existing officer corps became alienated from the new regime because of its political and social policies; and at the same time they found their authority over their troops disintegrating. Their reaction was widespread resignation and emigration which, within three and one half years, deprived the army of three-quarters of the officers of the Old Regime. Precisely when this exodus reached its peak, in late 1791 and early 1792, the national government found itself embroiled in a major European war. In these circumstances the process of professionalization was rapidly accelerated and modified to meet the exigencies of the moment, which demanded the most efficient officer corps that could be created in the shortest possible time.

The very rapidity with which the officer corps was renewed had important effects. For one thing, fully bureaucratic criteria had to be temporarily discarded for more empirical norms. An original emphasis on examinations, which presumed a special military education, gradually gave way to the more basic criterion of literacy. Simultaneously, emphasis on military experience, judged by length of service, increased. Moreover, the extent and the speed of the change made it essential, from a professional point of view, that some officers with prior experience in the higher echelons of the military hierarchy be kept in service, lest experienced leadership be totally eliminated. Thus, the very extensive and rapid turnover among officers which occurred between 1789 and 1793, while it expedited an acceptance of the new standards and aims by the new personnel, at the same time threatened the very process of professionalization itself. As it turned out, however, there was a sufficiently large number of officers, of field grade and above, who remained at their posts, out of conviction for the principles of the Revolution, a sense of patriotism or dedication to their military career, so that efficiency and continuity were maintained.

The government of the Revolution had, in the meantime, facilitated the pursuit of a military career. The abolition of venality and the opening of careers to talent would have been meaningless, if the government had not also provided officers with a sufficient income. The increased officer salaries which the National Assembly had voted in 1790 made it possible for men from all social classes to seek a career as an officer. Military service was a full-time occupation or profession for the new officer corps which had emerged by 1793.

One of the most striking changes in the army since 1789 was in the composition of the officer corps. The turnover in personnel had been greatest on the lowest officer levels, among lieutenants and captains. It was in these grades that most nobles had served before the Revolution; and because of this, *émigrés* from these ranks were the most numerous. At the same time, these were the grades most readily filled from the ranks of the non-commissioned officers of the Royal Army, who had adequate experience and the comparatively low skill levels to fulfil the functions of company officers. The superior grades of colonel and lieutenant colonel, which required a broader experience and more skill, were filled by men who had served as officers (majors, captains and lieutenants for the most part) before 1789. Many of these officers, at least 40%,[2] were nobles who had rejected the option of resignation or emigration and whose careers had benefited considerably from this decision.

As a group, general officers exhibited the least change in composition, although there had been a very large turnover in individual personnel. By 1793 nobles still constituted 70% of the generals; and the former court aristocracy was still the dominant social group among lieutenant generals. Men who had been at least field grade officers before the Revolution comprised most of the general officers, although a significant minority of brigadier generals had been company grade officers in 1789. The group of general officers in 1789 and 1793 was more similar in composition than was any other military echelon at the two dates. The basic reason for this was that of all echelons, general officers required the highest skill levels and were the most difficult to train and educate in a very brief time.

It was, therefore, necessary that men who had experience on regimental, brigade and division levels be kept in their functions or promoted to higher commands. If this had not been done the professional character, the military efficiency and, perhaps, the very existence of the French army would have been seriously jeopardized.

Of course, whatever the basic similarities within the various echelons in 1789 and 1793, the individuals were very different;[3] and this is not an insignificant change. Even more important, however, is that all personnel, new and old on all levels, were now subject to new professional criteria which were impersonal and blind to social origins, except in so far as these affected efficient functioning. By 1793 any similarities in the social composition of the officer corps of the Old Regime and of the Revolution were incidental to the professionalization of the officer corps and were not, as before 1789, an integral part of the political and social system.

 1. The criteria used to measure professionalization in this study are primarily empiri-
    cal and eclectic. However, Max Weber's description and analysis of bureaucrati-
    zation have provided a general theoretical framework which, although not explicitly
    followed, has greatly influenced my approach. See the section on 'Bureaucracy'
    in H. H. GERTH and C. WRIGHT MILLS, eds., *From Max Weber: Essays in Sociology*
    (New York: Oxford University Press, 1958), pp. 196–244.
 2. This, along with other factors, especially great regional variation, is an important
    reason why eighteenth century social history is often reconstructed from the local
    level up.

The officer corps of the old regime
 1. Raoul GIRARDET, *La société militaire dans la France contemporaine (1815–1939)*
    (Paris: Plon, 1953), p. 54.
 2. Louis TUETEY, *Les officiers sous l'ancien régime* (Paris: Plon, 1908), p. 153 and
    Louis DUSSIEUX, *L'armée en France: Histoire et Organisation depuis les temps
    anciens jusqu'à nos jours* (3 vols.; Versailles: Bernard, 1884), II, 312–13.
 3. TUETEY, *Les officiers*, pp. 134–37 and André CORVISIER, *L'armée française de la fin
    du XVIIᵉ siècle au ministère de Choiseul: Le Soldat* (2 vols.; Paris: Presses Univer-
    sitaires de France, 1964), I, 130.
 4. DUSSIEUX, *L'armée en France*, II, 301–04; Albert BABEAU, *La vie militaire sous
    l'ancien régime*; Vol. II: *Les Officiers* (Paris: Firmin-Didot, 1890), pp. 170–77; and
    Emile LÉONARD, *L'armée et ses problèmes au XVIIIᵉ siècle* (Paris: Plon, 1958),
    pp. 171–74.
 5. Chevalier DE MAUTORT, *Mémoires du chevalier de Mautort, Capitaine au régiment
    d'Austrasie, Chevalier de l'Ordre royal et militaire de Saint-Louis (1752–1802)*
    (Paris: Plon, 1895), *passim*, pp. 171–73.
 6. TUETEY, *Les officiers*, pp. 17–19.
 7. For an example of this, see MAUTORT, *Mémoires*, pp. 5–6 and 27.
 8. Further evidence of the intimate connection between nobility and military service is
    the phenomenon of noblemen serving in the ranks. See Samuel F. SCOTT, 'Les sol-
    dats gentilshommes au temps de la Révolution,' to appear in a forthcoming number
    of *Revue Historique de l'Armée*.
 9. BABEAU, *Les Officiers*, pp. 133 and 188; LÉONARD, *L'armée et ses problèmes*, p. 64;
    and Capitaine BACQUET, *L'Infanterie au XVIIIᵉ siècle: L'Organisation* (Paris:
    Berger-Levrault, 1907), p. 20.
10. TUETEY, *Les Officiers*, pp. 129–31 and CORVISIER, *L'armée française*, I, 142–43.
11. Arthur CHUQUET, 'Roture et noblesse dans l'armée royale,' *Séances et travaux de
    l'Académie des sciences morales et politiques*, CLXXV (1911), pp. 204–42 and
    TUETEY, *Les officiers*, pp. 88 and 90–94.
12. TUETEY, *Les officiers*, p. 99.
13. For a discussion of this problem, see *ibid.*, pp. 225–54.
14. *Ibid.*, pp. 281–88.
15. For a description of these aspects of officer life, see BABEAU, *Les Officiers*, pp. 222–
    56.
16. *Ibid.*, p. 188 and BACQUET, *L'Infanterie*, pp. 20–22.
17. Léon MENTION, *L'Armée de l'ancien régime* (Paris: Société française d'éditions
    d'art [1900]), p. 109.

51

18. Édouard DESBRIÈRE and Maurice SAUTAI, *La Cavalerie de 1740 à 1789* (Paris: Berger-Levrault, 1906), pp. 129 and 113.
19. MAUTORT, *Mémoires*, p. 351.
20. BABEAU, *Les Officiers*, p. 83 and GIRARDET, *La société militaire*, p. 51. The quotation is from Girardet (page 53).
21. TUETEY, *Les officiers*, p. 280.
22. *Ibid.*, pp. 37–38; LÉONARD, *L'armée et ses problèmes*, p. 178; and Hubert MÉTHIVIER, *L'ancien régime* (Paris: Presses Universitaires de France, 1961), p. 107.
23. BABEAU, *Les Officiers*, p. 68 and LÉONARD, *L'armée et ses problèmes*, p. 179.
24. LÉONARD, *L'armée et ses problèmes*, p. 195 and TUETEY, *Les officiers*, pp. 164–65 and 175.
25. CORVISIER, *L'armée française*, I, 131.
26. CHUQUET, 'Roture et noblesse,' p. 237 and Henri SÉE, *La France économique et sociale au XVIIIᵉ siècle* (4th ed.; Paris: Armand Colin, 1946), p. 77.
27. This breakdown was taken from a document dated 1775; see TUETEY, *Les officiers*, pp. 33-34.
28. Pierre VICTOR, Baron de BESENVAL, *Mémoires du Baron de Besenval* (2 vols.; Paris: Baudouin Frères, 1821), II, 189.
29. Quoted in Albert LATREILLE, *L'armée et la nation à la fin de l'ancien régime: Les derniers ministres de la guerre de la monarchie* (Paris: M. Imhaus & R. Chapelot, 1914), p. 167.
30. CORVISIER, *L'armée française*, I, 135–137.
31. *Ibid.*, II, 897–98.
32. LATREILLE, *L'armée et la nation*, pp. 6–7.
33. DESBRIÈRE and SAUTAI, *La Cavalerie de 1740 à 1789*, pp. 128–29.
34. P. CHALMIN, 'La désintégration de l'armée royale en France à la fin du XVIIIᵉ siècle', *Revue Historique de l'Armée* (February, 1964), pp. 76–79.
35. Général SUSANE, *Histoire de l'infanterie française* (5 vols.; Paris: J. Dumaire, 1876), I, 308.
36. LATREILLE, *L'armée et la nation*, p. 77.
37. Albert DURUY, *L'Armée Royale en 1789* (Paris: Calmann-Lévy, 1888), p. 75 and Henri CHOPPIN, *Les insurrections militaires en 1790* (Paris: L. Laveur, 1903), pp. 34–35.
38. TUETEY, *Les officiers*, pp. 180–81.
39. Albert SOBOUL, *La France à la veille de la Révolution*, Vol. I: *Économie et Société* (Paris: Société d'Édition d'Enseignement Supérieur, 1966), p. 84.
40. Despite the higher estimates (one-quarter to one-third) generally given for the proportion of commoners in the officer corps, the most recent research of David Bien and Charles Wrong both indicate that 10% is much closer to the truth and that these commoners were almost exclusively officers of fortune.

The revolution and the officer corps

1. Barthélemy PACQUET DU HAUT-JUSSÉ, *Les origines de la Révolution en Bretagne* (2 vols.; Paris: Perrin, 1885), I, 152.
2. For an eyewitness account of this phenomenon, see MAUTORT, *Mémoires*, p. 363.
3. Albert MATHIEZ, *The French Revolution*, trans. by Catherine Alison Phillips (New York: Grosset & Dunlap, 1964), p. 33.
4. L. HARTMANN, *Les officiers de l'armée royale et la Révolution* (Paris: Félix Alcan, 1910), pp. 78–80 and Spenser WILKINSON, *The French Army before Napoleon* (Oxford: Clarendon Press, 1915), p. 103.

5. Quoted in Georges SAGNIER, *La désertion dans la Pas-de-Calais de 1792 à 1802* (Blangermont, Pas-de-Calais: Chez l'auteur, 1965), pp. 20–21.

6. LÉONARD, *L'armée et ses problèmes*, p. 295; Ernest D'HAUTERIVE, *L'armée sous la Révolution, 1789–1794* (Paris: Ollendorff, 1894), p. 43; and Jules LEVERRIER, *La naissance de l'armée nationale, 1789–1794* (Paris: Éditions Sociales Internationales, 1939), p. 26.

7. Jules MICHELET, *History of the French Revolution*, trans. by Charles Cocks (Chicago: University of Chicago Press, 1967), pp. 129 and 136.

8. The best account of this whole episode is Pierre Caron, 'La tentative de contre-révolution de juin-juillet 1789,' *Revue d'histoire moderne et contemporaine*, VIII (1906–07), pp. 5–34 and 649–78.

9. Since 17 June 1789 the Third Estate, along with some deputies of the First Estate, had allocated this title for themselves. Reluctantly accepted by Louis XVI, this status was confirmed by the events of 14 July.

10. HARTMANN, *Les officiers*, pp. 98 and 104–07.

11. *Ibid.*, 108–26 and Donald GREER, *The Incidence of the Emigration during the French Revolution* (Gloucester, Massachusetts: Peter Smith, 1966), p. 23.

12. HARTMANN, *Les officiers*, p. 130.

13. MATHIEZ, *French Revolution*, p. 75.

14. GREER, *Incidence of Emigration*, p. 23.

15. D'HAUTERIVE, *L'armée sous la Révolution*, pp. 101–03; HARTMANN, *Les officiers*, pp. 134–35; and CHOPPIN, *Les insurrections militaires*, pp. 157–86.

16. There are numerous estimations of these numbers and some variations among all of them. There is, however, general consensus about the excessive number. See, for example, DESBRIÈRE and SAUTAI, *La Cavalerie de 1740 à 1789*, p. 89; HARTMANN, *Les officiers*, pp. 3–5; LEVERRIER, *La naissance de l'armée nationale*, p. 23; D'HAUTERIVE, *L'armée sous la Révolution*, p. 26; DURUY, *L'Armée Royale*, pp. 83–84 and 91; and Alphonse JUIN, *Trois siècles d'obéissance militaire,1650-1963* (Paris: Plon, 1964), p. 65.

17. According to the Law Gouvion-Saint-Cyr of 1818, to become an officer one had to either have two years service as an NCO or be a graduate of a military school; to be promoted to a higher grade, one had to have served four years in the next lower rank; and through the grade of lieutenant colonel two-thirds of the promotions were based on seniority and one-third was left to the king's choice. See Guillaume DE BERTIER DE SAUVIGNY, *The Bourbon Restoration*, trans. by Lynn M. Case (Philadelphia: University of Pennsylvania, 1966), p. 148.

18. HARTMANN, *Les officiers*, pp. 211–15.

19. Again, Mautort provides an eyewitness account: 'The most intriguing of our sergeants, the whole class of our officers of fortune, our greatest enemies, already saw themselves invested with our grades'. (*Mémoires*, pp. 396–97).

20. See, for example, the Maclure Collection of French Revolutionary Materials (University of Pennsylvania), vol. 842, 'Rapport fait à l'Assemblée Nationale sur l'état actuel de l'armée par M. BUREAUX DE PUSY.' This document is not dated, but certainly appeared in mid–1791.

21. GREER, *Incidence of Emigration*, pp. 24–25.

22. Sebastien JOSEPH, Baron de COMEAU DE CHARRY, *Souvenirs des guerres d'Allemagne pendant la Révolution et l'Empire* (Paris: Plon, 1900), pp. 44–45.

23. J. REVOL, *Histoire de l'armée française* (Paris: Larousse, 1929), p. 133 and HARTMANN, *Les officiers*, p. 288.

24. GREER, *Incidence of Emigration*, p. 26 and HARTMANN, *Les officiers*, p. 352.

25. Maclure Collection, vol. 842, 'Décret de l'Assemblée Nationale du 30 Juin 1791, Concernant le Changement des Drapeaux dans l'Armée Française'.
26. Mautort recounts his own experience with this in his *Mémoires*, pp. 397–98.
27. *Ibid.*, p. 403.
28. D'HAUTERIVE, *L'armée sous la Révolution*, pp. 167–70. The names of the regiments of the line army had been changed to numbers in January 1791, in another, minor application of bureaucratic principles.
29. Arthur CHUQUET, *La première invasion prussienne (11 août-2 septembre 1792)* (Paris: Léopold Cerf, 1886), p. 40 and Édouard DESBRIÈRE and Maurice SAUTAI, *La cavalerie pendant la Révolution, du 14 juillet 1789 au 26 juin 1794: La Crise* (Paris: Berger-Levrault, 1907), p. 41.
30. HARTMANN, *Les officiers*, pp. 440–41.
31. Paul-Marie DE GORCE, *The French Army: A Military-Political History*, trans. by Kenneth Douglas (New York: George Braziller, 1963), pp. 20–21.
32. On this point, see GERTH and MILLS, *From Max Weber*, pp. 224–31.
33. GREER, *Incidence of Emigration*, pp. 90, 112 and 33. Greer's estimate of the number of noble officers who emigrated is disturbing, since he classified all non-nobles as bourgeois and includes under this heading 'bourgeois or recently ennobled' (p. 90).

The new officer corps

1. The archival research which provided the basic data on regimental officers was done under the auspices of a Research Training Fellowship from the Social Science Research Council. In addition, many of the concepts and techniques employed in this study were developed when I participated in this program.
2. This information is preserved at the Archives de la Guerre (henceforth abbreviated as A.G.) in Ministère de la Guerre, État-Major de l'Armée, Archives Historiques, Série Xb, cartons 162–198. This very valuable series was brought to my attention by my friend and colleague, Jean-Paul Bertaud.
3. A.G., Contrôles des Officiers, Révolution et Empire (uncoded). The registers of cavalry officers were kept by regiment. They were begun in 1788 (except for units established after then) and continued through the Empire.
4. A.G., Série Xd, cartons 3, 7, 12 and 16.
5. For this purpose, the series A.G., Ministère de la Guerre, Archives Administratives, Classement Général Alphabétique: Officiers, 1791–1847 was used. This is a huge series, almost four thousand cartons, which contain assorted papers on various officers. Only a portion of the officers who served between 1791 and 1847 have any papers here, and these are often of little value.
6. François SICARD, *Histoire des institutions militaires Français* (4 vols. plus atlas; Paris: J. Corréard, 1834), II, 294–301; III, 16–20; and III, 247–50. These references give the authorized strength for units in the three major branches.
7. Georges SIX, *Dictionnaire biographique des généraux et amiraux français de la Révolution et de l'Empire (1792–1814)* (2 vols.; Paris: Saffroy, 1934).
8. This information on the ages of officers before 1789 is based primarily on the research of Charles Wrong. Prof. Wrong studied nine infantry regiments and one chasseur unit from 1775 to 1789. He has generously permitted me to use his findings.
9. Arthur Chuquet estimates that the artillery lost only half as many officers as the other branches. See *La première invasion prussienne*, pp. 40 and 82.
10. See A.G., Xb, 180.

11. See Contrôles des Officiers, Révolution et Empire, the register for the 4th Hussars, volume two, page 71.
12. In 1806, one quarter of all the regimental and battalion commanders in the Prussian army were older than sixty years of age. See Gordon CRAIG, *The Politics of the Prussian Army, 1640–1945* (Oxford: Clarendon Press, 1964), p. 26.
13. Samuel F. SCOTT, 'The French Revolution and the Line Army, 1787–1793' (unpublished Ph. D. dissertation, University of Wisconsin, 1968), pp. 163–64.
14. The research of Prof. Charles Wrong also substantiates this conclusion.
15. The proportion of foreigners among junior officers is comparable to the proportion of foreigners in the ranks in 1789. See SCOTT, 'French Revolution and the Line Army,' p. 164.
16. See the report on the civil and military status of officers in this regiment, prepared for the Convention in the spring of 1793, in A.G., Xb, 192.
17. This could not be done in the case of cavalry officers because their domicile was recorded too infrequently.
18. Marcel REINHARD, 'La population des villes: Sa mesure sous la Révolution et l'Empire', *Population*, IX (1954), pp. 281–283.
19. The basis for ascertaining the population of cities and towns in France in 1789 was the Archives Nationales, Série D^{iv} bis, Dossier 47 ('États de Population'). This very useful document was brought to my attention by Prof. Gilbert Shapiro of the University of Pittsburgh. In certain instances, this source was supplemented by Ministère des Travaux Publics, de l'Agriculture et du Commerce, *Statistique de France* (Paris: Imprimerie Royale, 1837), pp. 267–79.
20. The nearly complete absence of this kind of data on cavalry officers makes it impossible to reach any conclusions about the domiciles of these officers.
21. SCOTT, 'French Revolution and Line Army', p. 185.
22. Literacy had been higher in the urbanized areas of France since the seventeenth century. See Michel FLEURY and Pierre VALMARY, 'Les progrès de l'instruction élémentaire de Louis XIV à Napoléon III, d'après l'enquête de Louis Maggiolo (1877–1879)', *Population*, XII (January-March 1957), pp. 71–92.
23. SCOTT, 'French Revolution and Line Army', pp. 219–20.
24. For these two examples, see the reports on officers drawn up for the Convention in the spring of 1793 in A.G., Xb, 195 and 189 respectively.
25. See the same type of report in A.G., Xb, 173.
26. A.G., Xb, 198.
27. This information was in a report on officers serving in the Army of the West. It can be found in the register for the 14th Cavalry Regiment (later 23rd Dragoons) in A.G., Contrôles des Officiers, Révolution et Empire.
28. In the Year II (1793–94) an incomplete report on the cavalry indicated that in forty-nine regiments there were still 117 officers (of approximately 1450) who were nobles. See DESBRIÈRE and SAUTAI, *La cavalerie pendant la Révolution*, pp. 260–61.
29. An example of this kind of officer was Captain Meras of the 1st Artillery Regiment. Although a noble, he had joined this regiment in 1764 as an enlisted man and had worked his way through the ranks before being commissioned. In Nivôse of the Year II (December 1793-January 1794) the officers, NCO's and soldiers of his regiment wrote to the Minister of War to attest to his ability and loyalty. See the dossier for Meras in A.G., Classement Général Alphabétique: Officiers, 1791–1847, carton 2643.
30. This has been frequently stated; recently by Alfred COBBAN, who seems to regard this fact as something of a refutation of Marxist or sociological historians. See

The Social Interpretation of the French Revolution (Cambridge: The University Press, 1964), pp. 84-85.

31. During the period of the Revolution, less than 1.5% of the men in the ranks of the line army were clerks in public and private employment. See SCOTT, 'French Revolution and Line Army', p. 219.
32. *Ibid.*, 219 and 227.
33. *Ibid.*, 220.
34. FLEURY and VALMARY, 'Les progrès de l'instruction', pp. 84-89.
35. In almost half the cases there was no indication of literacy or illiteracy. However, in 1 142 cases the ability to read and/or write was indicated.
36. Samuel SCOTT and Jean-Paul BERTAUD, 'Le 104ᵉ Régiment de ligne: Gardes françaises et gardes nationaux parisiens aux armées de la Révolution (1792-1793)', *Études de la région parisienne* (October 1966), pp. 10-11.
37. Unless indicated otherwise, the data on all general officers serving as of 28 February 1793 is drawn from SIX, *Dictionnaire biographique*, vols. I and II.
38. All general officers who held the rank of lieutenant general were included in this category, even if they might have been at the same time generals in chief or commanders of armies.
39. Provisional brigadier generals (or *maréchaux-de-camp*) are treated in the same way as those whose rank had already been confirmed. These provisional generals were in fact serving as general officers on the sample date; and all but two of them were confirmed in their rank within the following three months.
40. SIX, *Dictionnaire biographique*, II, 499.
41. *Ibid.*, I, 502.
42. These are minimum percentages since only *explicit* references to combat experience by Six have been taken into consideration.
43. Of 142 generals in the Prussian army in 1806, sixty-two (43.6%) were over sixty years of age. See CRAIG, *Politics of the Prussian Army*, p. 26.
44. Georges SIX, *Les généraux de la Révolution et de l'Empire* (Paris: Bordas, 1947), p. 25.
45. The discussion of the noble colonels and lieutenant colonels of 1793 applies, in essence, to the generals drawn from this same social group. See above, p. 39.
46. For the numbers of general officers in the French army before the Revolution, see DURUY, *L'Armée Royale*, pp. 83-84.
47. It is impossible to adequately describe the social background of the commoners who were generals on 28 February 1793. Six's biographical dictionary provides explicit information on only fifteen such officers. Seven of these were from families connected with military service, sons of officers or of officials of the Ministry of War. Three were sons of civilian officials under the monarchy. Two were from the professional middle class, the son of a lawyer and the son of a doctor. And three were from the popular classes: a shoemaker, a brewer and a glazier.

Conclusion

1. The 'grassroots' character of demands for bureaucratization has been recently pointed out by Sasha R. WEITMAN in 'The Sociological Thesis of Tocqueville's *The Old Regime and the French Revolution*', *Social Research*, XXXIII (Autumn 1966), pp. 402-03. Weitman focuses on demands concerning the administrative apparatus; but such demands concerned other institutions as well, e.g. the military.
2. The reasons for this being a minimum estimate and given above; see pp. 37-39.
3. For the personnel changes among general officers, see above, p. 47.

Politics and Ideology

Elements of Military Conservatism: Traditional and Modern

B. ABRAHAMSSON

BENGT ABRAHAMSSON, born in Sweden in 1937, is Associate Professor of Sociology in Stockholm. During 1962–65 he conducted military sociological research at the Institute of Military Psychology in Stockholm. He is the author of *Military Professionalization and Political Power* (1971) and various papers on the military (see Jacques van Doorn (ed.), *Armed Forces and Society*, 1968, and *ibid.* (ed.), *Military Profession and Military Regimes*, 1969). Among his other fields of interest are exchange theory, the sociology of education, and organizational sociology. From January, 1972 he is the editor of the Scandinavian journal *Acta Sociologica*.

One of the most commonly noted characteristics of the military mind is a marked conservatism. It forms a cornerstone in Huntington's theory of civil-military relations[1]; it is a recurring theme in Alfred Vagts's historical account of militaristic thinking, and in Gordon Craig's analysis of the political interventionism of the Prussian military;[2] and it is a main element in Janowitz's treatment of the identity and ideology of American military leaders.[3]

Opinion surveys of the American, West German, and Swedish officer corps lend strong support to the hypothesis of military conservatism (table 1). The data show that as far as the Bundeswehr officers and their Swedish colleagues are concerned they deviate strongly in their political opinions from those of the population at large. No comparable population figures are available for the United States but, as Janowitz points out, 'it is clear that higher education is associated with a greater concentration of liberal attitudes in the population at large. Thus, the emphasis on conservative attachments is even more noteworthy, since they constitute a group in which higher education does not weaken conservative orientations.'[4]

It may be argued that officers show conservative attitudes because they constitute a socially privileged group; as is well known, professionals are more often conservative than liberal in their political tendencies.[5] This can be only a partial explanation, however, since occupational groups with an even more pronounced elitist character often show less conservative preferences. For instance, data on voting patterns among big businessmen, business managers, high officials in private service and higher grade civil servants in the 1964 election to the Swedish second chamber show that only 46 per cent voted conservative[6]. This may be compared to the military data collected in the 1962 survey. The fact that 85 per cent of the officers preferred the Conservative party suggests that the military group is strikingly homogeneous in its political sympathies. The high proportion of conservative officers in the Swedish military is even more noteworthy given its relatively egalitarian recruitment (59 per cent middle or lower class).[7] A pattern similar to the Swedish one is exhibited by data from West Germany, showing a much higher proportion of CDU/CSU sympathizers among Bundeswehr officers than among civilian self-employed and professionals (see table 1).

Explanations of why conservatism is particularly attractive to the military can be based only to a limited extent on social position; very few inferences with regard to political attitudes can be drawn from data on social background. Instead, we have to ask: how is it possible that such a high proportion of the officers have conservative sympathies when we know that the military is one of the most broadly recruited of professions? To answer this, we have to take into account, (a) the set of values that are functional to military professional performance, (b) the

Table 1. Military political preferences
Political identifications among U.S. Army officers. Year: 1954[a]. Per cent

	Conser- vative	Some- what conser- vative	Some- what liberal	Liberal	No answer	Total	Number
Academy Graduate	27.4	42.1	18.9	6.3	5.3	100.0	95
Non-Academy Graduate	23.3	46.6	23.3	4.3	2.5	100.0	116

Political identifications among soldiers in the Bundeswehr. Year: 1960[b]. Per cent

Question: Which of the political parties comes closest to your own position?

	CDU/ CSU	FDP	SPD	Other parties	No in- forma- tion	Total	Number
Recruit	47.5	6.4	24.0	3.7	18.0	99.6	1302
Corporal	55.7	3.6	24.1	1.9	14.4	99.7	1509
Sergeant	74.2	3.2	13.1	3.5	5.6	99.6	595
Senior NCO	76.9	4.3	11.6	3.3	3.5	99.6	309
Officer candidate	73.5	11.4	7.3	2.7	4.7	99.6	612
Officer (Lt Capt)	74.6	11.5	4.8	3.9	4.8	99.6	108
General population, 1964	34	6	34	2	24	100.0	
Self-employed and professionals, 1964	40	12	19	2	27	100.0	

Political identifications among Swedish officers. Year: 1962ᶜ. Per cent
Question: With which political party do you sympathize the most?

	Conservatives	Center Party (Agrarians)	Liberals	Social Democrats	Communists	Total	Number
Officers	85.1	1.7	9.3	3.9	0.0	100.0	781
Electorate, local election, 1962	15.5	13.1	17.1	50.5	3.8	100.0	

Conservative preferences among Swedish Army officers. By rank. Year: 1962ᵈ. Per cent
Base numbers within parentheses. Per cent sympathizing with Conservatives.

	Second lieutenant	First lieutenant	Captain	Major
Army: infantry	60 (16)	86 (64)	90 (80)	95 (20)
Army: other branches	— (7)	81 (88)	86 (139)	94 (37)

a. *Source*: Janowitz, *The Professional Soldier*, p. 240 (table 29). These figures relatively accurately also represent political identifications among Pentagon officers (1954) and among Navy and Air Force officers. Cf. *ibid.*, pp. 236–241.
b. *Sources*: Military, Eric Waldman, *The Goose-Step Is Verboten*, Glencoe, Ill., Free Press, 1964, p. 216, table 4. Population, Noelle and Neumann, *Jahrbuch der öffentlichen Meinung, 1958–1964*, pp. 3 ff, and EMNID, *Informationen*, Nos. 13 and 26 (1964). Quoted from Lewis J. Edinger, *Politics in Germany*, Boston, 1968: Little, Brown, and Company.
c. *Source*: Abrahamsson, *Anpassning och avgångsbenägenhet bland militärt befäl*, p. 69.
d. *Source*: Bengt Abrahamsson, 'The Ideology of an Elite', in J. A. A. van Doorn (ed.), *Armed Forces and Society*, The Hague, 1968: Mouton, p. 75.

historical traditions of the military and, (c) the relation of the military to other influential groups, particularly business and industrial elites.

As has been noted by Herbert McClosky, among others, the notion of man as fundamentally aggressive is an inherent part of conservative ideology. McClosky, in an article on the elements of conservatism, with reference to the works of Edmund Burke, Russell Kirk, Clinton Rossiter, and others[8], points to the agreement among them on the treatment of a number of topics, some of which are:

> Man is a creature of appetite and will, 'governed more by emotion than by reason' (Kirk), in whom 'wickedness, unreason, and the urge to violence lurk always behind the curtain of civilized behavior' (Rossiter). He is a fallen creature, doomed to imperfection, and inclined to license and anarchy.[9]

Since society cannot be held together under such generally hostile conditions, it has to impose certain restriction on the individuals:

> Order, authority, and community are the primary defence against the impulse of violence and anarchy. The superiority of duties over rights and the need to strengthen the stabilizing institutions of society, especially the church, the family, and, above all, private property.

McClosky supports his analysis with data from a sample of Minnesota residents. Conservatism is shown to correlate with certain personality variables, like dominance, alienation, hostility, and pessimism. Conservatives, oftener than liberals, tended to endorse items like 'duties are more important than rights', 'you can't change human nature', 'the world is too complicated to be understood by anyone but experts', and so forth. These tendencies remained when such factors as education, occupation, socio-economic status, and possible response set were controlled for. McClosky summarizes:

> These tendencies may also lie at the root of the conservative inclination to regulate and control man; to ensure that he will not violate the conditions necessary for order; to train him to value duty, obedience, and conformity; and to surround him with stabilizing influences, like property, church, and the family.
> The high values placed on authority, leadership, and natural hierarchy, and on an elite to guide and check the rest of mankind, apparently derive from the same set of psychological impulses.

McClosky's examination of the conservative syndrome coincides well with Huntington's analysis of the military mind, which is echoed also by Coates and Pellegrin in their *Military Sociology*:[10]

> The military man concedes that he holds a pessimistic view of the nature of man. He believes, however, that his conception is the correct one.
> As Huntington explains it, the military view of man emphasizes his propensity for conflict, violence is 'rooted in the permanent biological and psychological nature of men'. Man is weak, selfish, irrational. ... Man being what he is, conflict is inevitable.[11]

Low faith in people has been shown by Rosenberg to correlate with pessimistic attitudes towards the possibilities of avoiding war.[12] Table 2 shows a cross-classification of the variable 'faith in people' with answers to the statement 'The most we can hope to accomplish is the partial elimination of war'.

Table 2. Faith in people

	High					Low
	1	2	3	4	5	6
Agree	32	39	43	50	52	59
Disagree	51	43	44	40	33	36
Undecided	17	18	13	10	15	5
Total	100	100	100	100	100	100

Source: ROSENBERG, *op. cit.*, table 9.

The lower the position on the 'faith' variable, the higher the proportion of 'pessimists' on the matter of elimination of war.

Thus far, the data cited have served only to demonstrate the general interrelationships of conservatism with other variables for non-military respondents. But for professionals who are preoccupied with matters of war and war preparations, a pessimistic view of man and of the prospects of avoiding war seems to be fundamentally in accordance with daily occupational practices, and McClosky's findings seem relevant to the military setting. Conversely, an optimistic view of the possibilities of bringing about disarmament would threaten the basic professional values of the military. As has been shown above, alarmism (i.e., the belief in the high probability of war) among officers is positively related to military rank and to work adjustment, supporting the notion that a 'pessimistic' view tends to facilitate performance in the military role.[13] And a study on Swedish reserve officers showed that they less often than comparable groups agree to the statement 'Man can learn to avoid war'.[14]

McClosky also suggested that there is 'a conservative inclination to regulate and control man; to ensure that he will not violate the conditions necessary for order; to train him to value duty, obedience, and conformity'. The functional importance of such attitudes to the military role is substantiated in a study by Korpi, showing that Swedish Army NCO aspirants who planned to attend cadet school or who actually attended such schools were more authoritarian than comparable groups of non-aspirants.[15]

To summarize, military men as a professional group seem to be conservative partly because many of the values and attitudes that are part of the conservative syndrome appear to facilitate, and tend to support, adjustment to the professional role. Conversely, high faith in the rationality and reason of man, the belief that man is capable of eliminating war, and an 'optimistic' view in international relations tend to be incompatible with successful professional performance.

B. ASSOCIATIONS WITH RULING ELITES

As Mosca pointed out, one reason why officers in nineteenth-century England and the United States did not revolt against civil authority may have been that they were recruited from the very same stratum that made up the ruling elites.[16] Although the generality of this thesis is questionable – the Prussian military, for instance, was also recruited from the elite stratum but this did not restrain the officers to any great extent from political manoeuvring – we may expect the ruling elites and the military to agree with each other on the necessity of the social status quo, and to be suspicious about rapid and seemingly disorderly social transformations. As Vagts has asserted, the military have traditionally not been in the forefronts of revolutions, but rather the contrary:

As it takes many years to organize and equip an army, a long-time stability is necessary in the structure and functions of the society in which the preparation of the army is made. Hence the army by the very nature of things depends for its existence, honor, emoluments, and privileges upon the order in which it takes form; and in self-defence, if nothing more, it is conservative in relation to the order in which it thrives, whether that order be agrarian, capitalistic, or communistic.
The great modern revolutions have been foreign to and remote from armies; armies have been closely associated with suppressions, reactions, and counterrevolutions.
The resistance of armies and their leaders to such revolutions is based to some extent on their professional conservatism, which loves order, sees order merely in the established arrangements, and cannot discern a new one amid popular turmoil....
Clinging to tradition, which in itself is a means for him to maintain authority, the soldier is averse to acknowledging and embracing changes forced upon him, particularly if they do not appear to favor his immediate interests.[17]

66

The major internal values of the profession are in accord with the basic elements of the conservative tradition. These values stem from the feudal heritage of the military, its historical role as a guardian of the status quo, and its traditional ties with ruling establishments bent on preserving rather than changing existing social and political patterns. Many officers of the old French army chose to emigrate and to join the forces of the First Coalition, fighting the Revolution from outside; others stayed behind to work against the Revolution from within the regiments.[18] And the officers of the Tsarist Russian Army, in spite of the fact that the expansion during the First World War had brought in a large influx from the peasant class and the intelligentsia, were more often to be found among the ranks of the White than of the Red Army during the Civil War.[19]

When the fascist movements started to grow strong in Europe, officers were often eager to support them, since the policies favored by fascist leaders brought a number of seeming advantages to the military establishment.

Fascism fulfilled many an old daydream of officers everywhere; for instance, it abolished the politician, with his awkward queries on budgetary matters, and at the same time it effectively stopped criticism on the conduct of military affairs through press or books or from the platform. ... A further lure was the fact that military men were conceded the highest rank in society under fascism; military institutions furnished the examples for all other organizations in the state. ... Besides such apparent conveniences to army men, fascism provided enlarged armies, bringing rapid promotion.[20]

Although traditionally rightist movements and ideas have had a much greater appeal to military men than the movements and ideas of the left, there are some obvious exceptions. In countries where the struggle against landholding, industrial, and/or aristocratic elites has been carried out by armed revolutionary forces, the military leaders of these forces will typically exhibit a less conservative inclination than in countries where change has been more gradual and where it does not involve any part of the armies in the overthrow of long existing regimes. Thus, the military organizations of revolutionary France and of Russia during and immediately after the revolution contained considerable progressive elements.

But again, once the revolutionary struggle is over and the period of consolidation sets in, armies tend to acquire the role of supporters of the status quo, and the officer corps tends to become part of the social establishment. As Vagts says, the army depends 'upon the order in which it takes form'; and when that order becomes consolidated, the army will be its primary support.

An officer corps emerging from revolutionary war campaigns will be relatively unprofessionalized, partly because of its need to recruit officers from all possible groups, and partly because the joint revolutionary-military role counteracts the isolation of the military and its inclinations toward corporate autonomy. A case may therefore be made that professionalism and conservatism tend to develop together, and that professionalized post-revolutionary armies tend to loose their political heritage. For instance, according to Garthoff, there are a number of similarities between the Imperial Russian Army and the Soviet Army in 1935-65, both being more professionalized than the Red Army of the 1920's and early 1930's. Beginning with the mid-1930's, a number of demands from the new officer class were met. 'In 1935, ranks were restored, except for general officer grades, which were not given until 1940; moreover, the creation of the rank of marshal was an 'imperial' addition that had not even been found in the pre-revolutionary army. New salary scales not only favored the military, but also reflected the growing gap between officers and enlisted men, and between junior and senior officers. Hundreds of special stores, theaters, and clubs were established for military officers and their families. The emerging new caste of officers were given lessons in French, in polo, in dancing, and in the social graces'.[21] In 1942 the *pogony* (golden epaulettes) were reintroduced, and officers were granted the opportunity to send their sons to new exclusive cadet schools, established in 1943.[22]

In the face of such preferences for at least a partial return to earlier practices and privileges, intensive political education is employed as a means of retaining the revolutionary heritage. In the Soviet Army today, about twenty per cent of the soldiers' training time is devoted to political instruction.[23] Almost all officers (93 per cent) are members of either the Communist Party or the Komsomol.[24] But in spite of this, as the revolutionary experience recedes into history and as new technological and highly complex demands are put on the Soviet military, it is not unlikely that it will continue 'to develop as a technically-oriented, highly professional, and essentially apolitical instrument of the state';[25] 'apolitical' in this context being synonymous with 'de-revolutionized'.

To sum up, although armies may be successful instruments for popular revolutions, once their leaders develop into a professionalized officer corps they will be less than effective as a force for social change. The officer in a professional army is prone to prefer a political status quo and to view with suspicion attempts to rapidly transform the social structure. As Huntington has pointed out with regard to the u.s. military, professionalism fits well into a conservative political setting. 'Only an environment which is sympathetically conservative will permit American military leaders to combine the political power which society thrusts upon them with the military professionalism without which society cannot endure'.[26]

C. MILITARY TIES WITH BUSINESS AND INDUSTRIAL ELITES

Although the professional military man prefers traditional order and social stability to social change, it would be a mistake to infer that military conservatism applies equally strongly to *technological* change. On the contrary, one may with greater justification propose the thesis that the military profession from its beginning has been closely associated with technological innovations. In military education, as we have seen, technical schools were often established well before schools for the infantry and cavalry. In the United States, West Point was early in the forefront of technical education.

This thesis is not without qualification, however. A number of examples of resistance by military men to military inventions do exist, particularly with regard to the period of the first World War. In 1915 the French General Headquarters turned down a proposal of development of the tank weapon characterizing the new vehicles as 'engines not susceptible of lending themselves to any military use'. In England, Haig and Kitchener only reluctantly accepted the machine gun, Haig calling it 'a much overrated weapon'. The equipment of the English forces with the machine gun was to a large extent the effect of Lloyd George's concern about the waste of men being moved down by the Germans who had been more quick in adopting the new weapon[27]. Military men on the Allied side in the war were less prone to advocate the development of heavy artillery, which contributed to the superiority of the Central Powers in this field during the beginning of the war.[28] French politicians in 1910 pointed to the military use of aviation, getting the answer from Foch, Director of the École de Guerre, that 'for the army, the aeroplane is zero'.[29]

It is questionable, however, how far one can generalize from these cases. First, it seems that the resistance to weapons innovations often came from the older generation of officers while the younger took active part in the development of new weapons. For instance, while a few English generals were reluctant to adopt the tank as a weapon, junior officers played an important role in its development and promotion for war use.[30] Second, the resistance to new weapons by English military leaders may have been largely caused by a *déformation professionnelle*

69

resulting from their experiences in the Boer War, in which horsemanship had counted for more than trench warfare, barbed wire, and heavy artillery. As Lloyd George writes in his memoirs, when the First World War broke out the English generals had the most important lessons of their art to learn.

Their brains were cluttered with useless lumber, packed in every niche and corner. ... For instance, take their ridiculous cavalry obsession.
In a war where heavy artillery and engineering and trench work were more in demand than in any war in history we were led by soldiers trained in the cavalry. Haig was persuaded to the end of the war that a time would come when his troopers would one day charge through the gap made by his artillery and convert the German defeat into a headlong scamper for the Rhine. Needless to say, that chance never came. ... The Generals themselves were at least four-fifths amateurs, hampered by the wrong training.[31]

Third, there was no marked conservatism exhibited against some other new means of warfare, most importantly the U-boat and the poison gas which, in the judgment of Vagts, the Germans employed 'prematurely and too experimentally'.[32] And after all, perhaps the most epochmaking innovation of them all, the aeroplane, was making rapid headway. In France, the machine so scornfully turned down by Foch in 1910 was manufactured in no less than 50 000 units during the period of 1915-18; and at the armistice in 1918, the French plane factories employed 186 000 workers. Similarly, during the war Germany produced 48 000 planes in 33 factories.[33]

The situation after the Second World War has been characterized by continuous technological experimentation, witnessed in the developments of systems like the Nike-Zeus, Nike X, Sentinel (all three anti-ballistic missile systems), the Fractional Orbit Bombarding System (FOBS), the Ballistic Missile Early Warning System (BMEWS), Semi-Automatic Ground Environment air-defence system (SAGE), Multiple Independently Targetable Re-entry Vehicles (MIRV), missiles like the Polaris, Poseidon, Minuteman I, II, and III, and Titan, and aircraft such as the nuclear-powered plane (development cost $1 025 billion), the B-70 bomber ($1.5 billion), and the Seamaster jet-powered sea-plane ($361 million), the three latter now being judged as 'unfeasible and wasteful' development projects.[34]

With the increasing emphasis on technological development, the contacts and personnel alliances between the military and industrial establishments have tended to widen. In March, 1969, Senator William Proxmire released figures showing that the 100 most prominent defence contractors in the United States employ 'some 2 072 retired military officers of the rank of colonel or Navy captain or above' (compared to

70

721 in 1959).[35] The Sentinel ABM system alone has been estimated to involve more than 15 000 companies for its development and production.[36] The impact of such developments has caused the American debate on the military-industrial complex to change perspective. At the publication of Mills's *The Power Elite* the argument to a large extent was about whether the military-industrial complex *existed* or not; today, one more commonly finds arguments *for* or *against* it, and the question of its existence seems to be definitely answered in the affirmative.[37]

The far-reaching coincidence of military and industrial interests may be expected to cause a modification and 'modernization' of the traditional military conservatism. It should also be pointed out that the tremendous growth of logistical functions especially during the present century has made the military manager responsive to economic planning. He is now part of the administration of what is almost a replica of civilian society (but for certain production and reproduction functions). Hence it seems only natural that, as Janowitz has expressed it, traditional conservative identifications should become 'compatible with a belief in the need for continuous and decisive governmental intervention in the economic order', especially of course if such intervention is advantageous for the military establishment. 'The military approach to the economic system centers on the issue of the military budget, on what, theoretically, the nation needs and can afford for national security.'[38]

Today, to a large extent, major economic power-groups have replaced the old aristocratic elites as the primary supporters of the military system, and we may expect military conservatism to exhibit a more up-to-date profile as it becomes modeled upon the political outlooks of business and industry. However, the new outlooks do not necessarily guarantee a more liberal attitude to major social reforms since, as Janowitz emphasizes, the military's views of the economic system are primarily motivated by professional self-interest.

SUMMARY AND CONCLUSIONS

1. Military conservatism in part reflects dominant elements in 'classical' conservatism. It tends to emphasize order, hierarchy, and the 'stabilizing' institutions of society (church, family, private property). It maintains a pessimistic image of human nature and is dubious of the prospects of avoiding or eliminating war, such pessimism facilitating adjustment to the military professional role. Conversely, an optimistic image of man, optimism about the possibilities of avoiding war,

71

and radical values are at variance with successful professional performance.

2. The military's historical associations with ruling elites have tended to support and reinforce conservative values, with the exception of cases where armies have recent revolutionary experiences. Conservatism and professionalization may be assumed to be mutually supportive.

3. A third and more recent element in military conservatism stems from its ties with modern industrial and technological elites, leading to an acceptance of rapid technological developments. This does not, however, necessarily imply a more progressive attitude to major social reforms.

4. Managerial training and professional experiences in running the highly complex military establishment will increase the confidence of military leaders that they are competent to also administer the civilian sphere (since the military replicates a large number of functions found in civilian society). To the extent that they command enough power to bring about this transfer of skills and to intervene in the political process, military political ideology will adversely affect programs aiming at social equality. It will support technological research and development, particularly if such programs directly (through arms and weapons systems) or indirectly (through the development of transport, communications, etc.) favor the interests of the military establishment. The combination of military conservatism, technologism, and professionalism represents a formidable force in the political struggle over the utilization and distribution of national economic resources.

NOTES

1. Samuel P. HUNTINGTON, *The Soldier and the State*, Cambridge, Mass., 1957: Harvard University Press.
2. Alfred VAGTS, *A History of Militarism*. New York, 1959: Meridian Books, esp. chs. 9 and 12. Gordon A. CRAIG, *The Politics of the Prussian Army*, Oxford, 1955: Clarendon Press.
3. Morris JANOWITZ, *The Professional Soldier*, Glencoe, Ill., 1960: Free Press, ch. 12.
4. *Ibid.*, p. 238.
5. See, for instance, Seymour M. LIPSET and Mildred A. SCHWARZ, 'The Politics of Professionals', in H. M. VOLLMER and D. M. MILLS, *Professionalization*, Englewood Cliffs, N.J.: Prentice-Hall, pp. 299–310.
6. *Riksdagsmannavalen åren 1961–1964: II*, Stockholm, 1965: Statistiska Centralbyrån, p. 95.
7. Bengt ABRAHAMSSON, *Anpassning och avgångsbenägenhet bland militärt befäl*, Stockholm, 1965: Militärpsykologiska institutet. MPI report no. 37, p. 61.
8. BURKE, *Reflections on the Revolution in France*, New York, 1962: Holt, Rinehart, and Winston; Russell KIRK, *The Conservative Mind*, Chicago, 1953; Clinton ROSSITER, *Conservatism in America*, New York, 1955.
9. Herbert McCLOSKY, 'Conservatism and Personality', *American Political Science Review*, 1958, vol. 52, pp. 27–45.
10. Charles H. COATES and Roland J. PELLEGRIN, *Military Sociology: A Study of American Military Institutions and Military Life*, University Park, Maryland: The Social Science Press, 1965.
11. *Ibid.*, p. 50.
12. Morris ROSENBERG, *Occupations and Values*, Glencoe, Ill., 1957: Free Press.
13. Bengt ABRAHAMSSON, 'The Ideology of an Elite', in VAN DOORN, J. A. A., *Armed Forces and Society*, The Hague, 1968: Mouton, pp. 71–83; *ibid.*, 'Military Professionalization and Estimates on the Probability of War', in VAN DOORN, J. A. A., *Military Profession and Military Regimes*, The Hague, 1969, pp. 35–51.
14. Eva-Stina BENGTSSON, 'Some Political Perspectives of Academic Reserve Officers', *Journal of Peace Research*, no. 3, 1968, pp. 293–305.
15. Walter KORPI, *Social Pressures and Attitudes in Military Training*, Stockholm, 1964: Almqvist och Wiksell, pp. 83–91.
16. Gaetano MOSCA, *The Ruling Class*, New York and London, 1939: McGraw-Hill, Translated, edited, and revised by Arthur Livingston. Cf. also S. ANDRESKI, 'Conservatism and Radicalism of the Military', *European Journal of Sociology*, 1961, 1.
17. VAGTS, *op. cit.*, p. 30.
18. *Ibid.*, p. 106.
19. 'During the Civil War, between 50 000 and 100 000 officers of the old army were taken into the new Red Army (while some 200 000 entered the White Armies). ... By August, 1920, over 48 000 former officers of the Imperial Army had been taken into the Red Army – though, of course, many of these were wartime promoted officers. At the end of the Civil War, however, a large number of these officers were dismissed' (figure given for dismissals in 1921: 37 954). Raymond L. GARTHOFF, 'The Military in Russia, 1861–1965', in VAN DOORN, J. A. A. (ed.), *Armed Forces and Society*, p. 246. Also compare P. ZHILIN, 'The Armed Forces of the Soviet State', in VAN DOORN (ed.), *Military Profession and Military Regimes*, pp. 157–174.
20. VAGTS, *op. cit.*, p. 411.

73

21. GARTHOFF, *op. cit.*, p. 248.
22. *Ibid.*, p. 250.
23. *Ibid.*, p. 252.
24. ZHILIN, *op. cit.*, p. 167.
25. GARTHOFF, *op. cit.*, p. 256.
26. HUNTINGTON, *op. cit.*, p. 464.
27. VAGTS, *op. cit.*, p. 233.
28. *Ibid.*, p. 372.
29. *Ibid.*, pp. 372–373.
30. *Ibid.*, p. 232.
31. David Lloyd GEORGE, *War Memoirs*, Boston 1933–37, vol. VI, pp. 338–347.
32. VAGTS, *op. cit.*, p. 231.
33. J. BOUDET et al. (eds.), *Arméernas Världshistoria*, vol. IV, Stockholm, 1969: AB Svensk Litteratur, table 1.
34. Adam YARMOLINSKY, 'The Problem of Momentum', in Abram CHAYES and Jerome B. WIESNER (eds.), *ABM – An Evaluation of the Decision to Deploy an Antiballistic Missile System*, New York, 1969: Signet Books, p. 146.
35. *Ibid.*, p. 148.
36. *Ibid.*, p. 146.
37. The *Chicago Daily News*, April 16, 1969, carried the following news announcement:
Barry: 'Thank heaven'
Washington (UPI) – Sen. Barry M. Goldwater (R-Ariz.) said Tuesday that the United States 'should thank heavens' for the military-industrial complex as 'the bubble under which our nation thrives and prospers'.
'Its ultimate aim is peace in our time regardless of the aggressive, militaristic image that the left wing is attempting to give it', the 1964 GOP presidential candidate said in a Senate speech.
38. Morris JANOWITZ, *The Professional Soldier*, p. 246.

Justifying Military Action:
The Dutch Return to Indonesia
1945-1949

J. VAN DOORN

JACQUES VAN DOORN (1925) is Professor of Sociology in the Department of Social Science, Netherlands School of Economics, Rotterdam, Head of the Department of Sociology, Netherlands Military Academy, Breda, and consultant to the Netherlands Ministry of Defence. He is First Vice-Chairman of the Research Committee on Armed Forces and Society, International Sociological Association. His primary interests are in the field of the sociology of organizations, political and military sociology. He is author of a number of sociological books in Dutch, and has contributed articles to various international journals and readers. He is editor of *Armed Forces and Society: Sociological Essays* (1968) and *Military Profession and Military Regimes: Commitments and Conflicts* (1969).

I am grateful to William J. Hendrix for his kind permission to use part of the material contained in our publication: J. A.A. van Doorn and W.J. Hendrix, *Ontsporing van geweld: Over het Nederlands/Indisch/Indonesisch conflict* (Derailment of Force: On the Dutch/Netherlands Indies/Indonesian Conflict) (Rotterdam University Press, 1970).

76

The end of World War II in Europe in May 1945 completed the liberation of the Netherlands but left the Dutch East Indies still under Japanese occupation. At that moment thousands of Dutch troops from the southern provinces of the country were already in training and their numbers soon swelled to more than two infantry divisions. Though impoverished and exhausted by five years of German occupation, the Dutch lost no time in building an expeditionary force to join the Allies in the Pacific.

But they came too late. At the time of the sudden surrender of Japan (August 15, 1945) only very weak Dutch forces were operating in the Far East. They were totally incapable of taking over the Indies from the Japanese military administration, which they had to leave in control until some months later, when British and Indian troops were ready to move into the main cities of Java and Sumatra.

Those few months, however, had been sufficient for a group of Indonesian leaders to proclaim an independent Republic of Indonesia and to gain some popular support, especially from the people of Java. Attempts by the British troops to assume control in the main cities, and the return of the Dutch from the Japanese internment camps soon led to irregular fighting, which gave rise to bitter resistance by armed young Indonesians. A disastrous wave of anti-Dutch and anti-European feeling swept over the main islands, claiming thousands of victims among the Dutch and Chinese minorities. In some places, notably at Surabaya, British and Indian troops killed thousands of young Indonesian guerrilla fighters, thus broadening the gap between the young Republic and the British and Dutch interim administration.

When the British left in the autumn of 1946 a state of intermittent warfare and political bargaining continued for several years, until finally the Republic of Indonesia was recognized by the Dutch. The Dutch troops, by then increased to 150 000, tried to overrun the Republic in two campaigns, both of which were terminated by order of the Security Council and were followed by long periods of insurgency warfare throughout the whole of Java and in parts of the Outer Islands. At last, forced by international pressure and by its obvious inability to end the Indonesian guerrilla, the Netherlands decided to transfer sovereignty to Indonesia (December, 1949).[1]

The story of the conflict is a story of collective frustration. During the four years of Japanese occupation, the Dutch East Indies had undergone a fundamental change. The Dutch part of the population – about

250 000 people, 70% of them born in the Indies – returned in 1945 from the camps to a society in full political and social mobilization. Having only just survived the Japanese terror, they now had to face the fanatical attacks of a youth which was trained and indoctrinated by their hated foe and headed by radical nationalists who had been in Dutch internment before the war.

To their sense of alienation in their own country was added a feeling of bitterness about the critical attitude adopted by the Allies they had voluntarily joined in 1941 when Japan launched its offensive in the Pacific. The Dutch in the Indies felt 'the winds of change', now referred to as the era of decolonization, earlier than the French and the Belgians in their colonies.

Criticism was not confined to the international world; part of the national scene was critical too. During all the years of the conflict the home front was divided, with political parties overtly voicing the wish to give up the South East Asian part of the empire. The Dutch in the colony felt ever more strongly that they were aboard of a sinking ship.

Although the Indonesian Republic was acknowledged *de jure* at the end of 1949, the feeling of disappointment and humiliation did not vanish at once. The Dutch were to function as a scapegoat for a further 15 years. Even now, more than a quarter of a century later, there is a traumatic consciousness among a great number of the Hollanders who were connected in some way with the Indonesian drama.

Such a case of collective frustration must surely represent a case of collective justification, as in fact it does. The whole complex of conditions is there, varying from emotional bonds, social commitments, legal rights and economic interests, and providing in combination a most solid base on which to erect a monument of ideological definitions of the conflict.

In the following pages we shall discuss briefly the various patterns of ideology developed in the five years of the struggle, the empirical background of these evaluations, and the sources of the stubborn search for self-justification continued despite the widening credibility gap. The emphasis will be on the role of the military.

II. PATTERNS OF IDEOLOGY

Ideological justifications are often drawn from the situation at hand. Those concerned are trying to defend themselves by referring to the unbearable conditions which they feel will make their method of handling the problem more readily understood.

In major questions, however, past experience will be mobilized as well. If the problem has been a subject of discussion for a long time, it is not difficult to deploy old arguments in the search for adapted justification.

Both sorts of arguments were used in the Indonesian conflict. The dubious origins of the young Indonesian Republic and its inability to control the situation provided the Dutch with sufficient reason to intervene. The most important arguments, however, had long served traditional political claims. As a colonial elite, the Dutch policy-makers had defended their role and position against the rising tide of Asian nationalism. Now that stormy weather was ahead, they repeated all the old traditional arguments in a last effort to influence a disapproving international opinion.

The impossible nation. One of the strongest objections against the rise of the Republic of Indonesia was the denial that 'Indonesia' in fact existed at all, either ethnically or politically. It was claimed that it consisted of no more than an incohesive collection of peoples without common culture or race and without any political identity. The general standpoint of Dutch colonial policy had been voiced many times in the past century, including by the statesman and colonial expert Colijn in 1928:

The term Indonesia which is often used to express a national unity is without meaning. The isles of the East Indies archipelago are a unity for the simple reason that they constitute the *Dutch* East Indies, and for that reason only.[2]

So the name 'Indonesia' retained a revolutionary meaning, a sort of provocation used by radicals which was obviously intended to symbolize an independent and future unity against the colonial power.

In proclaiming the Republic of Indonesia in 1945 the nationalist leaders in fact proclaimed the rise of this non-existent political unity. The entire machinery of Dutch conservatism could be expected to oppose this claim:

There are at least seven nationalities on Java and Sumatra alone... This state is quite certainly predestined to desintegrate after a time.[3]

In speaking of the granting of independence to Indonesia one should not forget that it comprises 66 peoples totalling in all some 70 millions who inhabit an archipelago as vast as Europe...
Reference to Indonesia and Indonesians in any news bulletin can only be considered to be a means of propaganda intended to suggest that 66 peoples are one people, one nation, which of course presents a completely false picture.[4]

The flow of information to the Dutch troops was based on the same theme:

The Dutch East Indies with its numerous completely different races is not a
geographical area of homogeneous people called 'Indonesians' as the
anti-propaganda forces would like to have us believe. The many peoples of the
archipelago are so distinctive that any attempt to force them into a unity with the
collective noun 'Indonesians' is as foolish as the assertion that all Europeans are
one people.[5]

This was not an academic debate but the basis of the federal system, developed before the war and continued in the post-war period by the successive establishment of a number of Dutch-backed states in the Outer Islands.[6] The overt and consistently pursued goal was the reduction of the Republic of Indonesia to a 'Republic of Djocja', as it came to be called.

The contaminated Republic. A charge levelled with even greater frequency against the Republic was that it was a Japanese creation, the product of manipulation on the part of the Japanese regime.

A Dutch parliamentary delegation concluded after a visit to Indonesia in March and April 1946:

Thus the 'Repoeblik Indonesia' was born, made in Japan, under Japanese
supervision and under two leaders who during the years of oppression had served
the Japanese war effort and supported by a power which was instructed and
educated by the Japanese and was penetrated throughout by Japanese ideas.[7]

This argument was heard repeatedly in the following years. Its tremendous popular impact is hardly surprising, for in the post-war period there was no more damning accusation than that of collaboration with the enemy. The Indonesian objection to Dutch policy, namely that the federal states were 'made by the Dutch', was readily countered with the argument that the Indonesian Republic was 'made in Japan.'[8]

For the Dutch troops this propaganda had a very special significance. The first divisions were formed in the closing stages of World War II for the purpose of joining the Allies in the war against Japan. In addition, some of the troops were recruited directly among members of the resistance movement against the German occupation, which meant that they were extremely sensitive on the point of political collaboration.

Moreover, the argument was effective because the change in the war aims, i.e., the substitution of the Republican nationalists for the Japanese, was made easier in that the former could be labelled as accomplices. The

80

military operations were justified as being a purge of the Indonesian regime from traitors and war criminals. This interpretation was bound to find fervent support among the members of the Dutch colonial forces (KNIL), who had suffered a great deal at Japanese hands and who thus had many reasons for wishing to erase all Japanese influence.

Furthermore, the troop commanders were ordered to devote special attention to Japanese deserters who had joined the Indonesian army and who were sometimes taken prisoner. They were assumed to be the hard core of Republican resistance, though in actual fact there was only a small number of Japanese deserters in the Indonesian army.[9]

The idea of a Japanese-contaminated Republic seems to have been of durable ideological value. As late as October 1949, during the Round Table Conference which preceded the transfer of sovereignty two months later, Dutch-oriented Irian leaders pleaded in favor of an autonomous Irian Barat (West New Guinea) because, as they argued, the Indonesian Republic displayed 'Japanese tendencies.'[10]

Yet another infection seemed gradually to gain in value as an argument against the Indonesian cause: the penetration of communism. Communist Indonesian leaders and organizations had been actively involved in the struggle for independence from the time of its inception. On the internal front they made repeated attempts to overrule the nationalist government in Djocja.[11] These facts were eagerly exploited by Dutch propaganda, which suggested that independence for Indonesia could result in a communist regime.

A typical example of this approach was a pamphlet entitled '*Naar de Sovjet Republiek Indonesia*' (Toward the Soviet Republic of Indonesia) written by a prominent opponent of the official Dutch policy and published by the Information Service of a very influential pressure group, the so-called National Committee for the Maintenance of a Unified Empire.[12] The general tenor of this pamphlet was that Indonesian nationalism was no more than a smoke screen for international communism, and was supported by the Soviet Union. It suggested that the past political career of all prominent nationalist leaders – Sukarno, Hatta, Sjahrir – was a dubious one in that they had had relations with communist organizations.

This argument did not penetrate to the lower army echelons, but was acclaimed only at top level, especially among intelligence officers of the political branch.

Legitimacy and legality. The political debate about the Indonesian problem was to a large extent dominated by legal arguments. The main attack on the progressive Dutch politicians and parties was largely based on the argument that the constitution was at stake.[13] Throughout the whole of the conflict the Republic of Indonesia was assumed to have no rights whatsoever, and it was accorded only a hesitant *de facto* recognition.

This being the case, the Dutch army was free to label its military opponent 'subversive elements', 'extremists' and 'terrorists', operating in bands wrongly claiming to constitute a regular armed force. There could be only one army in Indonesia: the one serving the Dutch government.

This legalistic background explains the name given to the first and second military campaign against the Indonesian Republic (medio 1947 and end 1948), which were organized as large-scale military operations with tanks, artillery and bombers, but were nevertheless labelled 'politionele acties' (police actions). It was formally admitted that this was the usual term applied to all activity of the Dutch colonial army connected with internal conflicts.[14]

The attitude of the Dutch government made it possible for the troops to define the Indonesian armed resistance in terms either of insurrection or of crime. Often there was no distinction made between Indonesian regular forces, guerrilla units and bandits. This accounts for court-martialling and execution of regular Indonesian soldiers and officers taken prisoner in Dutch-controlled territory.[15] Although legally admissible, these and other sentences symbolized the fundamental difference in the legal position of the protagonists' forces. For after all, the Indonesian army was supposed to be an insurgency force, not a military opponent.

Law and order. Formally and informally the most frequently used and most popular argument employed by the Dutch was that it was by no means the intention for the Dutch forces to occupy the country; they were simply there to suppress the terrorists in order to protect the population. The tens of thousands of patrol orders all contained the same stereotyped wording: 'Destroy the enemy forces; arrest suspects; gain the confidence of the population'.

In the Dutch military ideology the only major distinction seemed to be the line drawn between the Indonesian population – victims of terror – and the enemy, i.e., the terrorists, who were first and foremost the enemies of their own people. The military mission was officially conducted in terms of 'Justice and Security' or 'Law and Order'.

All troops were indoctrinated with this pattern of justification, particularly those brought in from Holland. It often started with a letter from the commanding officer to the parents of the enlisted man, saying:

The Japanese occupation has caused a crisis which the population of the Netherlands Indies cannot resolve without the help of others. The Netherlands, which has been in contact with the inhabitants for more than 300 years, is the obvious country to provide such help. Our army has now been entrusted with the task of restoring law and order to the East Indies, which is incapable of performing this action alone.[16]

On disembarkation in Indonesia the soldiers themselves received a letter from the Commander-in-Chief himself:

The Japanese occupation and its consequences – lawlessness, terror, poverty, hunger – destroyed the foundations and disintegrated the social order. This situation did not end with the Japanese surrender. Too many irresponsible elements – unfortunately part of every nation – took advantage of the disorder and the lasting defencelessness of their own people.[17]

The second military action against the Republic of Indonesia was motivated in the same way. In the words of the Order of the Day issued by the Commander-in-Chief on December 17, 1948:

Remember that you are bearers of justice and security to a population that has long been subjected to terror and oppression.[18]

The final cease-fire in August 1949 necessitated cooperation between the Dutch and Indonesian forces. The Commander-in-Chief now had to give another interpretation of the army's maintenance of law and order:

We were termed 'the strange army' ... We came as a fighting force but nevertheless as a friend which was compelled to act as an enemy in a country whose population was seen as friends to be protected. Now we shall no longer fight against the Republican Army, but with it, since the Indonesian army shares with us a duty to protect the population against the marauding bands.[19]

For the military, and particularly for the KNIL, this part of the ideology was of major importance. Formally, as armed police supporting the ordinary police forces in the colony, their first task was to take action against the rebels. As long as it was possible to define the situation as a temporary state of disturbance there was no need to worry about a justification of armed action, which could be regarded simply as part of a police-and-judicial control pattern, and not a real military action.

It may be concluded that it is possible to differentiate between the social, political, legal and police arguments, all of which avoided any suggestion that the Dutch military were fighting a war. They were simply restoring the social and political order which in their view had proved to be the most appropriate system for the population of Indonesia. The Indonesian Republic lacked not only the legal basis needed to provide an acceptable alternative, but was moreover incapable of protecting its people from the consequences of the social disintegration following Japanese occupation. So the Republic was declared a failure on the double score of legitimacy and effectiveness.

This interpretation was formulated at the highest levels of Dutch policy, officially voiced and unofficially supported by an impressive number of colonial experts. The military establishment absorbed and accepted this evaluation and was provided with arguments from above. It played no substantial or autonomous part in the development of the pattern of justification; it simply made use of it.

III. HARD FACTS AND SELECTIVE PERCEPTION

Ideologies always contain an element of truth. They derive their special significance from their interwoven threads of empirical observations and distorted perception. So ideologies can be distinguished from outright lies and propaganda on the one hand, and from a serious intellectual approach to reality on the other.

For the ideological patterns discussed above the same sort of distinction has to be made between factual observation and selective perception. The centuries'-long interaction between the Dutch rulers and the Indonesian population and the thorough study of Indonesia by Dutch specialists guaranteed sufficient knowledge of the real situation in the colony, even taking into account the fact that the sudden political and psychological breakthrough which started in 1942 had changed the scene entirely.

On the other hand it was precisely this close contact, always from a position of absolute power and authority, that made it difficult for the Dutch to make judgements without being influenced by distortive emotions and shortsighted perception. Foreigners often tended to come closer to the truth than the Dutch insiders who stuck to their policy until its credibility was entirely exhausted.

Before proceeding to an attempt to explain this obstinate determination to justify the Dutch position, we shall deal briefly with the extent to which these ideologies found a more or less solid basis in the reality of post-war Indonesia.

84

The viability of the Indonesian Republic. The post-war federal policy developed by the Dutch had a history of at least fifty years. It might even be stated that the Dutch traditionally preferred decentralized administration to centralized control. The enormous distances were not the only factor here; of greater importance was the fundamental idea that the ethnic, religious and cultural heterogeneity of the population was far too great to allow of a uniform policy.

The system of indirect rule adopted had much to do with this standpoint, not only for the tactical political profit it promised but also as a means of keeping intact the plurality of Indonesian culture and society.

Both conventional wisdom and ethnographic knowledge contributed to the insight that it would be almost impossible to press the given heterogeneity into a common pattern. The Dutch had ample reason to assume that the idea of a unified Indonesian Republic would prove to be either a false claim of a small group of Java-centred leaders or an illusion that was symptomatic of the naivety of the revolutionary situation.

Now, twenty years later, it has to be acknowledged that Dutch pessimism has found support from recent political events and from newer studies of Indonesian culture. The unitary state was scarcely in existence (1950) when tensions arose between the Javanese centre and what the Dutch had termed 'the Outer Territories' (Buitengewesten), culminating in the late fifties in a civil war which continued for three years.

Specialists in Indonesian history and culture have since recognized the dichotomy between Java and Outer Indonesia which, though masked by colonial rule, is rooted in an older cultural matrix.[20]

Yet the arguments put forward at the time by the Dutch must be labelled as ideological in that they entirely under-estimated the impact of post-war nationalism as a unifying force and particularly as a force directed against Dutch intervention. What was ideological in the narrower sense was the hesitation to promote unification because the major argument employed stressed historical heterogeneity and not future politics, thus giving direct support to the interests of Dutch policy in the East.

The charge that the Republic of Indonesia was a Japanese creation was much weaker. It was quite true that the nationalist leaders had accepted Japanese help and owed their success in the initial stages of insurrection to Japanese manipulation. It was also true that the Republic, imitating the Japanese in many visible cultural aspects like the training, uniform and ritual of the armed forces, could not but arouse deeply-felt abhorrence among the Dutch ex-repatriates and ex-prisoners.

But the constant use of these points as a political argument against the rise of Indonesian nationalism was evidently insufficient. The Japanese were extremely unpopular, as evidenced by an armed Indonesian insurrection in the last year of occupation. The first attacks of the nationalist *Pemudas* (revolutionary youth) were primarily directed against the Japanese military.[21] Moreover, the argument lost its substance at the end of World War II, when Japan was eliminated as a political factor. It was not only untrue, but ineffective as well.

The suggestion of a communist infection of the Indonesian Republic had much more relevance and effectiveness, particularly in the years of the Cold War and the rise of Communist China. The *coup* engineered by Muso and other communist leaders in Madiun (September 1948) and supported by about 25 000 troops demonstrated once again the real danger of a communist regime in this part of the world.[22] It was speedily followed, however, by a demonstration of force by the central government, which soon succeeded in putting down the rebellion.

This event strengthened the international position of the Republic, particularly in the view of the United States, eager to support any regime that proved capable of controlling its communists at home. The Muso rebellion was a test-case whereby the Dutch argument lost its value in the eyes of the American government. Soon afterwards when it embarked upon the second military action (December 1948), the Dutch were to find that American support had changed sides.

Terrorist tactics against the civilian population. The rise of the Indonesian Republic followed a period of serious social disruption caused by the Japanese occupation. Millions were impoverished, largely owing to the closure of the big agricultural estates, hundreds of thousands experienced forced labor or served in the Japanese army as auxiliary soldiers.

In the last months of 1945, when Japanese authority had disappeared but not been replaced by either Allied or Dutch forces, revolutionary uprisings were accompanied by waves of mass criminality. After that terrifying time of suffering and humiliation the majority of the Dutch population there tended to identify the Indonesian cause with chaos and terror.

There is sufficient empirical evidence that in the years of the Dutch-Indonesian conflict the Republican forces did not succeed in controlling the considerable numbers of criminal bands in the countryside. In addition, guerrilla groups often employed force and even terror to obtain food and money from the population.

It is also quite true that the Dutch troops were often more effective in guaranteeing law and order. By providing massive material and technical aid and expertise, the Dutch military take-over of former Republican regions marked the start of economic progress for the population.

These facts made it fairly simple for the Dutch to obscure the difference between the Republican forces and the criminal elements. Because this difference was vague and gradual, it was easily to suggest that the Indonesian army could hardly be regarded as a respectable regular army and that it bore full responsibility for the hardships of the population.

The Dutch interpretation of affairs gave full emphasis to the fact – common in every revolutionary war – that the struggle between the opponents was for the loyalty of the population, so that in a sense the war was conducted like an agonizing and bloody election campaign.[23] In struggles of this kind terrorism is the weapon of the weak. Unable to withstand the attacks of the Dutch army in the open field, the Indonesian resistance concentrated on hit and run operations and on pressing the civilians to hide and supply the guerrilla fighters.

The accusation of terrorism might be justified in a large number of cases, but the reverse side of the medal was the Dutch use of counter-terror tactics, as in the southern Celebes (Sulawesi) where the notorious Special Forces of Captain Raymond Westerling killed at least several thousands of civilians to gain control of the chaotic situation.[24]

Even though actions of this kind were exceptional, the Dutch tolerated a general policy of intimidating the Indonesian population by mass arrests and the use of torture on suspect prisoners. It would be hypocritical to ignore this aspect of the struggle, as is usually the case in Dutch commentaries.[25]

The silence systematically observed on this 'terror-torture cycle'[26] is perhaps the most significant aspect of the Dutch justification of the military intervention. By comparing the pacification efforts of the Dutch army with the terrorist practices of scattered bands of Indonesian guerrilla fighters Dutch military authorities built up a real ideological picture. It is a picture requiring completion by reference to the official *Tentara Republik Indonesia* as a considerable pacifying force and to the widespread Dutch police brutality.

A last question still remains to be answered: how are we to account for the fact that for some four years the Dutch stuck to their largely false interpretation of the situation and to their distorted perception of the conflict and its gradual escalation? The question is especially important in view of the fact that the Dutch government succeeded in retaining the support of the majority of the Dutch population throughout the full period of the conflict. Public opinion polls showed that the hawkish approach to the problem never failed to find widespread support among the voters.[27] How are we to explain the absence of a credibility gap?

IV. SOURCES OF IDEOLOGY

Conditions for ideological distortion can be divided into two categories. The first concerns the factors which directly influence the perceptive process, like the amount of information provided and the degree of emotional commitment; the second category includes the indirect causes, such as the social basis of intellectual distortion (vested interests etc.). A lesser known third element, the self-propelling aspect of ideological justification, will be discussed separately in a later section.

Collective humiliation. It is clear from several elaborate studies that the revolt of the French army had definitely been provoked by long years of humiliation.[28] Though the Dutch KNIL suffered from similar frustration it never defied the Dutch government. A recent analysis by Kroes has made it amply clear that praetorianism played only a marginal role.[29]

Yet the Dutch East Indies army had many good reasons to feel angry and even desperate. In 1942 it had been defeated by the Japanese in a way that could hardly considered to be honourable. After only a few weeks the strong Dutch forces on Java and Sumatra had surrendered, in many places with little resistance. In addition, their defeat was plainly visible to the native population, traditionally prepared to accept the superiority of the Dutch and now suddenly confronted with a total breakdown of the rulers' apparatus under a single blow from a poorly equipped Asian force.

In the prisoner of war and internment camps humiliation was experienced even more deeply. A policy of continued submittance supported by harsh methods of punishment deepened the hatred of the Dutch military and civilian population for the Japanese. The internees, separated from their wives and children, waited four years for the moment when they would have the chance to avenge themselves.

The end of the war, however, did not end humiliation. Far from resuming their former position of power, they had to endure the street terror of young Indonesians and the rising tide of revolution. While the Japanese authorities and the new Indonesian leaders and their supporters struggled for control in the country, the Dutch military, unarmed and utterly exhausted, were ordered to stay in the camps.

When finally, many months later, they had gathered sufficient power to take the initiative a long and laborious bargaining process started between the Dutch government and the Indonesian leaders. Time and again the Dutch troops clashed with the less disciplined Republican army staffed partly by ex-KNIL-soldiers who could only be regarded as traitors. The first military action, in the summer of 1947, was stopped by order of the Security Council, and bargaining started again. The forced cease-fire was supervised by United Nations Military Observers, which was experienced as a national insult.

This story of continued humiliation at both the personal and institutional levels contains the first explanation of ideological defence. Unable to accept the new situation and prevented from restoring the old order of things, the military were very much inclined to seek unrealistic explanations. Their frustration and disgust were focussed on the scapegoats at hand: the Japanese, their Indonesian collaborators, the Allies not prepared to take a hard line, the Dutch politicians – some of them without colonial experience and therefore considered to be utterly naive – and, behind these personal failures, the invisible hand of British colonial interests and world communism. As far as emotional factors can provide an explanation of the distortion of social perception, all conditions were fulfilled.

Limited information. The perception of events was also distorted by a lack of information about what had happened during the Japanese occupation of the Indies. Even for a detached observer without emotional ties with the country the uprising of the Indonesians in the critical post-war months came as a complete surprise. The information possessed by the Allied and Dutch intelligence services had been scant in the extreme. They had been sufficiently informed about the activities of the Japanese and their efforts to mobilize the population against the Allied forces, but little was known about the success of this policy.

During the war the Dutch inside the colony were completely isolated in internment camps and were not permitted to have any contact with the Indonesian population. Little was known of the new nationalist organizations and their political claims, which were not considered to be a serious threat. Even left-wing camp groups proved to be conservative in their plans and proposals on their return to freedom and post-war Indonesian reality.

Separation of the Dutch- and Indonesian-controlled territories was effected in the second half of 1945. In the following years only small groups of Dutch politicians and journalists visited the Indonesian Republic. The Dutch were again isolated from the course of events in the nationalist camp, which meant that once again they lacked first-hand information.

This self-chosen isolation was reinforced by the governmental and military manipulation of what little information there was. The propaganda machinery of the Dutch was mobilized to minimize the achievements of the young Republic and to emphasize its failures, which were indeed considerable and frequent. Conservative groups in Holland obtained their information about the course of the conflict sometimes directly from the political intelligence services.[30]

The Dutch forces not only manipulated information but also suffered from its incapacity to interpret the nature of the developing guerrilla war and the immanent danger of its escalation into a scarcely controllable armed conflict. Right from the beginning the KNIL-generals underestimated the strength of the Republican resistance.[31] Their miscalculation now causes no surprise in the light of the later experiences of the French in Algeria and the Americans in Vietnam, neither of which managed a more realistic evaluation of their situation.

All in all, the limited amount of knowledge and the little understood failure of the Dutch politicians and military forces to gain control of the situation gave rise to a flow of justifications. Up to the end of the conflict stress was constantly placed on the distinction between the 'small group of irresponsible elements' which had seized control with the aid of force and even terror, and the mass of the population, eager to accept Dutch rule. The Netherlands only had to stand firm both politically and militarily, for it was in a position to offer an acceptable alternative to what was assumed to be a *va banc* policy of the regime in Djocja. It was not until the last year that, after having failed to overrun the heartland of the Republic, the Dutch were reluctantly prepared to acknowledge their various miscalculations. Bitter experience proved to be the only way of revealing the irrelevance of the false interpretations of the 'Indonesian question'.

Vested interests. Part of this miscalculation was inevitable. The Dutch were the first nation to experience the post-war decolonization process, and to be forced to decide how to cope with a major revolt inside their colonial empire. In 1945 and 1946, the crucial years in Dutch policy formulation, it was not easily to foresee that only fifteen years later even the African continent would have been decolonized.

Looking back, it is extremely difficult to reconstruct the collective outlook of the first post-war generation. Confronted with a highly incomprehensive and complex situation, they tended to rely on the judgment of insiders and experts. Because of the unexpected development of events, however, the solutions suggested by the specialists could only refer to earlier experience. As a consequence, many interpretations of the Indonesian conflict referred to historical situations rather than future developments.

The pattern of ideology presented by the Dutch may thus be classified as typically conservative, in fact as a plea for the *status quo*. The ideas put forward were supported by a general feeling of nostalgia, particularly among the Eurasian population which longed for *tempo doeloe* (old times).

Reference to vested interests as a major source of collective justification should therefore not be restricted to the field of economic advantages, but must be understood as covering the whole field of human experience. In colonial conflicts in particular, when part of the 'establishment' has an emotional investment in the existing order, the strong tensions generated express themselves in anxiety and distorted ideas.

Various sorts of vested interests were accumulated in the Dutch East Indies. The major cause of ideological distortion was the existential bond of at least half the Dutch minority with the country. These emotional investments also had social and institutional roots since nearly all key positions in the colony were in the hands of the Dutch. One might even say that the institutional superstructure – government administration, army, schools, plantations and churches – was above all part of the Dutch acculturation process and was consequently experienced as a Dutch achievement. This included the purely economic interests forming part of the existing order: the majority of the Dutch population felt that they were sure to be expelled sooner or later after independence.

This expectation or at least the general feeling of uncertainty about the future resulted in over-emphasis of the Dutch contribution to the colony. The traditional feeling of ethnic and national superiority developed into an overt ideology which manifested itself in strong paternalistic attitudes, the restoration of former Dutch positions and a general tenor of opinion that the future Indonesian state should in any case be integrated in a Dutch-controlled commonwealth.

The Dutch military establishment in the Indies was one of the main pillars of the colonial upper class. Kroes has shown that 40% of the senior officers of the KNIL were born in the colony and have to be classified as a group that had staked everything on a career in the Indies.[32] The lower ranks, the non-commissioned officers and the rank and file, were largely Eurasians and members of what was called in the British colonies 'the martial races' of the archipelago (Amboinese, Menadonese, and others), many of them Christian, and all of them ardently devoted to the Dutch cause.

So the hard core of the Dutch troops in Indonesia had ample reason to fear any change in the colonial *status quo*. Their social and professional existence depended on the continuity of the colonial situation. Among the military the idea of Western superiority and its concomitant contempt for the Indonesians took the form of a feeling of military superiority. Their corporate ideology, supported by their membership of certain ethnic minorities, resulted in a serious miscalculation regarding the rapid surrender of the Indonesian rebels.

In fact most Dutch military never felt serious doubts about the outcome of the armed conflict. They claimed superiority and, in a way, they were superior. Though it is true that they failed to cope with the guerrilla of the Republic, it is also true that the Indonesian forces never succeeded in gaining a victory, even a minor one, against Dutch troops. Viewed against this background it is clear that the military failed to adapt their ideas to the political reality of the moment, maintaining up to the last stage of the conflict that the Indonesians could easily be defeated by force, which was the only adequate answer in the circumstances.

'Point of no return'. Because a conflict is a process, the ideological interpretation of conflicts can only be adequately understood as a result of the process. A 'latent ideology'[33] is probably always in existence, but it only becomes manifest, and grows into a motivational force, in the course of action.

In virtually every preface to the records of Dutch divisions, brigades and regiments stationed in the Indies a highly characteristic statement expressing the feeling of the troops is found: 'de offers kúnnen niet vergeefs zijn geweest' (the sacrifices cannot have been in vain).

This feeling can be generalized. The Dutch population had suffered long years of hardship during and after the period of Japanese occupation. Many of them had lost relatives and all of them returned from the camps destitute, and exhausted by illness and hunger. Yet many of them felt obliged to pick up the threads of the pre-war years and did their utmost to restore the disorganized public services and the destroyed plantations, bringing in new machinery and vehicles that had been bought by groups of Dutch specialists in Australian exile.[34]

The technical, economic and organizational reconstruction continued for several years despite serious difficulties and setbacks. Stimulated by the enormous demand for raw materials a policy of expanding investments was pursued in the expectation of short-term profits from the world

market prices and a long-term restoration of the previous situation.
Politically the commitments were even stronger. The federal policy of the Dutch government led to the emergence of a number of Dutch-sponsored states which offered a wide variety of political and administrative positions to Indonesians. Many Indonesian aristocratic rulers, in particular, succumbed to the temptation to share power with the Dutch in the face of the rising influence of the nationalist middle class of the Republic.

It can be argued that the increasing efforts of the Dutch in the policial, military and economic fields constitute a major explanation of the ongoing justification of the Dutch presence in Indonesia. On the one hand, the investments in men and money – including two and a half thousand casualties – demanded a strong moral defence; on the other hand, the Dutch succeeded in regaining the political, military and economic initiative, and felt that each new step forward justified further progression along the same lines. Both the sacrifices and the successes, however limited the latter, constituted major reasons for the continued defence of the Dutch intervention. The ongoing conflict did not eliminate the need for justification but strengthened its ideological basis.

The fact that the military were among the last to accept the end of the empire is readily understandable in view of the strong military attachment to the Dutch position overseas. The conquest of the Indies completed in the nineteenth and early twentieth centuries was almost entirely the achievement of the KNIL, and therefore an important element in the Dutch military heritage.

Moreover, many Dutch military felt responsible for the Indonesian soldiers who served in the colonial army and for that part of the population which had developed ties of friendship with the Dutch. At this point the ideology became rooted in moral feelings of loyalty which changed to guilt at the idea of moving out and thus betraying the Dutch-oriented Indonesians.[35]

It is highly probable that revolutionary wars characterized by a process of escalation and a growing commitment, but without a decisive outcome, engender tenacious loyalties among the men who carry the burden.[36] When the point of no return is reached loyalty and honor will be cited as a last defence against the growing feeling of desperation.

NOTES

1. Van Doorn and Hendrix, *Ontsporing van geweld: Over het Nederlands/Indisch/ Indonesisch conflict* (Rotterdam: Rotterdam University Press, 1970), Chapters II and III (pp. 49 ff., 99 ff.); George McTurnan Kahin, *Nationalism and Revolution in Indonesia* (Ithaca, N.Y.: Cornell U.P., 1952).
2. H. Colijn, *Koloniale vraagstukken van heden en morgen* (Amsterdam: De Standaard, 1928), pp. 59 ff.
3. Ch. Kiès, *Het Indonesisch probleem* (Private publication 1948), p.12; also Ch. Kiès, *Wat de meeste Nederlanders niet weten omtrent Nederlandsch-Indië* (Deventer: W. van Hoeve, n.d. 1946), pp. 5 ff., 34.
4. D. J. Jongeneel, *Het spel, dat met Nederlandsch Indië gespeeld wordt* (The Hague: Van Stockum, 1946), p. 27.
5. M. van den Heuvel, 'Het Indisch Instructie-Bataljon', in: *De Militaire Spectator*, Vol. CXVI, 1947, p. 284.
6. Kahin, *op. cit.*, pp. 351 ff.
7. *Report of the Parliamentary Commission (States General) Dutch East Indies* (Chairman M. van Poll), May, 1946 (The Hague), p. 23.
8. Mas Slamet, *Japanese Machinations* (Batavia, Febr./March 1946), four pamphlets against the Japanese origin of the Indonesian Republic written by a Dutch-oriented Indonesian politician; Jongeneel, *op. cit.*, pp. 31 ff.; G. Gerretson, *Indië onder dictatuur* (Amsterdam and Brussels: Elsevier, 1946), p. 79; H. W. J. Picard, *De waarheid over Java* (The Hague: Van Hoeve, 1946); *Klare taal: Een bundel radio-redevoeringen van tegenstanders van de overeenkomst van Linggadjati*, with an introduction by W. K. H. Feuilletau De Bruyn (n.d., no publisher, 1947), pp. 17, 21, 23 ff.; P. M. Van Wulfften Palthe, *Psychological Aspects of the Indonesian Problem* (Leiden: E. J. Brill, 1949), pp. 1 ff., 10 ff.; P. S. Gerbrandy, *De scheuring van het rijk: Het drama van de Indonesische crisis* (Kampen: J. H. Kok, 1951), pp. 66–70.
   Of these authors Gerbrandy was the war-time Dutch prime-minister in London, and several were prominent colonial experts, former colonial senior civil servants, etc.
9. Of the total force of about 325 000 Japanese in the Indies, no more than 2 000 are assumed to have deserted at the end of the war, some because they had married Indonesian wives. Only part of this category served in the Indonesian army. H. J. Van Mook, *Indonesië, Nederland en de Wereld* (Amsterdam: De Bezige Bij, 1949), p. 134.
10. A declaration published in *De Locomotief* (Dutch daily in the East Indies), October 29, 1949.
11. Kahin, *op. cit.*, Chapters VI and IX.
12. W. K. H. Feuilletau de Bruyn, *Naar de Sovjet Republiek Indonesia* (1947, 1948²)
13. See the publications of Gerretson and Gerbrandy referred to above.
14. W. Drees, *Zestig jaren levenservaring* (Amsterdam: Arbeiderspers, 1962), p. 228.
15. Van Doorn and Hendrix, *op. cit.*, pp. 93 ff.
16. The present writer's personal experience as a conscripted soldier at the time.
17. Published in *Van Arnhem tot de Poentjak: Herinneringen aan het 421e Bataljon Garderegiment Prinses Irene. Nederland-Indonesië: Maart 1948 - Augustus 1950* (1951), pp. 68 ff.
18. Personal information obtained by the writer at the time.
19. Radio speech by Major General Buurman van Vreeden, August, 1949.

20. Harry J. BENDA, 'Decolonization in Indonesia: The Problem of Continuity and Change', in: *American Historical Review*, Vol. LXX, 1965, pp. 1062 ff.
21. KAHIN, *op. cit.*, pp. 112 ff., 122 ff., 134 ff.
22. KAHIN, *op. cit.*, pp. 292 ff.
23. Samuel P. HUNTINGTON, 'The New Military Politics', in: Samuel P. HUNTINGTON (ed.), *Changing Patterns of Military Politics* (New York: Free Press of Glencoe, 1962), p. 30.
24. See Dutch Government Publication *Nota betreffende het archievenonderzoek naar gegevens omtrent excessen in Indonesië begaan door Nederlandse militairen in de periode 1945–1950* (1949), a memorandum presented by the Prime-Minister to the Second Chamber of the Dutch Parliament on June 3, 1949, Supplement 2.
25. For an extensive analysis of this problem see VAN DOORN and HENDRIX, *op. cit.*, chapters III and IV.
26. George Armstrong KELLY, *Lost Soldiers: The French Army and Empire in Crisis 1947–1962* (Cambridge, Mass.: The MIT Press, 1965), pp. 197–199.
27. Cf. the Dutch public opinion polls on Dutch policy concerning the Indonesian conflict: *De publieke opinie over Indonesië in de jaren 1946–1950*, Newsletter NIPO, No. 1261 (Febr. 6, 1969). Arend LIJPHART, *The Trauma of Decolonization: The Dutch and West New Guinea* (New Haven and London: Yale U. P., 1966), pp. 122, 125.
28. Besides KELLY, *op. cit.*, see: John Steward AMBLER, *Soldiers against the State: The French Army in Politics* (Garden City, N.Y.: Anchor Books, 1968), Part I and II.
29. Rob KROES, 'Decolonization and Military: The Case of the Netherlands', in: Morris JANOWITZ and Jacques VAN DOORN (eds.), *On Military Intervention* (Rotterdam: Rotterdam University Press, 1971), pp. 93 ff.
30. Some publications of the Dutch opponents of the official agreement with the Indonesian Republic contained secret information.
    In 1949 the Head of the Military Intelligence Service (MID), Dr. J. M. SOMER, was dismissed because of his secret contacts with political opposition groups in the Netherlands.
31. VAN DOORN and HENDRIX, *op. cit.*, pp. 65 ff.
32. KROES, *op. cit.* For details of the Indonesian background of neval officers see C. J. LAMMERS, *Het Koninklijk Instituut voor de Marine* (Assen: Van Gorcum/Prakke & Prakke, 1963), pp. 400 ff.
33. Charles C. MOSKOS, Jr., *The American Enlisted Man* (New York: Russell Sage Foundation, 1970), pp. 146 ff.
34. For instance, the NIRUB (Netherlands Indies Rubber Fund) had ordered production equipment in the United States in 1945 to the value of 48 million Dutch guilders.
35. The Amboinese soldiers and their families, numbering 12 500 people, were evacuated to the Netherlands. *Ambonezen in Nederland*. Rapport Ministerie Maatschappelijk Werk (The Hague: Government Printing and Publishing Office, 1959), pp. 10 ff.
36. French observation by Raoul GIRARDET, 'Civil and Military Power in the Fourth Republic' in: Samuel P. HUNTINGTON (ed.), *Changing Patterns of Military Politics* (New York: Free Press of Glencoe, 1962), p. 140.

The West-German Bundeswehr as an Institution for Political Education

W. VON BREDOW

Wilfried Freiherr von Bredow, born in 1944 in Heinrichsdorf, is Akademischer Rat at the Seminar of Political Science of the Rheinische Friedrich-Wilhelms Universität, Bonn. His main fields of interest are military organization with special reference to civil-military relations, the different forms of conflict between capitalist and socialist countries, and peace research. He is author of *Der Primat militärischen Denkens: Die Bundeswehr und das Problem der okkupierten Öffentlichkeit* (1969) and co-author of *Bibliographie zur Politik in Theorie und Praxis* (1970). He is editor of a documentation on conscientious objection in West Germany and has contributed a number of articles to various journals.

In general, research concerning the organisational sociology of the military deals only superficially with the problems and difficulties of providing a political education to the soldiers. To be sure, the necessity of a 'moral armament' of the military personnel is unanimously recognized, and – of course – the difference between moral armament in a totalitarian society as opposed to that in a democratic society is pointed out. Generally, however, you will only find hints to the various elements of moral armament such as a) the professional code, b) the image of the enemy and c) the political objectives of the national security or that policy of security laid down within the framework of an alliance. According to Janowitz, military measures of education are more successful when trying to mold the soldiers by means of the professional code, while motivations on the basis of the 'what-do-we-fight for?' reasoning have failed without exception.[1]

If these findings were laid down in a set of principles, they would constitute the conception of a conservative military establishment. Due to the historical situation at the time of its founding, the basic conception of the Federal Republic of Germany turned out to be rather atypical – for here the political education within the *Bundeswehr* was initially meant to serve other purposes as well. The discrepancy between the initial conceptions and the actual development, which was decisively influenced by decisions and actions outside the military sphere, might stimulate several interesting discussions about the somewhat problematic relationship between the military establishment and the civilian society, but also about the difficulties arising in an international situation adequately characterized as 'organized peacelessness' (D. Senghaas) for a democratic society which in its own conception has the obligation to preserve and increase the democratic substance.

POLITICAL EDUCATION IN THE FRG

These briefly sketched outlines of the present paper require several deviations, for the discussions within the *Bundeswehr* can only be adequately understood in the context of the general situation, in which the conceptions for political education in the FRG have been formed by the relevant institutions, such as the schools and the universities, where the new discipline of 'political science' was introduced after the Second World War. Here, too, a reminder of the specific historical situation should help to prevent an all too easy generalization.

A review of the political education in the FRG leads to the conclusion that the postwar period of political education has been a period of drastic disappointments. Doubts about the effectiveness of political education have increased over the past years and – considering the student unrest of the late sixties, when a general dissatisfaction with politics and society was voiced – it seems justified to agree with all those critics who charge that the conceptions of political education have failed 'in their task to provide a democratic theory of education and to realize it in the schools (including the institutions of adult education). Instead, the application of authoritarian, conformistic patterns of socialization has been practised'.[2] According to the ideas of the 'Great Coalition' (1966-1969) of the Federal Government, political education has the following purpose: 'It has to provide information – which should be as objective as possible – about the factors and functional relationships between political processes; it has to broaden the political insight and to deepen the ability and willingness for political judgment; it has to promote the understanding of one's own place within the framework of the society; it has to lead to an acceptance of the fundamental values of a free democratic society; it has to develop the ability for political action and to teach a knowledge of the democratic rules and practise them'.[3] These purposes were formulated in consequence to the complaints voiced also by Parliament about the state of the political education. In order to explain its activities in this field, the Federal Government has accepted an important part of the criticism brought out in the scientific discussion of the political education. This criticism applies on the one hand to the historical development since 1945, on the other hand to the inability of pedagogues to overcome obvious shortcomings. Indeed, the activities in the field of political education after the Second World War were largely determined by a retroactive discussion on National Socialism, that is, the discussion dealt with the 'ideology' of National Socialism and far less with its structural premises. At the same time the ideology of Communism provided a new 'opponent', who could now, along with the first, be summarized under the term of 'totalitarianism'. The history of research on totalitarianism and its application to the activities of political education often provides an almost grotesque support for the theoretical concepts of the 'Frankfurter Schule'. Nevertheless, its actual effects can hardly be overestimated. The totalitarian ideologies and systems were simply placed opposite the democratic ones, and thus by discrediting the enemy, one's own merits were proved. It was mainly this 'strategy of ideological self-deception'[4] that led to an all too harmonizing, glorifying picture of democracy and thereby to an overestimation of values such as 'community', 'partnership' etc. This in turn led to a 'misconception of the nature of politics'.[5] The 'load' of the past was meant to stimulate a rise of democratic consciousness in the whole population – but instead the result was a meaningless proclamation of phrases that very soon turned away those to whom democracy was to be taught, and finally caused them to rebel.

Political education in those days was no more than the repeated condemnation of National Socialism, a rigid preaching of anticommunism and the painting of an idealistic picture of a well-functioning democracy that attracted and integrated the young generation into the society.

THE ARMED FORCES AND POLITICAL EDUCATION

It is commonplace to say that the law and the self-conception of a military apparatus are strongly linked with the civilian society surrounding it. *One* of the important channels through which the social and political conceptions of the civilian society are transmitted into the military is the institution of political education. The transmission takes place in two directions: for a strong military is also quite capable of transmitting its social and political conceptions to the soldiers, for example the draftees, through political education.[6] It would be altogether inadequate, though, to do no more than to formally compare these two groups of a society and to restrict the discussion to the question of primacy of either political or military objectives in certain decisions. This frequently occurs in German discussions of the problem and inevitably leads to an attitude which excuses the actions of Hitler's *Wehrmacht* by pointing out that the total subordination of military officers under the primacy of a political leadership is a rule also in a democratic society. It is obvious that formal argumentation of this sort will not lead anywhere.

NATIONAL POLITICAL INSTRUCTION IN THE THIRD REICH

This example seems worth a discussion. In the winter of 1933/34 the Minister of the *Reichswehr*, Blomberg, introduced the National Political instruction. The basic book of instruction consisted of a collection of laws, official orders, quotations from Hitler as well as speeches and writings of leading National Socialists.[7] This book was constantly revised and brought up to date, so that as early as 1935 the sixth edition was already in circulation. The contents of the book included the main ideas of the national-socialistic ideology, the party's own interpretations of

Hitler's politics as well as fundamental discussions about the relationship between the *Wehrmacht* and the national-socialistic society, whereby the strong kinship between them was repeatedly stressed. From April 1, 1934 on, the 'Conceptions for the Instruction on Current Political Affairs' were published once or twice a month and added to the so-called 'Stepping Stones of the National Political Instruction'. The instructions had to be delivered by the company commander. *Reichswehrminister* Blomberg explained this new institution: 'During the first year of the national-socialistic leadership, the foundations were laid for the political and economical renewal of the nation. During the second year it became an utmost necessity to instill the leading ideas of the national-socialistic state into the people. An education of this kind is therefore an important task for all those organisations which support this new state with their convictions. This especially applies to the *Wehrmacht*'.[8]

The further development up to the installation of national-socialistic leading-officers shall not be dealt with here. In this connection it seems above all important that the highest military officers deliberately promoted National Socialism, a fact which was greatly favoured by the partial identity of the two ideologies.

Soldierly behaviour was carried into the whole society through 'civilian' institutions. The militarism of the national-socialistic society seems to be based on premises not sufficiently considered in Wildenmann's definition. This means that the institution of political education is caught between the political and strategic conceptions of the legislature on the one hand and the military leadership on the other, so that its obvious success can be seen as a consequence of the large identity of the two, while its obvious failure arises from certain conflicting positions. Provided that one is not of the irreversible conviction that the peculiarity of the military organisation does not permit the use of the term 'success' for an anyway marginal political education[9], then one will have to deal intensively with the amount, the contents and the different kinds of political education within the Armed Forces in order to determine the amount of agreement between the values and norms of the civilian and of the military sphere of society.

Concerning the national-socialistic type of regime this task should be somewhat simpler than would be expected from the memoirs of those directly involved. Also in regard to the communist regime there seems to be this large identity, although the content is quite different here. 'In the socialist state, the solution of the problem of the relationship between the civilian and the military power is based on the principle of party-leadership within the Armed Forces. This question, which presents such diffi-

102

culties for the class-society, is solved here through the realization of the principle of integration.'[10] This principle of integration is based on the leadership of the Communist Party, on the political education of military cadres according to the directions of the Party, and on the constant integration of military and civilian life – i.e. on carrying politics into the Armed Forces. Opinions may differ as to the factual realization of this principle of integration, but it is widely agreed that this principle is of great importance.

But how is this question solved in the 'class-society', as Wiatr calls it, that is in the bourgeois governed western industrial nations? It is questionable whether or not the West German example justifies general statements in this respect, but it should nevertheless be interesting to investigate this question.

THE POLITICAL EDUCATION IN THE BUNDESWEHR

The founding of the *Bundeswehr* in 1955 was prepared for and accompanied by an extremely bitter discussion about the moral and political justification of rearmament and its possible benefits. The Federal Government carried out these discussions with immense propagandistic efforts. Finally the rearmament took place, mainly because of outside pressure, which was cleverly used by the Federal Government.

When the principal question of rearmament was settled, there still remained the question of which model or example would provide a suitable pattern for the establishment of the new Armed Forces. The mortgage of the past, which had to be taken up after an interruption of ten years, influenced the integration of the Armed Forces into the society and state in such a way that the degree of potential controls through the civilian society was greatly expanded. Indeed, the creation of the laws concerning the military organisation must be considered quite a legislative achievement: a number of reform-oriented soldiers as well as nonmilitary individuals regulated the relations between the military organisation and the society in such a way, that the values and norms of a democratic society would bind the soldiers as far as this was possible. It must be realized of course, that the political pressure in this direction was so strong at the time that a great many of those involved, initially adherent to reforms out of a purely opportunistic attitude later turned back to their old conceptions. To many conservative officers the reform in the structural organisation meant no more than a temporary mimicry that could soon be given up again.[11] Details of the laws concerning the military organisation need not be discussed here; in the 'Soldier's Law of March 19th, 1956' it stated as a matter of principle that a soldier should have the same right as any other citizen and that he should recognize and preserve the free democratic order established through the West German constitution.[12] The moral values of the West German constitution became binding also for the Armed Forces.

Considering these constitutional intentions, the reality of legal practice looks far less favorable.[13] Nevertheless the challenge of these laws remains alive.

The constitutional reorganization of the Armed Forces into a 'Force for Democracy' was meant to signal the beginning of a sociological program of reforms, centered around the political conception of the 'citizen in uniform', that is the democratic soldier.

THE CONCEPTION OF THE 'CITIZEN IN UNIFORM'

Professional soldiers and draftees serve in the West German *Bundeswehr* as citizens and not as a group taken out of its political context through over-or-underprivileges; that is the meaning of 'citizen in uniform'.[14] Such a scarce and slightly polemical definition could express all or nothing – but it does not do justice to the original conception. On the other hand, the original conception cannot be easily outlined because of certain inner contradictions, which ultimately caused it to fail, although it served as a pretext for a long time. According to the opinion of Graf Baudissin, one of the exponents of this conception, the main objective was to make the newly drafted young soldiers see why and for what they were making these sacrifices. 'Without instructions in civics, they would never understand the meaning and the limitation of their military service. Without this (civics education), they will not be soldiers, but mercenaries, they would be tools of any regime or technician of force without a conscience'. In answer to a question about the meaning and the purpose of political education of the Armed Forces, Baudissin said in 1954: 'There are but two alternatives: freedom and an existence guaranteeing basic human dignity or subjugation under a totalitarian apparatus'.[15] Therefore the democratic consciousness can be regarded as the qualitative characteristic of a soldier in the Armed Forces of a democratic society. This demand should be met above all by the members of the officer corps of the *Bundeswehr*. Again and again Baudissin expressed this central idea: 'Only he can defend a society who cherishes it, has grown into it, and who knows that his very existence depends on the continuance of his

104

order'.[16] The 'citizen in uniform' very quickly turned into a reality of a citizen filled with anticommunism. Political education within the Armed Forces has parallelled the development of political education within the society since 1945. According to § 33 of the 'Soldier's Law', the *Bundeswehr* pledges responsibility for the political education of the soldiers: 'The soldiers will be given instructions in civics and international law. The officer conducting the class may not restrict the discussion of political questions to the portrayal of only one type of political view. Instead the classes must be held in such a way that the soldiers will not be influenced either in favor of or against certain political opinions. The soldiers must be instructed about their civic and international responsibilities and rights in peace and war.'[17]

The amount of political education in the West German Armed Forces, its contents, and its structure are laid down in the 'Central Official Orders 12/1,' concerning 'moral armament', and also apply to the field of political education.[18] In these obligatory regulations, the conception of the 'citizen in uniform' is set down as the main idea for education and training in the *Bundeswehr* and portrays a soldier who will stand up for freedom and democracy with a firm moral and political conviction, and who will be prepared to defend these principles even at the cost of his life. In this connection it is the aim of the 'moral armament' to firmly convince the individual soldier that his moral convictions, his conceptions of freedom and democracy, are values worth fighting for. For this he needs an inner firmness based on the knowledge of fighting for a just cause, faith in his own abilities, faith in his fellow soldiers and his leadership. After this brief outline of the function, which 'moral armament' serves within the frame of the military establishment, the official regulations continue to give a detailed account of its further tasks.[19] As has been pointed out, the knowledge of the rights and duties of citizenship is considered the foundation of the 'moral armament' and consequently the soldier has to be taught civics.

Along with the relevant activities of public organizations, the military provides the so-called 'Information for the Armed Forces', a part of which consists of the civics instruction, carried out by the group leader (company level). According to § 33 of the 'Soldier's Law', the instructor is called upon to refrain from letting his personal views determine the outcome of the instruction. 'The instruction in civics increases the appreciation of the free society, deepens the political consciousness and provides

Table 1

Das totalitäre System
„totus" = ganz, allumfassend

A) Fluchtgründe

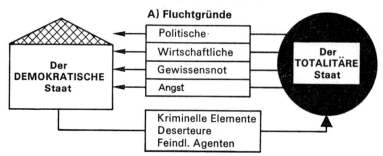

| | Der DEMOKRATISCHE Staat | → | Politische | → | Der TOTALITÄRE Staat |
| Wirtschaftliche |
| Gewissensnot |
| Angst |

Kriminelle Elemente
Deserteure
Feindl. Agenten

B) u. C) Aufbau des totalitären Staates und seine Zwangsmittel

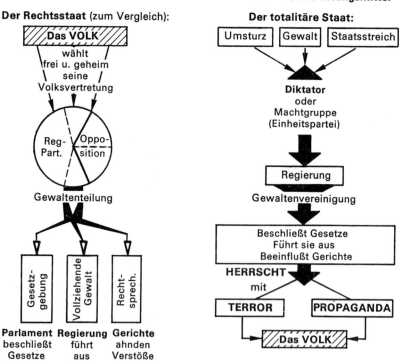

Der Rechtsstaat (zum Vergleich):

Das VOLK

wählt
frei u. geheim
seine
Volksvertretung

Reg-Part. / Oppo-sition

Gewaltenteilung

Gesetz-gebung — Vollziehende Gewalt — Recht-sprech.

Parlament **Regierung** **Gerichte**
beschließt   führt   ahnden
Gesetze   aus   Verstöße

Merkmale:
1) „Alle Gewalt geht vom Volke aus"
2) Gewaltenteilung
3) Grundrechte garantiert

Der totalitäre Staat:

Umsturz Gewalt Staatsstreich

Diktator
oder
Machtgruppe
(Einheitspartei)

Regierung

Gewaltenvereinigung

Beschließt Gesetze
Führt sie aus
Beeinflußt Gerichte

HERRSCHT
mit

TERROR   **PROPAGANDA**

Das VOLK

Merkmale:
1) „Der Staat bin ICH"
2) Gewaltenvereinigung
3) Mißachtung der Grundrechte

106

information about the character, types, and the dangers of totalitarianism'. Because the main burden of providing 'moral armament' rests on the greatly overworked responsible officers, the official regulations give an extremely detailed account of the basic ideas and the teaching aids for the instructions in civics. Pertaining to the aims of 'moral armament' the teaching procedure stresses three main topics:

— the free democratic society and its basic values;
— forces and conceptions endangering the free democracy; the reality of life under totalitarian rule;
— means and methods of totalitarian threats; the psychological strain in battle.

These basic ideas are further explained: 'The conception of a free democratic society, the teachings of the nature and values of democracy should make the moral foundations and the aims of the Free World an integral part of the soldier's personality. The value of the European and Atlantic alliances and its power should be established in his views, and the importance of integrating our state into the great community of the free nations should be made clear.

The soldier should be brought to see the advantages and characteristics of our order of life, as they present themselves in our state, our laws, our economy, and our society. These characteristics should be illustrated during the lecture through examples occurring in every-day life. Here too it is not enough to simply provide theoretical knowledge. Instead, our order of life, our belief of freedom, justice, and human dignity have to be brought to life through the practice of modern human guidance within the soldierly order in the every-day experience of military service and through the example set by the officers.' Similar explanations were issued for the two topics of 'moral armament.' After a reminder to the officers to thoroughly acquaint themselves with the subject to be discussed and not to distort the information through exaggeration and hatred, the official regulations then discuss the available teaching aids. Publications for the 'inner guidance' are pointed out, especially the monthly booklets called 'Information for the Armed Forces', which indeed furnish enough suitable material for the instructions.[20] Apart from this, a number of teaching aids were available through the libraries of the *Bundeswehr*.[21] Greatly appreciated for the civics instruction in the *Bundeswehr* are also a certain type of illustrated tables that can be projected before the class and on which different topics are clearly outlined. An example of such a table is shown here (Table 1)[22].

Concerning the civics instruction, the official regulations provide the following obligatory schedule:

1. Basic Course of Instruction (1 to 3 months of service), a total number of 12 lectures on the topics that follow:
   - The divided Germany (end of the Second World War and the divided Germany from 1945 until today)
   - Our basic rights
   - Life under a Communist regime (political terror, suppression of the freedom of consciousness)
   - The basic duties of the soldier (meaning of the Oath and Pledge of Allegiance, the moral conception of justice and freedom – necessity and meaning of the military service; the duty of loyalty and bravery)
2. Main and Special Course of Instruction (4 to 18 months of service), total number of 46 lectures on the following topics:
   - What do we defend? Germany (territory and borders, population, countryside, economy and traffic; causes and military development of the Second World War, capitulation 1945, expulsion from Eastern territories, division of Germany, the German Eastern regions, creation of the Federal Republic of Germany, the countries, Parliamentary Council, *Bundestag* and *Bundesrat*, the Federal Government, Berlin – island of freedom, Four-Power administration, division of the city, protecting forces, Berlin Ultimatum 1958, August 13, 1961; claim for the unity of Germany, right for self-determination as the basis for a reunification, the FRG within free Europe, European unity since 1945)
   - What do we defend? Our free order of life (parties and elections, political freedom of conscience, forms and meaning of elections; our democracy, the organisation of the state, our constitutional state organs of jurisdiction, obligation to law and justice, the citizen in the constitutional state; our economic order; our free order of society, the social structure, nature of the pluralistic society, press, radio, television; the nature of the free order of life: summary)
   - The defence of freedom and one's own country (the *Bundeswehr*, founding and development of the West German contribution to the defence of freedom, NATO, development and purpose, political and military structure, the armed forces of the Allies, Europe and the Atlantic partnership; the example of great soldiers, conduct and achievement of German soldiers in war and peace; our national anthem and our symbols; the defence of freedom as a task for the whole people: summary)
   - What threatens us? National Socialism as a historical example

(the downfall of freedom, the end of the Weimar Republic; the seizure of power in 1933 and its consequences, total adjustment, dictatorship of the Party, the annulment of freedom, justice and security)

— What threatens us? Communism as shown in the example of the Soviet occupational zone (the communist dictatorship; the courts in the service of the Party, the annulment of the citizens' rights; the communistic planned economy, the plan, the bureaucracy; exploitation of manpower)

— What threatens us? The world revolution (the communist teachings of the World revolution, theory and realisation, examples: CSSR, the civil war in Greece, Baltic states; suppression of rebellions in the sphere of Soviet rule, examples: Berlin, June 17th, 1953, Hungary, 1956)

— The threat to freedom from within (misuse of freedom in the state and society, Art. 18 Basic Law, indifference of the individual toward the community)

— Which mental and psychological strains occur in battle? (the modern scene of war, psychology as a weapon, temptation, threats, undermining of faith, methods of the communist psychological attack: part 1 – propaganda and agitation, examples of communist slogans, means: pamphlet, radio, television, film, literature, letter campaign; part 2 – infiltration, agents, voluntary and involuntary helpers; – overcoming of a crisis, individual initiative, preventing and overcoming panics, overcoming of the ABC-complex; conduct as prisoners of war, tactics and methods of psychologically influencing prisoners in communist custody, rules of conduct, 'I shall not be intimidated!' – (repeating and summarizing: intentions, means and methods of communist psychological warfare)

The 'moral armament' of the soldiers is not only carried out through the civics instruction; a second means of instruction and guidance is the information for the Armed Forces. The contents correspond to those of the civics instruction. The term 'information for the Armed Forces' includes three kinds of information: the 'general information', the 'current information' and the 'brief information'. This differentiation is easily recognized; special importance is attributed to the 'current information', for which a certain amount of time is reserved in the schedule: at least 30 min. a week for current events of the day, 60 min. a month for the 'topic of the month', and 60 min. a month for the *Bundeswehr*-film-performance. The 'topic of the month' was published for several years in the 'Information for the Armed Forces' along with methodical advice.

In a class on current information, the following topics should be dealt with: important events of the day, memorial days, regional and local events. Material on these topics is also published in the daily 'Messages to the Soldier', which is edited by the Ministry of Defence.[23] It is apparent that the task of 'moral armament' is not an altogether easy one for the unit leaders, especially if one considers that neither at the officer-training-schools of the Army nor at the respective institutions of the other branches of the military forces[24] are the prospective officers given special training for this job.

This fact points to a first obvious contradiction in the practice of the political education in the West German Armed Forces. Even without a far reaching analysis of the ideological implications underlying the Official Regulations of 1966, one feels inclined to doubt the credibility and the power of conviction of these conceptions[25]: a black-and-white picture is painted here, and strong efforts are made to cover up the by now obvious shortcomings on one's 'own' side.

DIFFICULTIES AND CONTRADICTIONS

The problematic confrontation, the rigidity of the enemy's image and above all the constant attempts to cover up the discrepancy between the proclaimed self-conception and the reality give rise to a number of contradictions and difficulties, which, in turn, influence the reality of political education in the every-day practice of the military forces.

First, the discussion about the actual aims of political education in the Armed Forces has never unequivocally been decided in favour of one attitude or another. It is true that these attitudes only vary in their different accentuations, although these should not be underestimated.

P. Balke, who has given an analysis of political education in the *Bundeswehr* on the basis of empirical findings, follows a similar argumentation to Graf Baudissin's. He interprets these aims above all from the viewpoint of the whole society and its civilian self-conception: 'With the creation of an army based on the draft, a new additional opportunity presented itself to the Federal Government, to introduce every young citizen at a relatively late stage of his mental development to questions concerning the structure of the state, the rights and duties of a citizen, the knowledge of basic political connections, and the role of the military forces in the German postwar democracy. This was made possible through a kind of "graduate course" that initially lasted for twelve months, later for eighteen.

110

An additional, legitimate and promising pedagogical possibility of influence has appeared, and a conscientious and adequate fulfilment promised to increase the democratic potential of the FRG considerably'.[26] The temptation of labelling such an interpretation with 'sancta simplicitas' seems great: but even he who considers himself a realist should withstand it for the time being.[27] Indeed, political education in the Armed Forces would have to be organized and planned along different lines if it were to fulfil this aim.[28] The majority of the officer corps of the *Bundeswehr* and also of the top officials in the Ministry define the objective of political education in a different way. Statements issued for instance by von Hassel, the former Minister of Defence, are characteristic of this fact. In a speech, he pointed out the necessity of political education as an 'especially important task' for an army based on the draft; the spirit and the fighting will of the soldiers have today become even more important than in the past. And they are both founded on insight and conviction. 'It is the task of the civics education in the *Bundeswehr* to achieve this'.[29] In the same way, Walter Loch, *Regierungsrat* in the Federal Ministry of Defence, defines the civics education in the *Bundeswehr* as a 'means of guidance'.[30] He continues to explain this: 'Civics education in the *Bundeswehr* is neither an end in itself, nor a "democratic adornment". It is a necessity in a modern fighting force'.[31] According to Loch, this necessity derives from the aim of such an education, in which the defence motive is explained and the inner structure of the units stabilized and secured, so that even small formations or the individual soldier are able to act 'in accordance with the aims of the whole'. For a thinking type of obedience calls for a citizen, as only he is able to preserve the necessary enthusiasm of freedom.[32]

These not altogether identical explanations are clearly dominated by the military aspect: here political education aims at integrating the military norms and values into the society not so much by making the soldier pledge to them as by integrating the soldier into the military forces. The term of the 'thinking type of obedience', that was introduced here, is so obviously misplaced that one is inclined to suspect a mistake on the part of the printer. The true aim of the author and all those whose conception he expressed is to increase the morale and thereby the effectiveness of the military forces. This soon leads to conceptions, according to which the integration of the military establishment and the civilian society takes place not on the basis of an increasing democracy, but on the basis of the formation of the people according to the needs of military planning. From time to time statements to the effect have been made by high ranking officials: for instance in cases when they believed that they were able to judge the democratic substance and the extent of political education in the civilian society by the actual manifest willingness for military service.[33] This somewhat dangerous misunderstanding of a democratic consciousness by high ranking officials was made apparent through the publication of the so-called 'Schnez-Study' in 1969. This much discussed report on the conditions of the Army, which was written by a number of conservative officers, held the conditions within the society responsible for the stated shortcomings. 'Only a reform of "head and body", of the *Bundeswehr* and the society, can get to the root of this evil and can decisively raise the morale and the effectiveness of the Army.'[34] This frightening return to the mentality of many officers in the early thirties has been sufficiently criticized in the public discussion of the 'Schnez-Study'.

In connection with the general uncertainty about the aims of a political education in the military forces, this incident demonstrates the necessity of a clarifying discussion that takes into consideration the actual practice of political education in the *Bundeswehr*. That practice is in effect very much different than is imagined by the exponents of one or the other conceptions.[35] As was pointed out in the beginning, the activities of political education in the civilian sphere are also not in an admirable state, and this fact alone leads to certain conclusions in regard to the 'moral armament'. In the opinion of those who are professionally involved in the *Bundeswehr*, there is hardly the danger that the *Bundeswehr* will develop into the reactionary 'school of the nation', but rather into a second-grade national institution.[36] This somewhat exaggerated view holds true at least insofar as the majority of young draftees[37] have far less knowledge of civics and, what seems worse, far less interest in it than should be expected of a 'democratic soldier'. This failure on behalf of the general societal efforts concerning political education makes it difficult to effect 'moral armament' in the Armed Forces. On the other hand it places the military in a position of monopoly as regards political education. 'Political education in the Armed Forces should actually be just *one* part in the large system of political education that neither starts nor ends with the military service. Public schools as well as youth organizations should have already fulfilled their part by the time the young man becomes a soldier, and equally, adult education should set in once the soldier returns to civilian life. In reality political education in the Armed Forces presents the *only* and the *last* systematic and planned political information given to the young citizen.'[38] In addition, one could doubt whether indeed the part of political education in the Armed Forces is carried out in a systematic and planned way. According to the trustworthy accounts of many who are directly involved, this is not so at all. 'In no other field of training in the *Bundeswehr* is the situation as bad' as in the field of civics education, declared a batallion commander.[39] Pöggeler also states that in spite of the technical possibilities, political education in the military forces is considered boring and tedious. This is partly blamed on the fact that the unit leaders are overworked and can therefore reserve only inconvenient times for the political instructions, and partly on their old-fashioned didactic methods. Seen in this light, the statistical data given by Eric Waldman[40] as proof of the successful civics instruction of soldiers must be regarded differently. The same applies to the following research, carried out by the Institute of Demoscopics, Allensbach, in May 1965.

Question: 'This question concerns the civics instruction in the *Bundeswehr*: Did you enjoy these classes or did you not enjoy them so much?' The answers of the reservists were as follows:

41% 'enjoyed'
28% 'satisfied'
24% 'not enjoyed'
7% 'no comment'

Question: 'If you could decide – would you reserve more time for these classes or less?'
Answers:

58% 'more time'
29% 'no change'
9% 'less time'
4% 'no comment'[41]

The results should not be overestimated.

What now would be the balance drawn up for the political education of the military forces in the FRG, from which viewpoint can it be judged as effective, successful, indispensible, or the contrary?

CONCLUSIONS

Can the effectiveness of political education in the military forces be measured? Are its actual and/or hoped for results so important that an attempt would be justified?

To answer these questions, it is necessary to once more consider the whole relationship between the Armed Forces and the Western democratic society, for it first has to be decided from what perspective the possible

113

success or failure of political education in the military forces should be seen. Those liberals defending the thesis of an incompatibility of the capitalistic industrial society and military forces[42] are usually inclined to think, that an 'objective control' of the military forces through the civilian society would be the best of all temporary solutions to the fundamental conflict, and that, therefore, the ideological integration of the military could best be achieved through the accentuation of the special military professional code.

This 'integration at a distance'[43] might optimally link an officer corps of veteran specialists to the Western industrial society – although that too needs further discussion. For an Army based on the draft and for the multitude of sergeants and other personnel, it seems to be an inadequate means.

To be sure, political ideology has but an incidental importance in the whole of fighting motivations.[44] But is it not true that in almost all the Western industrial nations there exists a confusion as to the sense and purpose of soldiers and that to an ever larger degree the defence motivation of the civilian society is questioned?

Only veteran higher officers[45] and politicians whose ideas were formed in the fifties could regret the resumption, as a result of the recruiting difficulties of the military forces, of the political and strategical discussion about the sense and purpose of the military forces in the whole of the society. On the other hand this discussion needs to be taken seriously, and this in turn requires, that those who lead it should know their subject. One surely has to agree with Janowitz when he points out the ambiguity of anticommunist indoctrination of Western soldiers.[46] And equally, one cannot agree with the opinion voiced by Ludwig Schulte, who recently made the following statement about the political education in the *Bundeswehr*:

'Contrary to all those foreboding calls from leftist sociologists and leftist intellectuals, who accuse the *Bundeswehr* of stereotype manipulative and antidemocratic educational activities, the official regulations and decrees make it clear that the *Bundeswehr* has as a matter of principle given up the trend of using psychological influence in the educational activities... Without objectivity in educational work it simply is impossible to reach an understanding of the meaning of the military purpose'.[47] A somewhat coarse polemic (mainly against Wido Mosen), and a naive interpretation of 'objectivity', this does not lead anywhere.

On the other hand, there is an increasing call for an ideological and strategic inventory of the Federal Republic. What in our society, that is looked upon so critically by a strong minority of the young generation,

114

has to be defended, against what threat coming from where? These questions have to be answered by the whole of our society, including the soldiers.

So actually, the conceptions and aims of political education in the military forces should not be above all, adjusted to the requirement of the military organization, but rather to those of the society.

'Once of the most important political goals of education, also in the military forces..., should lie in teaching the soldiers to pay attention to the condition within one's own state'.[48] In this way civics education could make an important contribution to the democratic influence of the military consciousness. And who could deny that this would be a very effective way of working against the primacy of military thinking?

1. Morris JANOWITZ and Roger W. LITTLE, *Militär und Gesellschaft*, Boppard 1965, p. 158 ff. (German translation of: *Sociology and the Military Establishment*).
2. K. P. WALLRAVEN, Politische Bildung, in: Axel GÖRLITZ (ed.), *Handlexikon zur Politikwissenschaft*, München 1970, p. 315.
3. Answer given by the Federal Minister of the Interior to the official inquiry of the party fractions of the FDP, CDU/CSU, SPD, Drucksache V/3297 des Deutschen Bundestages, 23-9-1968, p.3.
4. WALLRAVEN, *op. cit.*, p. 316.
5. The answer given by the Federal Minister of the Interior, *op. cit.*, p. 3 f.
6. See the more general statement by R. WILDENMANN, 'Militarism as the transfer of "soldierly" behaviors to "civilian" interactions and decisions, is the latent consequence of any military education', in: *Politische Stellung und Kontrolle des Militärs*, in: R. KÖNIG (ed.), *Beiträge zur Militärsoziologie, Sonderheft 12 der Kölner Zeitschrift für Soziologie und Sozialpsychologie*, Köln/Opladen 1968, p. 61.
7. See M. MESSERSCHMIDT, *Die Wehrmacht im NS-Staat. Zeit der Indoktrination*, Hamburg 1969.
8. MESSERSCHMIDT, *op. cit.*, p. 18.
9. M. JANOWITZ, *op. cit.*, p. 161.
10. Jerzy J. WIATR, Sozio-politische Besonderheiten und Funktionen von Streitkräften in sozialistischen Ländern, in: *Beiträge zur Militärsoziologie, op. cit.*, p. 108.
11. Rather strong statements to this effect were made to a group of prospective officers of the *Generalstab* in spring 1969 by the Vice Inspector of the Armed Forces. His statements became publicly known through indiscretion and were widely discussed at the time.
12. Law on the Legal Position of the Soldier, §6, §8, München, undated, p. 43.
13. See: W. VON BREDOW, Der Wehrbeauftragte. Konzeption und Verfall einer Kontrollinstitution, in: *Blätter für deutsche und internationale Politik*, 1968, no. 9.
14. H. GROSSE, Soldat und politische Bildung, in: *Aus Politik und Zeitgeschichte*, no. 8/1968, p. 5.
15. Wolf Graf BAUDISSIN, Staatsbürgerliche Bildung und Erziehung zur politischen Verantwortung in der Truppe (1954), in: *Soldat für den Frieden, Entwürfe für eine zeitgemässe Bundeswehr*, München 1969, p. 260.
16. BAUDISSIN, Das Leitbild des zukünftigen Soldaten (1955), in: *Soldat für den Frieden, op. cit.*, p. 213.
17. Law on the Position of the Soldier, *op. cit.*, p. 51.
18. This official instruction dates back to January 1966; it has replaced a less detailed one. I quote from a copy of the 'Centre for Information and Press' of the Ministry of Defence, January 1968.
19. The term 'moral armament' has caused some critical discussions within the *Bundeswehr* just as the preceding term 'psychological armament'; at present the tendency exists to replace it by the term 'Information for the Armed Forces and civics education'.
20. Critical analyses can be found of the contents of the 'Information for the Armed Forces in: Hartmut LÜCK, *Zur politischen Bildung in der Bundeswehr. Eine Analyse zweier Jahrgänge der 'Information für die Truppe'*, München 1969 (*Gestern und heute*, 40); also W. VON BREDOW and A. HEIMANSBERG, Gesinnung bei der Bundeswehr, in: *Liberal*, II, no. 7, 1969, pp. 500–513.

21. Also e.g. the Monthly Review of the *Bundeswehr* as well as its educational films and collections of illustrated tables.
22. Taken from: Oberstleutnant S. HEYD and Oberst J. JAITNER, *Der Offizierunterricht in der Bundeswehr. Eine Sammlung ausgewählter Unterrichtsbeispiele*, Darmstadt 1967, 4th edition, p. 156.
23. The above mentioned information is intended mainly for use in battle.
24. Information given by a speaker of the Federal Ministry of Defence in May 1970.
25. The present version of the Central Official Regulations 12/1 originates from the leader of the department for psychological armament from 1962–1964 who was a strong representative of the Cold-War-Course. Since then language and style of the department have become somewhat milder. See: P. BALKE, *Der politische Unterricht in der Bundeswehr. Auswertung einer Fallstudie*, Diss. Kiel 1969, p. 115 ff.
26. BALKE, *Der politische Unterricht, op. cit.*, p. 1 f. On another page (p. 360) the author points out that the civics education in the *Bundeswehr* has not lost its experimental character up to this day.
27. That could also be said to those leftist critics, who like Wido MOSEN (*Eine Militärsoziologie*, Neuwied/Berlin 1967, p. 116) accuse the 'citizen in uniform' that its main function lies in the dishonest reconciliation of two institutions which are actually incompatible, namely the undemocratic military forces and the democratic society.
28. BALKE has made concrete suggestions for an alternative of the existing conception: elimination of the term 'moral armament', abolishment of the scheme 'for what-against what', mental and psychological strains, replacement of the present instructions through an education for alert, informed and critical citizens. See: BALKE, *Der politische Unterricht, op. cit.*, p. 345 ff.
29. K.-U. VON HASSEL, *Verantwortung für die Freiheit. Auszüge aus Reden und Veröffentlichungen in den Jahren 1963/64*, Boppard 1965, 2nd edition, p. 308.
30. W. LOCH, Staatsbürgerlicher Unterricht in der Bundeswehr, in: *Dokumente und Kommentare*, Suppl. to no. 1/1965 of *Information für die Truppe*, p. 3.
31. LOCH, Staatsbürgerlicher Unterricht, *op. cit.*, p. 5.
32. See also the farfetched and simply curious differentiation: 'civics education has nothing in common with the propaganda that was carried out by the national socialistic leading officers of Hitler's *Wehrmacht* and is today continued by the polit officers of the National Peoples Army in the Soviet Occupied Zone. Civics Education does not aim at creating a fanatical soldier'.
33. See: E. WAGEMANN (Oberst i.G.), *Staatsbürgerliche Erziehung in Schule und Bundeswehr*, Bad Boll 1964.
34. Quoted from: Abdruck der 'Schnez-Studie' in: *Blätter für deutsche und internationale Politik*, 15, 1970, no. 3.
35. See: Karl BAUER, Der Staatsbürger in Uniform, in: *Dokumente und Kommentare*, Suppl. to no. 3/1966 of *Information für die Truppe*, p. 10 ff.
36. See: General VON DE MAIZIERE, Erziehung zum Staatsbürger in Uniform, in: *Dokumente und Kommentare*, Suppl. to no. 3/1966 of *Information für die Truppe*.
37. At least as far as high school graduates are concerned, this might have changed during the last years – even though in an opposite direction as the outdated but still practised directives of political education in schools.
38. F. PÖGGELER (Mitglied des Beirats für Innere Führung), Politische Bildung in den Streitkräften. Praxis, Wirkung, Reform, in: *Wehrkunde*, 18, 1969, no. 8, p. 394 f.
39. G. KIESSLING, Der staatsbürgerliche Unterricht in der Truppe. Erfahrungen eines Bataillonskommandeurs, in: *Information für die Truppe*, no. 2, 1969, p. 94.

40. E. WALDMAN, *Soldat im Staat. Der Staatsbürger in Uniform. Vorstellung und Wirklichkeit*, Boppard 1964, 3rd edition.
41. These figures have not been published up to now.
42. Cf. L. VON FRIEDEBURG, Zum Verhältnis von Militär und Gesellschaft in der Bundesrepublik, in: G. PICHT (ed.), *Studien zur politischen und gesellschaftlichen Situation der Bundeswehr*, Vol. 2, Berlin/Witten, 1966.
43. Cf. S. P. HUNTINGTON, *The Soldier and the State. The Theory and Politics of Civil-Military Relations*, Cambridge (Mass.) 1967, 4th edition.
44. Cf. Ch. C. MOSKOS Jr., Eigeninteresse, Primärgruppen und Ideologie. Eine Untersuchung der Kampfmotivation amerikanischer Truppen in Vietnam, in: *Beiträge zur Militärsoziologie, op. cit.*, p. 199 ff.
45. Cf. B. ABRAHAMSSON, Military Professionalization and Estimates on the Probability of War, in: J. A. A. VAN DOORN (ed.), *Military Profession and Military Regimes. Commitments and Conflicts*, The Hague/Paris 1969, p. 35 ff.
46. M. JANOWITZ, *Militär und Gesellschaft, op. cit.*, p. 161 f.
47. L. SCHULTE, Innere Führung – ein dynamisches Prinzip. Versuch einer Systematisierung, in: *Wehrkunde*, 19, 1969, no. 5, p. 244.
48. P. BALKE, *Der politische Unterricht, op. cit.*, p. 361.

Career Motivation
and Military Ideology:
the Case of Chile

R. A. HANSEN

Roy Hansen is an Associate Professor in the Department of Sociology at the University of South Florida. He is a graduate of UCLA and was an Assistant Professor at the University of California, Berkeley (1964–1968). His doctoral dissertation was an analysis of the Chilean Army: *Military Culture and Organizational Decline* and he has subsequently authored several papers on the topic.

Two types of explanatory variables have been generally utilized in the analysis of internal differences in the ideology and identity of the military officer: (1) social origins (such as class, regional, ethnic, or religious background), and (2) differential career patterns. The former appears to be of decisive importance when the social origins of the officer corps are highly diverse and professional institutions poorly developed. Since social class differences frequently encompass a number of these factors, it has been the most widely utilized variable of this type. Despite current trends toward increasing professionalization and middle class monopolization of the military establishment of Latin America, social class remains a significant explanatory variable in the culture area.[1]

Homogeneity of social origin or highly developed professional institutions may so reduce the impact of other factors that internal differences in military sub-culture can derive in great part from differential career patterns.[2] Career patterns also assume major significance during transitional periods in the history of the organization and profession. Alba, for example, distinguishes between three types of contemporary officers in Latin America on the basis of changing patterns of military education and professional experience: 'the barracks groups,' 'the school officers,' and 'the laboratory men.'[3]

Neither social origins nor differential career patterns alone were judged to be suitable independent variables in the analysis of differences in ideology among the elite of the Chilean Army. Military careers of the elite were essentially all of a prescribed pattern and their social origin (and that of the officer corps in general) was overwhelmingly middle class.[4] However, an examination of civilian attitudes with respect to the meaning and role of the military in Chile demonstrated intra-class variance to generally be larger than mean inter-class differences. This suggests the possibility that differences in professional military ideology may significantly derive from the selective recruitment of specific 'social types' (such as the super-patriot or the status seeker) from the population-at-large.

A substantial body of research has demonstrated the existence of a meaningful relationship between selected personality dispositions, values, and career choice.[5] Moreover, a number of studies have demonstrated the significance of such characteristics for role performance and hence for institutional functioning.[6] These studies suggest that investigation of modal personality types characteristic of any given organization or institution might contribute significantly to a better understanding of policy formation and effectiveness. Inkeles, for example, states:

While accepting the crucial importance of the objective factors which determine social behavior, we must recognize that recruitment into occupational and other status positions, and the quality of performance in the roles people are thus assigned, may, to an important degree, be influenced by personal qualities in individuals. It may be assumed, further, that this happens on a sufficiently large scale to be a crucial factor in determining the functioning of any social system. To the degree that this is true, to predict the functioning of a particular institution, of a small- or large-scale system, we need to know not only the system of status-positions but also the distribution of personality characteristics in the population-at-large and among those playing important roles in the system.[7]

Inducements offered by a military career include economic benefits, a particular life-style, patriotism, comradeship, social status and prestige, and satisfactions based upon an identification with the goals of the military. *We propose that specific social types from the population-at-large will be attracted to the military by distinctive sets of career motivations and that differences in military ideology are thus significantly related to career motivation.*[8] In the first part of the paper, a typology is developed based upon patterns of career motivation. Three major orientations are proposed: the 'careerist,' the 'idealist,' and the 'traditionalist.' The remainder of the paper utilizes this typology in investigating differences in orientation within the elite to the meaning and role of the military as the profession responds to pressures generated by the rapid social change of Chilean society. Specifically we hypothesize that the views of 'careerist' officers will be the most civilianized, 'idealists' least civilianized, with 'traditionalists' occupying an intermediate position.

Data for the study was gathered during a series of three field trips to Chile between December, 1964, and June, 1965. Interviews with retired generals form the primary empirical data for the analysis of the orientations of the military elite. Thirty-nine of the fifty-eight generals retired since 1953 were located and a standardized interview administered to thirty-eight of them. This interview was extensive (2 to 5 hours) and covered a variety of subjects, from general social and political philosophy to specific questions on personal background and career patterns. Fourteen of the retired generals were interviewed a second time using a less structured format in order to further elaborate issues of particular interest raised in the first interview.

TYPES OF CAREER MOTIVATIONS

Stated career motivations were utilized to operationally classify officers with respect to their career perspectives. Three major orientations to the military were identified: the 'careerist,' the 'idealist,' and the 'tradition-

122

alist.' Careerist officers are concerned chiefly with the economic benefits, social status, and security offered by the career. The idealist officers' motivations emphasize 'boyhood ambition,' military life-style, or patriotic values. Traditionalists follow almost mechanically the interests of their parents.

Of the thirty-eight retired generals interviewed, thirteen were classified as careerists. Classification as a careerist did not imply that no other career motives were important, but rather that what we have defined as 'careerist' inducements appeared to be most potent. These comments illustrate the careerist perspective:

General of Division: 'It is sad to say but (the decision to become an officer) was due to the economic situation of my father. Instead of going to work in a bank, since I couldn't go into medicine, I came into the Army. *I didn't want to work at the bank.*'

General of Division: 'I became an orphan when I was six years old and lived practically from the good will of my uncles. In the third year of secondary school, a well-situated uncle wanted me to enter to work in a bank. *I wanted to be a professional* and since I could not do it, because of my situation, I entered the military school that was located near my house.'

General of Division: 'My father died when I was seven years old, and I promised him to educate my brothers. Thus, in spite of the fact that, in year 1921 or 1922 when I entered the service, the salaries were very low, *at least I was able to obtain (some) money in a rapid way.* This is very important since I had other qualities and perhaps in another activity I would have been more useful to the country. What I want to say is that even now many young men enter the Army because of the need of a rapid economic position and that perhaps they could be more useful in civilian activities.'

General of Brigade: 'I believe I entered the military school *more by opportunity than by vocation.* There were few possibilities of success in my town.' (All italics added.)

Note the essentially negative elements in these cases. The first went into the Army to avoid working in a bank. The second wanted a professional career – in *any* profession. The third needed money in a hurry. And the fourth joined simply because the opportunity was present. The central feature of the careerist orientation was that the unique character of the military profession was not crucial to the career choice.

In contrast to this lack of prior commitment to the profession, the major inducements of the idealists were based upon a strong positive attraction to the major characteristics of the military profession and/or to a belief in the importance of the military role in society. Twelve generals were placed in this category. These responses were typical:

123

General of Division: 'I had an innate vocation since I entered military school when I was fourteen years old. In my childhood games I was the leader and they were always of a military type. *Thus, it is a vocation of the spirit.*'

General of Brigade: 'I observed when a little boy the work and effort of the military and the disinterested form with which *they gave their services to the country.* I lived in a military residential district.'

General of Brigade: 'I liked it from *the sporting and masculine point of view; in all aspects of the physical culture.* Also by my boyhood image that I have of the uniform, parades, etc.'

General of Brigade: 'Since I was a little boy I played with toy soldiers. Now, when did I decide (to be a soldier)? It was when my father took me to military ceremonies – marches, parades. Outside of this, the talks with my school friends about heroes, looking at photographic albums of important soldiers. *Thus I felt this impulse toward the life of a soldier, in order to protect my country,* in spite of the adverse image of the military that my father had. He was so much in opposition that he refused to help in paying for military school which was very expensive.'

Of the thirty-eight generals interviewed, thirteen were classified on the basis of their initial motivations as careerist, and twelve as idealists. Of the remaining thirteen, twelve were from military families (their fathers were officers and/or there was a family tradition of military service). These twelve were designated 'traditionalists' and comprised the third and last category of our typology.[9] On an a priori basis, the orientations of traditionalist officers toward the meaning and role of the military might be expected to fall somewhere between those of careerist and idealist officers. Family tradition undoubtedly served to inculcate them with traditional military values and perspectives. Yet, what appeared more crucial was that relatives in the military service facilitated their entrance into the profession. Hence, selection of a military career was fundamentally the path of least resistance rather than deriving from a strong, personal commitment. The relationship between idealist and traditionalist officers was in this respect analogous to that of a convert and a member born into a church.

The career perspective of the officer, as reflected in his initial career motivations, was apparently present in large measure throughout his career.[10] Idealists remained most strongly committed to the career. Eighty-three percent of these officers (N = 12) as compared to 58% (N = 12) and 54% (N = 13) of traditionalist and careerist officers, respectively, would have recommended to a son or grandson that he enter the profession. Even more striking were the differences in criteria by which they made these judgments (see table 1). Two-thirds of idealist officers cited only idealist criteria of evaluation; most importantly, whether or not the career was a calling for the individual involved. The

Table 1. Criteria of Evaluation for Recommending a Military Career to a Son or Grandson

| | Type of Career Orientation | | | | | |
| | Careerist | | Traditionalist | | Idealist | |
Type of Criteria	%	N	%	N	%	N
Careerist Only[1]	46	6	33	4	0	0
Mixed Criteria	46	6	17	2	33	4
Idealist Only[2]	8	1	50	6	67	8
	100	13	100	12	100	12

1. Careerist criteria include evaluation of economic benefits, job security, career mobility, and social status.
2. Idealist criteria include vocation (i.e., the career is a 'calling'), military life-style, or service to the country.

remaining idealist officers mentioned at least some careerist criteria such as pay and benefits, job security, promotion opportunities, but none cited these criteria only. In contrast, almost half of the careerist generals utilized only careerist criteria and all but one mentioned one or more in their evaluation. Differences between idealist and careerist officers in this respect were significant, $p < .01$ (Fisher's Exact Test). Traditionalist officers, as expected, were less homogeneous with respect to these criteria of evaluation than either careerists or idealists.

GOAL RE-ORIENTATION OR ISOLATION: TWO PATTERNS COMPARED

Organizations decline when the social functions they perform decrease in importance to their clientele. This can occur when either its specific functions decline in relative importance or when, although the functions remain important, another organization performs them more effectively.

As a consequence of over three-quarters of a century of peace and the then current state of friendly relations with neighboring countries,

defence issues were no longer defined as of immediate and urgent importance in Chile. In addition, the National Police had assumed an increasingly greater responsibility for maintaining internal order. Thus, both of
the major traditional goals of the Chilean Army, i.e., national defence
and internal order, had decreased in significance to the society.

At the time of this study, the Chilean Army could be characterized as
an organization in decline. This decline was reflected in its budget,
growth pattern, and technological deterioration as well as in the dimin-
ishing prestige of the career. Furthermore, the officer corps was acutely
aware of the decline and of its implications for themselves, their profession, and the goals of the institution.

Since organizations consist of persons who have strong investments
in the fate of the system, organizational decline tends to produce some
form of adaptive behavior. Potentially available to the military were at
least three modes of adaptation: (1) decline may act as an incentive for
active political intervention; (2) decline may lead to a redefinition and/or
reorientation of military goals to increase their relevance to their clientele;
or (3) decline may result in a retreat into professional isolation. Most
frequently, accommodation might be expected to involve elements of all
three modes in some proportion.

Military decline inevitably generates hostility and resentments, especially toward political institutions, and so acts as an incentive for political
involvement. The means employed and the success of these efforts in
dealing with organizational decline will depend upon factors such as the
legitimacy and effectiveness of the nation's political institutions, the
conditions, if any, which the citizens of the society perceive as justifying
political intervention by the military, the coercive power of the military
vis-à-vis other social institutions, the degree of homogeneity of attitude
toward involvement among the military elite, and the significance of the
military's functions to its clientele. Democratic development must set
limits on the political influence of the military in the society. Chile's
democratic development appeared to have reached a stage where, under
normal conditions, the political influence of the military was insufficient
to intimidate the government.

As the environment increasingly limits the effectiveness of direct
political pressure, the choice of adaptation to decline is correspondingly
restricted to either a redefinition and/or orientation of military goals or
a retreat into professional isolation. This choice, as with most social
trends, is only seldom a deliberately planned strategy. Rather, it represents a series of day-to-day decisions the implications of which are
usually not clear even to those who make them.

126

A common response of civilian bureaucracies to organizational decline is to seek to undertake new and more viable functions and/or to change their clientele. Therefore, what we called a civilian bureaucratic mode of adaptation would require that the Chilean military redefine and broaden their professional role and/or reorient their goals around the interests of new social groups. However, this solution necessarily implies that two conditions obtain: (1) the socio-cultural environment must be receptive to and provide opportunity for this goal transformation, and (2) the military must demonstrate a willingness to recognize and accept social change within the society and seek to accommodate itself to their changing environment. The existence of these conditions should be reflected in a broad and flexible definition of what constitutes legitimate military functions, both within the civilian sector of society and in the professional ideology of the officer corps.

Demands for economic development and the emergence of the lower class as increasingly effective participants in the political process appear to have provided respectively an alternate goal and a powerful new social group around whose interests military goals could be reoriented. However, for the military itself, a bureaucratic mode of adaptation entails significant costs to their self-image as military professionals and to their own evaluation of the meaning and worth of their careers. Not only does this path transform them from military professionals into engineers or teachers, but also it invites comparison and competition with civilian organizations and institutions specializing in their functions. In addition, a substantial modification is involved of what is for many a highly valued life-style.

An unwillingness or inability of the military to accommodate themselves to this process of greater involvement in the internal social problems of the society may lead to an alternative mode of adaptation, that is, to *professional isolation and the development of a distinctive professional military ideology.* For example, the United States military experienced an extended period of rejection and decline between the Civil War and World War I. Politically impotent and repudiated by the prevalent business pacifist ideology of American society, the military retreated into professional isolation. The consequences were described by Huntington thusly:

The military officer who, at the end of the period of isolation,
rejoined civilian society in World War I and World War II, was a fundamentally
different creature from his ancestor who had withdrawn in the 1860's.
When he left, he was a citizen-soldier, an accepted member of the liberal family.
When he returned, he was a stranger in his own household. His membership in

127

the national family was no longer free, easy, and relaxed. The years of
isolation had remade him into a professional with values and outlook basically
at odds with those of the mass of his countrymen.[11]

The isolation of professional military establishment from the society,
viewed in this perspective, was a group solution to a common status
problem, i.e., their rejection by the civilian sector.[12] Elements of their
ideology may be derived from previous military tradition, international
patterns of military ideology, or be generated in reaction to unfavorable
civilian orientations. Isolation reduces the dissonance between their
orientations and those of civilian society and so makes for an increasingly distinctive professional military ideology. Taken together, professional isolation and the development of a supportive professional ideology
protect the self-image of the military and their own favorable perception
of the meaning and worth of their careers. In addition, these measures
facilitate the retention of the traditional life-style of the officer. We term
this second mode of adaptation to organizational decline the 'professional'
strategy.

A professional mode of adaptation, like the civilian bureaucratic
method, entails considerable costs. A retreat into professional isolation
reduces the relevance of the military to society, which (all else equal)
will result in further organizational decline. Reductions in the size and
budget of the Armed Forces, in addition to damaging their personal
interests, will be viewed as dangerous to the national security. Furthermore, the institution and profession may suffer serious loss of public
prestige by appearing reluctant or refusing to assume those functions
defined by society as legitimate and appropriate.

The civilian bureaucratic and professional modes of adaptation are not
necessarily mutually exclusive, i.e., the military may still attempt to
increase their relevance to society although already undergoing a process
of professional isolation and the development of a distinctive professional
ideology culture. However, they are essentially conflictive strategies since
one requires a broad and the other a narrow definition of military professionalism. Needless to say, these two adaptations should appeal to different segments of the military elite.

CAREER MOTIVATION AND PROFESSIONAL ORIENTATION

The extent to which military institutions differentially recruit particular
social types from the population-at-large is a function of the relative
importance in career motivation of inducements unique to the military
profession as compared to those which it shares with civilian careers.

128

Officers attracted to the military career primarily by inducements closely related to the traditional meaning and role of the military in Chilean society (such as patriotism, comradeship, life-style, goal of national defence) might be expected to differ most distinctly from civilian norms. In particular, their commitment to the traditional role and meaning of the military could generate resistance to a redefinition and/or reorientation of military goals as a means of adaptation to organizational decline. In contrast, officers whose primary career motivations are similar to those of civilian bureaucrats (such as economic benefits, social status, job security, and organizational mobility), being less committed to the traditional role and meaning of the military, might be expected to favor a civilian bureaucratic mode of adaptation if such a course of action would contribute to the welfare of the organization. Thus, applying the analysis of these modes of adaptation presented in the previous section, the idealist officer might be expected to be more isolated from civilian society, less favorable to changes in the organization's goal structure, and more resentful of and hostile to civilian authority than officers with a careerist perspective. Traditionalist officers should demonstrate less homogeneity than either group on these modes of adaptation.

Table 2. Number of Civilian Friends (Of Five[1] Best Friends of Generals During Final Years of Active Service)

| | Type of Career Orientation | | | | | |
| | Careerist | | Traditionalist | | Idealist | |
Number	%	N	%	N	%	N
None	23	3	42	5	75	9
One	31	4	25	3	0	0
Two	15	2	33	4	25	3
Three or More	31	4	0	0	0	0
	100	13	100	12	100	12

1. Number of selections vary for a few officers who could not select exactly five 'best' friends.

Table 2 displays the number of civilians among the five best friends of the retired generals during their last years of active service. As hypothesized, idealists were by this criteria more isolated from civilian society than were careerists. Only 23% (N = 13) of careerists as compared to 75% (N = 12) of idealists had no civilian 'best' friends ($p < .05$; Fisher's Exact Test). Traditionalist officers fell between these extremes having less civilian friends than careerists but more than idealist officers.

The relationship between type of career perspective and favorability to redefinition of military goals is displayed in tables 3, 4, and 5. Careerist officers are shown in table 3 to have been most favorable and idealist officers least favorable to an increase in civic action programs. Sixty-nine percent (N = 13) of careerist officers as compared to 42% (N = 12) of idealist officers favored such an increase ($p < .20$; $\chi^2 = 1.89$, $df = 1$). Traditionalist officers again fell between these extremes with 58% (N = 12) favoring an increase in the programs.

The Carabineros (National Police) performed a number of functions (e.g., border patrols and rural law enforcement) which had been in the past in Chile, and were presently in many Latin American nations, assigned to the military. To the extent to which the officer corps sought to expand military functions in these areas, the Carabineros were a competitive organization. As shown in table 4, careerist officers were most likely to view the Carabineros as assuming tasks which legitimately belong to the military. Ninety-two percent (N = 13) of careerist officers as compared to 41% (N = 12) of traditionalist and 55% (N = 11) of idealist officers agreed with the statement: 'The Carabineros act too much like an Army. They ought to concentrate on police tasks and leave military jobs to the Army.' Differences between careerists and both traditionalists and idealists are significant, $p < .05$ and $p < .10$, respectively (Fisher's Exact Test).

Table 3. *Attitude Toward Civic Action Programs*

| | Type of Career Orientation | | | | | |
| | Careerist | | Traditionalist | | Idealist | |
Programs Should Be:	%	N	%	N	%	N
Increased	69	9	58	7	42	5
No Change	15	2	25	3	25	3
Decreased	15	2	17	2	33	4
	99	13	100	12	100	12

130

Table 4. Attitude Toward Competition With Carabineros: 'The Carabineros act too much like an Army. They ought to concentrate more on police tasks and leave military jobs to the Army.'

| | *Type of Career Orientation* | | | | | |
| | *Careerist* | | *Traditionalist* | | *Idealist* | |
	%	N	%	N	%	N
Strongly Agree	46	6	33	4	36	4
Somewhat Agree	46	6	8	1	18	2
Somewhat Disagree	0	0	8	1	0	0
Strongly Disagree	8	1	50	6	45	5
	100	13	99	12	99	11

An index of favorability to a redefinition of military goals was constructed based upon orientations to civic action programs and perception of the Carabineros as performing military tasks. The relationship between type of career perspective and favorability to a redefinition of military goals as measured by this index is presented in table 5. Sixty-two percent (N = 13) of careerist officers ranked 'most favorable' to a redefinition of goals as compared to 25% (N = 12) of idealist officers. No careerist officers ranked 'least favorable' but one-third of idealist officers did so. (These differences were significant, $p < .10$, Fisher's Exact Test.) Traditionalist officers occupied an intermediate position but in this respect their orientations were closer to idealists than careerists. Differences in favorability to a redefinition of military goals between careerist officers and the combined idealist and traditionalist officers are significant, $p < .02$ ($\chi^2 = 6.0$, $df = 1$).

Finally, we hypothesized that idealist officers would tend to be more resentful of and hostile to civilian authority than careerist officers. Table 6 displays the relationship between career perspective and perceived cause of disagreements between military and political elites. Seventy-five percent (N = 12) of careerist officers believed these disagreements were due either to mutually limited perspectives or inadequate institutional arrangements, i.e., indicated a lack of hostility to civilian authority. Only 25% (N = 12) attributed them to civilian indifference, ignorance, or fear of the military. In contrast, 64% (N = 11) of idealist officers believed the cause to lie in civilian indifference, ignorance or fear of the military and only 9% (N = 11) to reasons indicating a lack of hostility to civilian authority. (These differences are significant, $p < .02$, Fisher's Exact Test.)

Table 5. Attitude Toward Redefinition of Military Goals

| | Type of Career Orientation | | | | | |
| | *Careerist* | | *Traditionalist* | | *Idealist* | |
Index of Favorability[1]	%	N	%	N	%	N
Least Favorable (0)	0	0	17	2	33	4
Intermediate (1)	38	5	67	8	42	5
Most Favorable (2)	62	8	17	2	25	3
	100	13	101	12	100	12

1. The index was constructed as shown below:

| | Score Assigned | |
	1	0
Orientation to Civic Action	Increase	No Increase
Carabineros Perform Military Tasks	Agree	Disagree

The scores of each respondent were added for a total score on the index ranging between 0 and 2.

Traditionalist officers, although in an intermediate position, again appeared in this respect to approach more closely the orientations of idealist rather than careerist officers.

SUMMARY AND CONCLUSIONS

Differences in career perspective appeared to derive from a process of selective recruitment into the military of officer candidates of specific social types who were attracted to the profession by distinctive patterns of career motivation. These initial career orientations were maintained in large part throughout the individual's career. The career perspective of

Table 6. Perceived Cause of Disagreements Between Military and Political Elites

	Careerist		Traditionalist		Idealist	
Type of Career Orientation						
	%	N	%	N	%	N
Mutually Limited Perspectives	33	4	9	1	0	0
Inadequate Institutional Arrangements	42	5	18	2	9	1
Civilians Lack Knowledge (Due to Training Responsibilities, etc.)	0	0	9	1	27	3
Civilians Indifferent, Ignorant, or Fear Military	25	3	64	7	64	7
	100	12	100	11	100	11

the officer has been shown to have been a significant factor in shaping his personal image of the meaning and role of the military in society. In particular, we have demonstrated a significant relationship between type of career perspective and the response of the officer to organizational decline. It was the idealists who tended to adopt the isolationist stance and the careerists who were the most civilianized and adaptable to change.

To a certain extent internal dissension in the military can contribute to democratic stability by politically neutralizing their overall influence. Military policy can be more easily manipulated by civilian authorities when the officer corps does not present a united front. Furthermore, although most officers, irregardless of career perspective, believed that the military should act as constitutional guardian, their tendency to favor intervention in civilian politics was influenced by their political identification. Careerist officers were predominantly leftist in orientation and idealists tended to hold rightist sentiments. Fifty-eight percent of the twelve careerists identified themselves as leftists, but not one of eleven idealists did so ($p < .01$, Fisher's Exact Test)!

A continued decline of the military would not necessarily enhance the strength of the careerist influence. To enter military school, the prospective officer candidate must meet a number of requirements, including completion of a secondary education. As 'careerist' inducements offered by the profession continued to decline vis-à-vis alternative civilian careers, the military would be increasingly less attractive to potential officer candidates with careerist perspectives. Recruitment into the profession will be motivated increasingly by inducements unique to the military. Hence, the proportion of idealists could increase relative to that of careerists. As a consequence, not only would the officer corps develop a more consistent and rigid ideology and self-image, but these orientations may be expected to become increasingly isolated from the perspectives and needs of the general public and hostile to civilian political institutions. Thus, the decline of the military could pose a distinct threat to the future development of Chilean political institutions.

POSTSCRIPT: MILITARY RESPONSE TO A MARXIST GOVERNMENT

The stability of Chile's democratic political institutions was shaken by the election (to the Presidency) in 1970 of Salvador Allende, the candidate of a six-party coalition led by Communists and Socialists. Threatened by Allende's call for the mass expropriation of estates and the nationalization of major industries, the political right sought to bargain with military commanders. Extremist elements turned to acts of terrorism intended to force (and perhaps justify) military intervention. These activities culminated in the assassination (during a badly managed kidnapping attempt) of General René Schneider, who, in his position as Commander-in-Chief of the Army, had taken a firm non-interventionist position.

A vast majority of officers were clearly anti-communist and many had friends or relatives whose interests were threatened by Allende's election. However, although a number of active and retired officers were apparently involved in various designs to upset the election results, the military as an institution rigidly adhered to its constitutional role. The motives underlying this decision were undoubtedly complex and at least in part (such as the shock of General Schneider's assassination) highly situational. On the other hand, a number of basic grounds for non-intervention are readily identifiable.

First, the officer corps was highly committed to the Constitution and to their traditional role as its guardians. However, Allende had not only been legally elected but repeatedly stressed his adhesion to democratic

134

political institutions. Thus, despite their uncertainty about his long-range intentions, no immediate justification existed for military intervention which would not violate their oaths to uphold the Constitution.

Secondly, anticipation of the possible consequences of military intervention would have certainly acted to deter that action. Allende had massive, well-organized support, particularly in the labor unions. Military intervention, even if successful, would have almost inevitably led to wide-spread violence and perhaps civil war.

A third reason for non-intervention, i.e. internal divisions within the officer corps, relates most closely to the topic under consideration in this paper. Idealist officers might have been expected to be most favorable to immediate intervention. In addition to their more conservative personal political ideology they tended to have closer ties with members of those elites (landowners and businessmen) most endangered by a Marxist government. Furthermore, distrustful and hostile to politicians in general, they were undoubtably most sceptical of Allende's promises to respect the Constitution.

Careerist officers, on the other hand, could have been expected to favor a wait-and-see attitude. Many aspects of Allende's social and economic reforms were compatible with their own inclinations. More open in their attitude toward politics and politicians, they perhaps were more inclined to question his intention and/or ability to destroy Chile's democratic institutions. Finally, their general orientation to an orderly career development would have made the risks associated with military intervention highly unattractive.

The adherence of the military to its constitutional role during the critical period of transition to a Marxist government does not necessarily imply their unwillingness and/or inability to act in the future. Should Allende's programs be manifestly failing (particularly if met with widespread violent opposition) or his government seek to grossly violate the Constitution, the military could well intervene. The likelihood of intervention would also increase should Allende pursue policies toward the military which would alienate the careerist officers and thus unite the military in opposition to his government. (Such policies would include attempts to gain control of the military by selective promotions and retirements based upon political criteria, attempts to weaken the military through cuts in manpower or budget, or the creation of a rival armed force such as a workers militia to act as a counterbalance.) In the absence of such circumstances, however, the military can be expected to continue in its tradition of non-intervention.

NOTES

1. JOHNSON, for example, states: 'Particular attention is paid to the socio-economic background of the officers, because until the services become considerably more professional, officers will often make decisions on the basis of personal rather than their institutional experiences.' John J. JOHNSON, *The Military and Society in Latin America* (Stanford: Stanford University Press, 1964), p. vii.
2. The significance of career patterns in this respect has been most carefully documented by Janowitz in his study of the United States military. See Morris JANOWITZ, *The Professional Soldier* (Glencoe: The Free Press, 1960).
3. Victor ALBA, 'The Stages of Militarism in Latin America,' in *The Role of the Military in Underdeveloped Countries*, edited by John J. JOHNSON (Princeton: Princeton University Press, 1962).
4. Discrimination of social class differences on a continuum between lower-middle and upper-middle class, although potentially significant, was difficult in practice.
5. See Anne ROE, *The Psychology of Occupations* (New York: John Wiley and Sons, 1956); Morris ROSENBERG, *Occupations and Values* (Glencoe: The Free Press, 1957); and Victor H. VROOM, *Work and Motivation* (New York: John Wiley and Sons, 1964).
6. See, for example, Doris C. GILBERT and Daniel J. LEVINSON, 'Role Performance, Ideology and Personality in Mental Hospital Aides,' in *The Patient and the Mental Hospital*, edited by Milton GREENBLATT, *et al.* (Glencoe: The Free Press, 1957); and George C. STERN, Morris J. STEIN, and Benjamin S. BLOOM, *Methods in Personality Assessment* (Glencoe: The Free Press, 1956).
7. Alex INKELES, *What is Sociology?* (Englewood Cliffs: Prentice-Hall, Inc., 1964), p. 57.
8. Janowitz noted the significance of career motivation in his distinction between heroic leaders and military managers among the United States military elite. See Morris JANOWITZ, *The Professional Soldier* (Glencoe: The Free Press, 1960), Chapter 8.
9. The remaining general could not be classified within the framework of the typology on the basis of his stated career motivation, i.e., the selection was attributed to the lifelong determination of his father (a lawyer) that his sons be officers.
10. The career perspectives held at the time of the interview may, of course, influence the respondents' recollection of their original career motivation. However, the relationship of these motivations to their objective social position at the time (i.e., family background and socio-economic status) indicated the significance of this factor was minimal.
11. Samuel P. HUNTINGTON, *The Soldier and the State* (New York: Vintage Books, 1964), pp. 229–230.
12. A similar process of sub-cultural solution to commonly-shared status problems was central to Cohen's analysis of delinquency. See Albert K. COHEN, *Delinquent Boys* (Glencoe: The Free Press, 1955).

136

Recruitment and Career

Dysfunctional Consequences of
Military Professionalization

G. HARRIES-JENKINS

GWYN HARRIES-JENKINS was educated at the University of Wales, Collège d'Europe, Bruges, and the University of East Anglia, and served as a regular officer. He is now a staff tutor in Social Studies at the University of Hull, England. The author of numerous papers on professionalism, he is currently working on a study of the British military elite in the nineteenth century.

In common with other large-scale organizations, the Royal Air Force employs a considerable number of specialists whose activities contribute to the attainment of the organizational goal. A minority of these, in common with their civilian counterparts, are *achievement* professionals. They are trained outside the organization in an institutionalized educational process. They are full members of the appropriate professional qualifying association, and their work activities are orientated towards the performance of a narrowly defined task. Doctors, dentists, lawyers and clergymen thus occupy a special position within the Royal Air Force.[1] Essentially, they are civilians who happen to perform their professional function within a military environment. As peripheral members of the organization, they retain close associations with their civilian colleagues, and, in common with the latter, their work activities are characterised by the exercise of expertise, autonomy, commitment and a sense of responsibility.[2]

In complete contrast, the majority of Air Force officers are ascriptive professionals.[3] They are trained within the organization in predominantly military skills. Their work activities are carried out in a monopolistic environment which determines their status, evaluates their ability, and delineates, through a rational process of selection and designation, the precise area within which particular tasks will be performed. Professional status is thus the result of an organizational decision, and its retention is subject to continual review and reassessment. These officers demonstrate an exceptional degree of dependence upon, and loyalty to, the employing organization. Aircrew, secretarial, equipment and regiment officers accept that imperative co-ordination ensures their obedience to the specific commands of a hierarchical superior, and it is this, in conjunction with their pronounced status dependency, which characterises their activities as *ascriptive* professionals.

Because the fusion of profession and organization is almost complete in the military environment,[4] intra-group strain is often conceptualized in terms of the potential conflict between professional and bureaucratic authority. Both have many characteristics in common. Parson's pattern variables – universal standards, specificity of expertness, and affective neutrality – are indicative of both forms of authority.[5] The contrast in their respective frames of reference, however, is believed to lead to conflict, for the tension between military obedience and professional competence is derived from two distinct structural patterns. To a certain extent, these patterns reflect the distinctions between the achievement and ascriptive professional. In general terms, the former, in taking his standards and norms from the professional community of which he is a member, acknowledges only professional authority. In contrast, the latter, on the basis that the officer corps is both a bureaucratized profession and a bureaucratized organization,[6] recognizes that the priority of the hierarchy of rank over the hierarchy of office necessitates acknowledgement of the superiority of bureaucratic authority.

The problem which arises is that while the majority of Air Force officers are ascriptive professionals, a number of officers occupy a position intermediate between the dichotomized extremes of wholly ascriptive or wholly achievement professionals. Officers in these sub-groups, or 'branches' in military terminology, may or may not be members of the relevant civilian professional associations. In the same branch, some members are trained wholly within the employing organization; others are trained outside the organization. The degree of their status dependency is directly related to the pre-military experience which they have enjoyed. This, in turn, affects their willingness to accept, without question, hierarchical commands. Consequently, within the same branch, some members tend towards the behavioural patterns of the achievement professional, while others accept the patterns of the ascriptive professional. Intra-branch strain is then a continuing problem, for potential conflicts which are derived from the contrast between the demands of professional and bureaucratic authority, are concentrated within relatively limited parameters.

Among these officers, engineers demonstrate particularly ambivalent attitudes. Some, in common with other ascriptive professionals, accept that the military organizational structure is an integrated hierarchy of specialized offices, defined by systematic rules. Certain specific organizational attitudes, noticeably the extent to which the vestigial power of the central sanctions mechanism is accepted, are indicative of an *autocratic model* of organizational behaviour.[7] Other characteristics, especially the way in which the relationship between the individual and his immediate hierarchical superior exhibits evidence of paternalism and organizational dependency, suggests that the pattern of behaviour follows that of the *custodial* model. In either case, attempts made by the organization to move away from the traditional form of military authority, based on coercion, to a form based on managerial persuasion, do not change the attitudes of these officers. The criteria of the *supportive* model of organizational behaviour, in which power is subordinated to leadership, and in which organizational dependency is replaced by a sense of individual responsibility, are unacceptable to these ascriptive engineers. The recognized need to secure complete organizational homogeneity in battle conditions, leads them to support the continuation of the bureaucratic pattern of authority, and to reject changes which could weaken the dominance of this pattern.

142

Other engineers, whose behavioural attitudes are similar to those of the civilian achievement professional, refuse to accept this thesis. In accepting orders, their reactions are part of a normative consensus, for these engineers contend that they retain, even within the military environment, a certain right of choice. In rejecting the validity of unitary concept of obedience, they imply that the only orders which are wholly acceptable to them, are those which come from a hierarchical superior in their area of specialization. Other orders are considered to be unacceptable, or to be on the borderline of acceptability, or if they are unquestionably acceptable, to fall within their zone of indifference. Hierarchy remains a component of their organizational system, so that they reject the neoteric model of organizational behaviour,[8] but, in common with other achievement professionals, these engineers support the development of a viable *collegial* model, in which bureaucratic authority is used only as a means of ensuring group integration. Legitimate authority is accepted, not because it implies a psychological submission to a set superior-subordinate relationships, but because it is based on professional authority. A latent authority structure, derived from the influence of external professional practice, modifies pure bureaucratic authority and reinforces the manifest structure associated with the exercise of professional authority. Adjustments to the demands of the formal bureaucratic organization are thus made by both superior and subordinate, for the achievement engineer recognizes the need to provide for the maximum degree of personal freedom and professional autonomy compatible with the aims of the organization. In this context, fresh appraisals of the strategic force of world power blocks, whereby these officers conclude that the main purpose of the profession of arms is not to win wars but to avoid them, are used to justify modifications to the inherited bureaucratic pattern of authority. The latter is considered to be out-moded, and there is a persistent demand from these engineers for the creation of a new basis of military authority, in which the achievement professional exercises autonomy, in participating with fellow professionals in formulating organizational goals.

The contrast between these two attitudes is thus the source of considerable role-strain and potential role conflict. Primarily, it is an intra-branch strain, although, since the engineer is part of the larger group of Air Force officers as a whole, an alternative form of potential conflict is associated with the employment of the engineer, as a professional, in the bureaucratic organization. This latter form resembles the classic type of strain which has been well documented,[9] but the purpose of this paper is to examine more closely the intra-branch strain which is apparent in the Air Force, rather than the classic form.

Initially, the structure of the Engineer Branch in the Royal Air Force was examined to identify the effects of contemporary recruitment policies. Second in size only to the General Duties Branch of aircrew officers at the 'centre' of the organization, the Engineer Branch at a date in 1969 totalled 3 135 officers. Of these, over 54 % were full career officers, that is, they could serve to the age of 55, the compulsory retiring date, and could be promoted to ranks at the apex of the hierarchical structure. The remainder were serving on a restricted career, characterised by a complex permutation of limiting factors. For all these officers, the rank which they could attain was limited, for this was a reflection of their restricted employment opportunities. Some officers were serving to the age of 38, or to complete sixteen years active service, when, on retirement with a pension, they would transfer to a second career in a civilian environment. Others, 1.5 %, had opted for a nonpensionable engagement for a limited number of years. The rank differentiation within this structure is shown at Table 1:

Table 1. Ranks of Engineer Officers in the Royal Air Force[10]

	Full Career		Limited Career		
	N	%	N	%	
Air Marshal	2 ⎫				
Air Vice-Marshal	10 ⎬	2	—	—	Top Management
Air Commodore	22 ⎭				
Group Captain	88	5	—	—	
Wing Commander	305	18	3	—	Middle Management
Squadron Leader	671	39	289	21	
Flight Lieutenant	360	21	689	48	
Flying Officer	177	11	401	28	Junior Management
Pilot Officer	77	4	41	3	
	1712	100	1423	100	

The different career opportunities, inherent in the distinction between these two categories of officers, were, in themselves, a source of strain. Although, in general terms, officers serving on a limited career accepted that full career officers would enjoy the benefits of higher rank, more attractive employment opportunities and a 'fuller' military life, a small number suffered from a sense of deprivation. These were, primarily, officers who possessed the academic qualifications necessary for selection for a full career, but who, for a variety of reasons, had either chosen, or had been selected for, the limited career. The force of their reaction was, however, limited. They were a small percentage of the total complement of the Engineer Branch. If they had selected the limited career, they were often motivated by a reluctance to commit themselves fully to the organization, so that they were rarely interested in organizational activities which might have been a source of strain. If they had not been selected for the full career, the reasons for their rejection often reflected a lack of such professional qualities as commitment or sense of responsibility, so that their reaction was derived from personal rather than professional attitudes.

A more pertinent source of strain was associated with the position of junior officers, serving on a full career in the ranks of pilot officer to flight lieutenant (subaltern to captain), who were under the hierarchical control of limited career officers. In many cases, this strain was associated with the difference in behavioural attitudes between the achievement professional and the ascriptive professional. The full career officer, if he were an achievement professional, failed to understand the attitudes of the ascriptive, limited career officer. The converse was also true, and it was equally evident that some limited career officers in junior ranks, were subjected to a situation of strain when they were controlled by achievement professionals, who were more senior in the hierarchical structure. This type of strain was not limited to observed differences in the organizational structure, for it was also present among full career officers, as a separate sub-group. Indeed, in this instance, the degree of strain was increased, for it could not be rationalised, nor explained away, as a characteristic of the differences between the full career and the limited career officer.

The sources of this strain were complex, although, in the first instance, it could be attributed to differences in attitudes which were derived from contrasting pre-recruitment experience. In common with other large-scale organizations, recruitment policy in the Royal Air Force has been amended to take into consideration such external factors as supply and demand, changes in educational and training programmes, the requirements of an increasingly complex technology, and the recognized need for increased professionalization. For the contemporary aspirant to a full career in the organization, the barriers which are raised to reject unsuitable applicants are initially educational in character. Pending the introduction of an announced policy of exclusive graduate entry, three different levels of entry qualifications are acceptable. Candidates who possess qualifications which would qualify them for entry to university, can apply for entry to the Royal Air Force College at Cranwell to read for a CNAA degree in engineering, or for a university cadetship. Alternatively, older

145

candidates must possess a degree in a suitable engineering subject, or be members, by examination, of a relevant professional institution. In both cases, the appropriate educational course with its emphasis on the study of the systematic base of theory, and the post-graduate assimilation course undertaken at Cranwell, are designed to ensure achievement professional status.

In contrast, serving officers who possess a Higher National Certificate in engineering, can apply from the limited career list for transfer to a full career. This qualification, usually obtained through part-time study outside the universities, is of a technician rather than a professional standard. Holders of this certificate must undertake a further period of study before they can sit the examinations set by the professional institutions. Accordingly, since they are not professional engineers by examination, these officers can be categorised as ascriptive engineers, for their professional status is conferred upon them by the employing organization, not by an independent external body.

Concomitantly, a more liberal recruitment policy which was adopted in the past, has created a situation in which a large number of officers, at all rank levels, lack any of these educational qualifications. Commissioned on the basis of their loyalty to the organization and their demonstrated ability in task performance, such officers are, again, ascriptive engineers. The numerical groupings of these ascriptive and achievement engineers are shown in Table 2.

Table 2. Qualifications of Full Career Engineers: 1969

	Achievement				Ascriptive	Totals
	Degree	PG	PG Dip	PI		
Air Commodore	11	—	1	6	4	22
Group Captain	14	—	11	34	29	88
Wing Commander	34	1	22	98	150	305
Squadron Leader	108	6	46	202	309	671
Flight Lieutenant	138	5	5	32	180	360
Flying Officer	50	—	—	—	127	177
Pilot Officer	12	—	—	—	65	77
	367	12	85	372	864	1700

PG: A higher degree, that is, M.Sc. or Ph.D
PG Dip: A post-graduate diploma.
PI: Membership of one of the relevant professional institutions.

Although 51 % of the total of 1700 full career officers are categorised as ascriptive engineers, there is a marked difference between the qualifications of the junior and senior officers in this category. At junior rank level, that is, Flight Lieutenant to Pilot Officer, the boundary between ascriptive and achievement engineer is blurred. Many of these officers are qualified, educationally, for membership of the appropriate professional institution, but lack the practical experience which is a prerequisite for their admission. Thus while they are currently ascriptive engineers, since the employing organization has conferred their professional status upon them, these officers are continually moving to an achievement professional status. Their behavioural attitudes approach those of the achievement professional, but they can still be distinguished from the latter. In contrast, senior officers who are ascriptive professionals, are ineligible for membership of the relevant professional institution, and external recognition of their status is derived exclusively from their membership of the organization.

An initial source of strain was associated with the presence within these more senior ranks of a large number of ascriptive professionals. The 614 full career junior officers, the majority of whom were either achievement professionals (39 %) or were moving towards this status, were subject to the hierarchical control of 960 squadron leaders (671 full career officers and 289 limited career). Of these, 38% were achievement professionals. It was therefore probable that a young achievement professional would be under the direct supervision and control of an ascriptive professional. To a lesser extent, achievement squadron leaders of whom there were 362, were controlled by 305 wing commanders, a half of whom were ascriptive professionals. Again, the achievement professional could be subject to the directions of a senior officer whose behavioural attitudes differed considerably from his own.

The intensity of this strain was accentuated by noted variations in promotion to higher rank. An established promotion policy ensures that, at each rank level, officers of a certain seniority are considered for promotion. Although the Royal Air Force does not specify promotion 'zones', an officer must have demonstrated his competence and fitness for promotion over a minimum period of time, before he can be considered for advancement. For the promotions made in 1968 to 1969, the minimum period for advancement to squadron leader and wing commander was five years in the rank of flight lieutenant and squadron leader respectively. In contrast, the maximum potential seniority of a promoted squadron leader was eighteen years, and of a flight lieutenant, twenty-two years, although in practice, the maximum was fifteen years and sixteen years respectively. The pattern of this promotion is shown in Tables 3 and 4.

Table 3. Potential and Actual Promotion to the rank of Wing Commander
1st July, 1968 to 1st January, 1969

Seniority	Potential					Actual				
	D	PG	PI	AS	T	D	PG	PI	AS	T
1951–1953	—	—	12	11	23	—	—	—	—	—
1954	—	—	11	23	34	—	—	1	—	1
1955	—	1	12	24	37	—	—	—	3	3
1956	4	—	16	43	63	—	—	—	4	4
1957	4	—	1	8	13	1	—	—	1	2
1958	—	1	5	14	20	—	—	2	1	3
1959	3	—	8	18	29	1	—	—	3	4
1960	1	—	5	23	29	—	—	—	2	2
1961	2	2	10	25	39	—	—	—	1	1
1962	6	3	18	23	50	2	1	3	—	6
1963	11	9	16	13	49	4	2	6	—	12
1964 (Part)	3	5	4	2	14	—	—	1	—	1
	34	21	118	227	400	8	3	13	15	39
1964–1969	82	34	97	97	310	—	—	—	—	—
	116	55	215	324	710	8	3	13	15	39

D: Primary Degree in Engineering
PG: Post-graduate qualification in Engineering
PI: Membership of a professional association
AS: Ascriptive Professional
The totals shown under the heading of 'Potential' promotions represent the totals of
Table 2 plus the totals of those who were promoted, and who are shown in Table
2 as wing commanders.

One source of noted strain was derived from the different expectations of
the achievement and ascriptive professional. The former could expect
promotion at an earlier point of his career; the ascriptive professional was
older and had served in the rank of squadron leader for a longer period.
Concomitantly, the passed-over achievement professional recognised
that his subsequent chances of promotion were less than those of his
ascriptive counterpart. The intensity of the associated strain was, however,
reduced, because the achievement professional in this situation, could
choose to leave the organization and transfer to a second career in civil life.
Indeed generous retirement benefits, whereby an officer after the completion of sixteen years service, could receive retired pay for the rest of his

life, accentuated the significance of the close links between the achievement professional and his civilian colleagues as motivating factors which often induced the officer to leave the military organization. Those officers who had decided to remain in the Royal Air Force, irrespective of their promotion prospects, had usually evaluated the comparative merits of the military career before making a decision which, because of its basis of rationality, limited or eliminated future organizational strain.

In contrast, the ascriptive professional whose sense of career commitment to the organization was more positively established, refused to accept that the criteria of an evolved pattern of promotion could, or should, affect his prospects of advancement. The degree of strain was often considerable. Passed-over officers resented the promotion given to younger achievement professionals whose general military experience and specific rank seniority were less than their own. In emphasizing the extent of their loyalty to the organization, these ascriptive professionals failed to distinguish between the concepts of bureaucratic and professional career commitment. Seniority was accepted as the sole criterion of importance, to the exclusion of all other factors. Consequently, many of these officers resented the promotion which was given to other ascriptive professionals of a comparable seniority, for, in excluding the consideration of other factors, they tended to assume that advancement was dependent on extra-occupational criteria. In extreme cases, the feeling of resentment and deprivation was so highly developed, that there was a considerable reduction in the level of career commitment. An unwillingness to accept the full obligations of a military career, an attitude which, in itself, was indicative of a low level of professionalization, thus created a further intra-organizational strain.

The smaller group of flight lieutenants exhibited less evidence of these types of strain. Primarily, this was the result of the blurring of the boundary between the ascriptive and achievement professional, but noted strain was again associated with the established pattern of promotion. The shape of the pyramidical structure, however, suggested that the majority of flight lieutenants serving on a full career, stood every chance of being promoted to the much larger group of squadron leaders. Strain, therefore, was often of a transitory nature, for as is shown in Table 4, few officers (approximately 6 %) had remained in the rank for more than seven years. This was in contrast to the position of squadron leaders, where 35 % of the officers were of this seniority. It was also in contrast to the position of limited career flight lieutenants, where 22 % of the officers had served in the rank for periods varying between seven and twenty-four years.

Transitory strain arose when some officers in a particular year of senior-

149

Table 4. Potential and Actual Promotion to the rank of Squadron Leader 1st July, 1968 to 1st January, 1969

Seniority	Potential					Actual				
	D	PG	PI	AS	T	D	PG	PI	AS	T
1947–1958	—	1	2	4	7	—	—	—	1	1
1959	1	—	1	1	3	1	—	—	1	2
1960	1	1	—	2	4	—	1	—	2	3
1961	5	—	3	2	10	3	—	1	2	6
1962	9	—	5	10	24	3	—	1	6	10
1963	11	1	7	16	35	4	1	2	6	13
1964	22	2	12	28	64	12	—	6	11	29
	49	5	30	63	147	23	2	10	29	64
1965–1969	112	7	12	146	277	—	—	—	—	—
	161	12	42	209	424	23	2	10	29	64

ity were promoted, while others were not. Delay in promotion, at this stage, often had a cumulative effect: since seniority in the rank of squadron leader, and thus the possibility of promotion to wing commander, depended on the date of promotion from flight lieutenant. Where the delay was of minimal length, that is, for six months or one year, dissatisfaction was not acute and it usually disappeared on promotion. During its existence however strain was primarily derived from the pre-entry educational and training experience of officers. It was the result of the contrast in the attitudes of those officers who had been trained as achievement professionals outside the organization, and those who had been trained within the organization. The latter were ascriptive professionals, but they were not technician engineers.[11] They had been trained at the Royal Air Force College, Cranwell to the Higher National Diploma standard, a level commensurate with a pass degree. External recognition by the relevant professional institution of their training and experience as a prerequisite for corporate membership of the institution, depended on a complex, but flexible, assessment of their suitability. Nevertheless, until they were admitted to this corporate membership, and the rules of the institution required these officers to be at least twenty-five years of age, they remained ascriptive professionals. Trained entirely within the organization, they lacked the independence of the achievement professional. The concept of professional autonomy was foreign to them, for the process of profession-alization in their case, had been orientated towards the integration of their professional activities in the military organization. The contrast was between functional autonomy and functional integration. The former emphasized the importance of concepts such as free inquiry, scientific objectivity, creativity and community responsibility. The latter was associated with task attainment, administrative efficiency, scientific utility, and organizational responsibility. Although more experienced officers accepted the interdependence of autonomy and integration, thereby modifying the extremes of either the ascriptive or achievement pattern of professional behaviour, these junior officers retained dichoto-mized attitudes. The achievement professional thus saw only the negative consequences of the authoritarian rank structure. The ascriptive profes-sional stressed the need to incorporate externally orientated engineers into the organization, ignoring the effects of organizational pressures on pro-fessional norms and occupational performance. Each related his lack of promotion to these distorted conceptualizations of group activities. The achievement professional thus deplored the effects of a system which subordinated professional autonomy to the need for integration. The ascriptive professional, in contrast, complained that a contemporary de-mand for increased group professionalization, had overlooked the need for the rational exploitation of existing group resources.

The strains which were evidenced in the pattern of recruitment and in the pattern of promotion, were more clearly defined in the contrast between varying types of occupational activities. The latter were examined under five headings: *Command, staff, advisory, operational* and *research*. None of these categories were entirely exclusive. In the Royal Air Force, as in many other occupations where the concept of specialization is not fully developed, there was a considerable blurring of the boundary between each category. Nevertheless, there were certain identifying characteristics associated with each category, and each was orientated towards a parti-cular objective of the organization. *Command* activities included the formulation of organizational policy, and the exercise of a decision-making function. This was characterised by the need to control and co-ordinate the activities of hierarchical subordinates, and a major criter-ion of this determinate functionalism, was the ability of the individual to make decisions which affected the work activities of other role practition-ers. Because of the power and authority derived from their exercise, command activities were considered to be indicative of elite functions within the organization. Both ascriptive and achievement professionals aspired to them, for the interdependence of rank and the exercise of these functions was so pronounced that 'rank' and 'command' were almost synonymous terms.

In the military organization, the term 'staff' was not used in the sense in which it is often employed to contrast *staff* functions with *line* functions.[12] It was associated with those activities which implemented organizational policy, after the latter had been formulated by the 'commander'. Primarily, staff activities were concerned with matters of internal organization and control, particularly where these ensured the settlement of broad questions of organizational policy, or where they were directed to the responsible conduct of military operations. Staff activities could be described as 'applicative functionalism',[13] for they were designed to ensure that the accepted plan of operations was implemented. In carrying out these activities, both ascriptive and achievement professionals served hierarchical superiors, but they did not have their authority over the occupants of other rank positions within the military organization, for this would have been an assumption of the command function. Nevertheless, the staff frequently acted for, and on behalf of, the exerciser of this command function, and it often appeared that the individual officer, in this situation, exercised some form of non-professional authority.

Professionals who performed *advisory* functions in the Royal Air Force, carried out particular engineering activities which required specialised knowledge and experience. An increasingly technological military organization requires a large number of specialists whose functions mirror the whole range of activities which are part of the civilian engineering system. The employment of these individuals enabled the organization to provide specialized skills at minimum expense for all parts of the Air Force. Accordingly, engineers helped others, performing a wider range of activities, in reaching their decisions, or in ensuring that the plan of operations was carried out. In addition to carrying out these advisory activities, that is 'to advise, counsel, suggest, guide and consult',[14] professionals who acted in this capacity, also performed service activities, whereby they carried out specific commitments for the commander. In this situation, they exercised a limited decision-making function, for they could only meet this commitment by determining task priorities. This extension of the normal characteristics of advisory activities, did not, however, counteract their limitations, for the individual practitioner was primarily involved in providing functional guidance to other individuals, in matters which fell within his sphere of competence.

In contrast, the professional who was employed in the implementation of *operational* activities, was directly involved in accomplishing occupational objectives. The precise nature of his task was most accurately defined in terms of the accepted goals of the organization. He was concerned with central, rather than peripheral, activities, and he had established close links with other professionals in the organization. Nevertheless, the engineer, irrespective of whether he was an achievement or an ascriptive professional, remained a part of a rigid, formal hierarchy. An explicit, rational, superior-subordinate relationship was created. This was used as a means whereby task commitments could be met, and, in this situation, autonomy was positively subordinated to the need for bureaucratic control.

Research activities were closely allied to these operational activities, for they were used to help the operational practitioner realize, more effectively and more efficiently, the goals of the military organization. Applied research could, however, be distinguished from operational activities, other than in terms of their respective functions. While operational practitioners were often involved in questions of organizational policy, engineering officers engaged in research, had surrendered their right to be consulted on matters of broad policy concerning their work.[15] Their demand for an autonomous professional authority was derived from a wish to establish a viable collegial model of organizational behaviour, and this hindered their participation in a system based on bureaucratic control. An emphasis on the need for organizational consensus was associated with the reluctance of these officers to integrate themselves fully into the military structure, and, in consequence, they were often peripheral members of the organization. They retained particularly close links with their colleagues in external occupations, and, in stressing that a common claim to professional status was based on a narrow field of specialist knowledge, these engineer officers refused to accept organizational definitions of ascriptive professionalism.

The existence of five separate categories of occupational activities was a primary source of some of the strains which were associated with the employment of both ascriptive and achievement professionals in the military organization. In general terms, the ideal-type of achievement professional was defined by characteristics, such as *expertise* and *autonomy*, which were compatible only with his employment in research and advisory activities. Employment in the remaining categories meant that officers were expected to possess qualities which were basically antithetical to these characteristics. This was particularly noticeable where achievement professionals were employed in *command* activities. Successful role performance depended upon the exercise of depersonalized bureaucratic authority. A considerable body of law and convention legitimized actions which were carried out, on the basis of formalistic impersonality. The dominant norms were concepts of duty, loyalty, career commitment and total involvement in organizational informal structures. A developed rank structure accentuated the importance of the relationship between power and experience gained within the military organization. A set of relationships was established, as is shown in Figure 1, which was based on the characteristics of the ascriptive, rather than the achievement, professional.

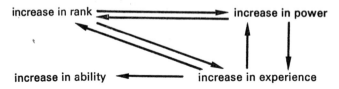

Figure 1

This set of relationships was designed to ensure the homogeneity of the organization, but the achievement professional often found it difficult to fit into this pattern. Experience was essentially 'military' experience, that is, a special knowledge of organizational facts, and it was by no means certain that the achievement professional had acquired this experience during his military service. Similarly, the derived ability was wider in its scope than mere 'professional ability', for it was concerned with the exercise of pure military skills. As a result, some achievement professionals found it difficult to achieve an acceptable standard of occupational performance, and their failure was a source of further intra-organizational strain.

Concomitantly, few engineer officers were prepared to withdraw from participation in command activities. Since the pattern of military promotion was designed to select potential commanders, a refusal to accept the responsibilities of command roles meant that the individual officer could not expect to be considered for promotion. Accordingly, achievement professionals, consciously or unconsciously, made adjustments to their attitudes. Where this was a conscious process, the departure from the behavioural attitudes of the achievement professional was rationalized in two ways. Firstly, it was argued that an increase in rank, and the associated increase in power, brought the individual into a position of bureaucratic authority where he could exercise a concomitant professional authority. In this situation, the individual could institute reforms and thereby ensure that a process of professionalization increased the participation of the achievement professional in command activities. Secondly, it was

154

argued that changes in the basis of military authority whereby the latter was dependent on the exercise of a managerial control rather than on the use of coercion, encouraged professional participation in military command activities. Here, the training process which the achievement professional had undergone, was claimed to be a more than adequate introduction to those management principles which were the claimed basis of an amended military authority.

In both cases, the achievement professional failed to take into account the advantages possessed by the ascriptive professional who had been trained within the organization. A complex military induction and assimilation programme was specifically designed to meet the need for management education. The military programme not only satisfied the requirements of the relevant professional institutions in this context, but went further to consider specifically the direct relationship between managerial control and military authority. Moreover, the ascriptive professional, by virtue of the greater length of his military service, was able to offer, as his qualifications for promotion, not only his formal academic training, but evidence of his practical experience, in management over a period of time. As a result, the achievement professional, as is shown in Tables 3 and 4, was not guaranteed automatic promotion, and the ascriptive professional with suitable military experience and ability, was considered equally by the organization for advancement in rank, and for employment in a command role. This was a further source of strain, particularly where the individual achievement professional had made a conscious adjustment in his behavioural attitudes. He regretted the steps he had taken, since these had not led to his promotion, and a sense of deprivation oftenled him to a position of potential conflict, in which the achievement professional reacted forcefully to control by the ascriptive professional acting in a command role.

The participation of these professional engineers in *staff* activities produced less evidence of role strain. With the exception of those achievement professionals who were interested only in employment in research and advisory activities, the remainder of this category, and the larger group of ascriptive professionals, accepted that employment in staff appointments was a rational extension of their military experience. Both categories of professionals were able to establish informal relationships with other engineers, the achievement professional on the basis of the principles of the collegial model of organizational behaviour, the ascriptive professional on the basis of the custodial model. Where this produced strain, because the recipient of staff instructions reacted against the established model of behaviour, the staff officer could resort to the otherwise latent, hierarchical form of control. Even where this was used, the achievement professional who employed this method, could justify his amended behavioural attitude on the grounds that he was not exercising direct bureaucratic authority, but was merely acting for, or on behalf of, the commander.

Employment in staff activities was therefore attractive to many engineers. It provided them with peripheral participation in the decision-making process, whilst permitting them to retain their innate behavioural attitudes. Moreover, staff activities were seen to be a 'testing' period, during which individuals were evaluated for future promotion, so that staff experience was considered to be a prerequisite for organizational advancement. Accordingly, there was very little direct strain associated with this type of employment. Conversely, a persistent latent strain became manifest when actual practice differed from this ideal-type pattern. This occurred when disappointment, caused by the failure of a promotion expectation, accentuated the stresses of an ambivalent position. The passed-over achievement professional, in particular, in performing his more usual operational or advisory activities, reformulated his concepts of professional behaviour. In doing this, he tended to over-emphasize his commitment to those characteristics which distinguished the achievement from the ascriptive professional. In extreme cases, he used his dichotomized position as an excuse for seeking freedom from both staff and command control, arguing that his experience of staff activities had made him aware of the extent to which the exercise of this control was the antithesis of a true professional ethos.

This latent strain was, perhaps, inevitable. The need to ensure a planned career for fully committed officers meant that officers, irrespective of whether they were ascriptive or achievement professionals, could not expect to be employed exclusively in performing staff activities. In the absence of a special 'Staff Corps' to which officers were appointed for lengthy periods of their military career, engineers could expect to alternate between staff and other appointments. The problem which arose was that officers who considered that they had been rejected, criticised a system which employed untrained officers in staff appointments. They argued that this suggested a situation which was admirably summed up in the Duke of Cambridge's dictum: 'I prefer for the staff to have regimental officers. I am quite satisfied that the best staff officer is your regimental officer...'[16] The strain which arose, was derived from their fear that the failure of the military organization to establish a policy of exclusive graduate entry for staff appointments, reduced employment opportunities and thereby affected chances of promotion.

156

This fear was no new phenomenon in the military organization. In the British Army during the nineteenth century, officers complained that while it was recognised that a 'College, or Senior Department, for the Staff is the completion and may be termed the strongest encouragement of General Military Education,'[17] published figures showed that few Staff College graduates were selected for these elite appointments.[18]

In the case of both the nineteenth century Army officer and the contemporary Air Force engineer, there was an apparent justification for this complaint. The number of full career engineer officers who had attended a Staff College, or who were qualified for entry to the College, is shown in Table 5. Of the 1064 officers who were in the relevant rank levels, 20% had undertaken a formal staff college course. Of the remainder, a further 16% were qualified for admission to the college, the majority having followed a two year part-time course in military subjects, which was designed to be an introduction to their subsequent formal college course.

Table 5. Military Qualifications of Full Career Officers

Rank	PSC	QSS	Nil	Total
Group Captain	47	16	25	88
Wing Commander	97	40	168	305
Squadron Leader	75	129	467	671
	219	185	660	1064

PSC: Graduate of a Staff College
QSS: Qualified for Entry to Staff College.

Published figures of staff appointments at the Ministry of Defence and at various Royal Air Force Command Headquarters, showed that some 210 posts were available for these officers. As Table 6 indicates, the greater number of these were filled by 'unqualified' officers, that is, officers who had neither attended a formal course of study in staff duties nor were eligible for admission to the Staff College.

Table 6 is incomplete and only indicative of trends, for an unknown number of officers were employed on other unspecified staff duties. It suggests, however, that the low participation rate of Staff College graduates in staff appointments, particularly at the lower rank levels, justified

157

Table 6. Military Experience of Staff Officers

Rank	Achievement Professional				Ascriptive Professional				Totals
	PSC	QSS	Nil	T	PSC	QSS	Nil	T	
Group Captain	4	3	5	12	5	0	1	6	18
Wing Commander	11	7	7	25	5	3	15	23	48
Squadron Leader	8	6	40	54	0	7	83	90	144
	23	16	52	91	10	10	99	199	210

the complaints of those officers who contended that the system of selection and appointment, reduced their employment opportunities. It was, however, significant that the degree of strain, associated with this complaint, varied according to the rank of the officers concerned. For officers who had attained the rank of wing commander, the amount of strain was limited. At this level, qualified individuals who were not currently employed on staff duties, often exercised command responsibilities commensurate with their status in the military hierarchy. It was also evident that more than 50% of the available posts were filled by the qualified or eligible officers, and an appreciation of this fact produced a concomitant reduction in the degree of possible strain.

The degree of strain was most noticeable among officers of the rank of squadron leader. There were a number of reasons for this. It was partly attributable to the very size of the group, which was bigger than the combined total of full career wing commanders and flight lieutenants. At squadron leader rank, the competition for promotion was most acute, not least because the transition from this rank level to the one above it, marked out those officers who could be considered for promotion to the apex of the hierarchical structure. Accordingly both achievement and ascriptive professionals sought to establish their claim for an exclusive entry into elite positions, such as staff appointments, which might lead to their subsequent promotion. In preferring this claim avalified achievement professionals were joined by those ascriptive professionals who had been trained at the Staff College or who were eligible for entry into the College. Accordingly three mutual interest groups were formed: (*a*) Staff trained or qualified achievement and ascriptive professionals; (*b*) other achievement professionals; (*c*) other ascriptive professionals. These were dynamic associations of segmental interests, although officers could not cross freely from one group to the other. From Table 7, it can be seen that achievement professionals and staff trained ascriptive professionals totalled 204 officers, other achievement professionals 213 and other ascriptive officers 254.

Table 7. Professional and Military Qualifications of Engineer Officers Full Career Squadron Leaders

	Degree	PG	PI	Total	Ascriptive	Total
PSC	21	14	28	63	12	75
QSS	22	14	50	86	43	129
Nil	65	24	124	213	254	467
	108	52	202	362	309	671

Of the total of 671 officers of this rank, only 254 (38 %) formed the third mutual interest group, yet this group supplied the majority of squadron leaders employed in staff activities (58 %). As a result they had a particular interest in ensuring that these elite positions remained open to them, justifying their selection for these staff appointments on the grounds of their military experience, their proven ability and their membership of homogeneous military organization. In contrast, the almost equal sized interest group of staff trained achievement and ascriptive professionals, in rejecting the validity of these claims, contended that they alone had the requisite professional ability, specific training and sense of career commitment.

The potential dichotomy associated with the presence within a single military collectivity of three distinct interest groups was, however, limited by the emergence of other associations based on common affinities. Several of the latter arose to meet the particular requirements of officers employed in *operational* activities. In many ways, these were the most arduous of all engineering activities and officers who were thus employed for any period of time, irrespective of whether they could be categorised as ascriptive or achievement professionals, considered that engineers could be dichotomized as 'them' and 'us'. The former were seen to be part of an 'In-group', whose members, enjoying roles as part of the centre of the organization, attempted to restrict the participation of other officers, currently employed in operational activities, in elitist activities. In contrast, the latter were considered to be members of a more broadly based peripheral association, whose participation in, and access to, the centre, was limited. The members of the 'In-group' were the carriers of positive dominance roles. Their aim was to preserve the organizational *status quo*, and to avoid participating in operational activities. Members of the 'Out-group' on the other hand, were negatively orientated officers who, excluded from participation in staff or command activities sought to change the *status quo*.

It was argued, in justification of proposed changes, that the 'In-group' did not use power as a facility for the performance of function in the military system, but as a means of authoritarian control. Members of the 'Out-group' considered that this type of control was outmoded, and that it was necessary to replace it by an alternative which was based on managerial persuasion. Since participation in *operational* activities, in which the majority of engineering tradesman were employed, had given these officers ample management experience, they stressed that they alone were capable of exercising the form of control which was needed in a technological military organization. Their inability to participate in elite activities despite their self-evaluated management ability, then became a source of role strain which was most noticeable where the relationship between staff officers and operational practitioners was based on the autocratic or custodial models of organizational behaviour.

This 'Out-group', however, was not a homogeneous entity. It contained both ascriptive and achievement professionals, particularly those of the latter who had not been selected for promotion. Consequently, the group rarely demonstrated a common attitude, and the contrast between the behavioural attitudes of the ascriptive and achievement professional engendered a multivariate reaction to universal problems. The former often considered that the particular operational activity in which he was engaged, was the only organizational goal of importance. Other goals which interfered with task attainment were rejected as irrelevant. To control the activity, the ascriptive professional made use of the theoretical training and practical experience he had gained in management, although, since he lacked an understanding of the more complex theoretical aspects of management, his approach was frequently pragmatic rather than planned. This type of approach could, and did bring him into conflict with the achievement professional, particularly since the ascriptive professional whose management approach to a problem had failed, tended to rely subsequently on the latent sanctions authority at his disposal. This reversion to a traditional type of authority then weakened the claim of the ascriptive professional to be given power in other spheres of military activity, on the basis of his managerial expertise, and this, again, created a situation of residual strain.

In contrast, the achievement professional formulated a more widely based interpretation of organizational goals. A specific operational activity was related to more general military objectives, but a concomitant search for professional autonomy often created a situation in which the achievement professional, in failing to understand the degree of importance attached by the organization to the activity, came into conflict with his hierarchical superiors. The force of the associated strain was accentuated by the lack of practical management experience which many of these professional engineers demonstrated. A wish to introduce changes, based on theoretical rather than proved management principles, created uncertainty which made it more difficult to attain maximum efficiency, so that this, combined with the lack of practical experience, weakened the claim of the achievement professional to promotion and to a transfer into more central military activities. As a result, the engineer remained a member of a self-defined 'Out-group', unless he was prepared to adjust to the demands of the employing organization.

The type of strain which was associated with the employment of both ascriptive and achievement professionals in *advisory* and *research* activities, took a different form. Since the nature of these activities was completely compatible with the behavioural attitudes of the achievement professional, the latter readily accepted this type of employment. His *extrinsic* interests, that is, his status, reputation, professional authority and reward, were satisfied. His *technical* interests were furthered by the development and recognition of his specific skill within the employment environment. His *cultural* interests, associated with the maintenance of the values, symbols and norms of the professional association, were ensured through the close links which he maintained with his civilian colleagues.[19] The ascriptive professional, in contrast, frequently found difficulty in adjusting his behavioural attitude to the requirements of an advisory or research environment. The military organization needed his practical experience; in addition he was often called upon to exercise his acquired management expertise in the performance of these functions. An initial degree of strain was derived from the exercise of these dual functions, for they were carried out in an atypical military environment which while recognising the importance of all aspects of the achievement behavioural attitude, appeared to denigrate the value of practical experience and management expertise. In consequence, the ascriptive professional who was employed in these quasi-civilian advisory and research roles, believed that he was excluded from full participation in organizational activities. This was particularly noticeable in those instances in which decision-making processes involving technological considerations, seemed to encourage the participation of junior achievement professionals to the exclusion of more senior ascriptive officers. Moreover, even on the numerous occasions when the practical experience of these ascriptive officers was used as a rational basis for future planning, it was apparent that they resented a situation in which while the achievement professional was able to increase the boundaries of his knowledge by drawing on the reserve of the ascriptive professional's experience, no reciprocal exchange or feedback took place. As a result, and in an attempt to re-assert his formal hierarchical status, the ascriptive professional often over-emphasized the significance of occurrences which he considered were infringements of his notional position within the military structure. Concomitantly, a similar form of reaction was apparent in the manner in which officers of this type, particularly those of senior rank, stressed the importance of military virtues, and attacked the manner in which the behaviour of achievement professionals in research establishments failed to conform to the traditional model of military attitudes.

The types of strain which have been considered are not peculiar to the military organization, and their counter-parts can be seen in other large-scale organizations, particularly in those in which a large number of participants are ascriptive professionals. Local government administration in Great Bitain, the Civil Service and industrial units particularly those which are organismic rather than mechanistic in form, display evidence of similar patterns of occupational strain. There are, however, several factors which are peculiar to a military environment. The desired wish to create a homogeneous organization does not encourage the development of critical self-analysis, with the result that the military organization is slow to accept that strains of the type which have been described, are natural and expected characteristics of large-scale organizations.[20] Similarly, the significance of strain within the military establishment is accentuated by the inability of the organization as a traditional bureaucracy to accommodate conflict. [21] Whereas professional organizations are structured to permit a great deal of internal strain and conflict, either potential or actual, the military, perhaps because of the high proportion of ascriptive professionals among its members, is unable to adopt this attitude. Accordingly, the military in rejecting the compatibility of strain, also tries either to deny its existence, or to rely over much on a highly developed centralized control, through an emphasis on leadership roles, to mitigate its effects.

162

The importance of these strains in the military organization cannot be minimised. Internally, strains and dysfunctions derived from the presence within the same sub-system of ascriptive and achievement professionals may have negative consequences for the performance of the organization. Externally their importance is derived from the readiness of the civil power to use evidence of noted strain as an excuse for increasing the amount of civil control, either direct or indirect, over the military establishment. Since this form of control is irrational and illegitimate, dysfunctional strain within the military organization then distorts the true pattern of civil-military relationships. It is for this last reason, above all, that evidence of strain within the military is a subject demanding further research and analysis, for the monopoly of violence which the military has at its disposal is so absolute, and the dangers associated with its abuse so great, that inadequate civil control is unacceptable in modern society.

1. See National Board for Prices and Incomes: *Standing Reference on the pay of the Armed Forces*, Second Report. Report No. 116 (London, HMSO, 1969), Cmnd 4079, Chapter 9, pp. 35–40.

2. These characteristics of professionalism are those accepted by W. KORNHAUSER, *Scientists in Industry: Conflict and Accommodation* (Berkeley, University of California Press, 1962), p. 1, and by George STRAUSS, 'Professionalism and Occupational Associations', *Industrial Relations* II, No. 3 (May 1963), pp. 8–9.

3. For an elaboration of the criteria of the *ascriptive* professional in a military environment, see M. D. FELD, 'Professionalism, Nationalism and the Alienation of the Military', in Jacques VAN DOORN (ed.), *Armed Forces and Society* (The Hague, Mouton, 1968), p. 56.

4. See Jacques VAN DOORN, 'The Officer Corps: A Fusion of Profession and Organization', *Archiv. Europ. Sociol*, Vol. VI (1965), p. 264.

5. Peter M. BLAU and W. Richard SCOTT, *Formal Organizations – A Comparative Approach* (San Francisco, Chandler, 1962), pp. 60 et seq.

6. Samuel P. HUNTINGTON, *The Soldier and the State, The Theory and Politics of Civil-Military Relations* (Cambridge, Mass., Harvard University Press, 1959), p. 16.

7. These models are based on those conceptualized by Keith DAVIS, 'Evolving Models of Organizational Behaviour', *Academy of Management Journal* (March, 1968), pp. 25–34.

8. See L. L. WADE, 'Professionals in Organizations: A Neoteric Model', *Human Organization*, Vol. 26, Nos. 1/2 (Spring/Summer, 1967), pp. 40–46.

9. See W. Richard SCOTT, 'Professionals in Bureaucracies – Areas of Conflict', in Howard M. VOLLMER and Donald M. MILLS (eds.), *Professionalization* (Englewood Cliffs, Prentice-Hall, 1966), pp. 265–275. J. BEN-DAVID, 'The Professional Role of the Physician in Bureaucratized Medicine. A Study in Role Conflict', *Human Relations*, II (1958), pp. 255–274. W. KORNHAUSER, *op. cit.* D. G. MOORE and R. RENCK, 'The Professional Employee in Industry', *Journal of Business*, Vol. 28 (January, 1955) pp. 58–66.

10. This table, and those which follow, are based on data calculated from the *Air Force List*, Spring 1969, and the *Air Force List*, Autumn 1969 (London, HMSO, 1969).

11. In the absence of a strictly legal definition of the professional engineer in the United Kingdom, it is necessary to distinguish between the *chartered* engineer and the *technician* engineer. The former is a member, by examination, of one of the professional associations affiliated to the Council of Engineering Institutions. The latter is educated and trained to a lower standard, usually that of the Higher National Certificate in Engineering (HNC), a qualification obtained by part-time study over a period of five years. The *technician* engineer may belong to one of the lesser associations, but this membership is no indication of engineering competence, nor can it be interpreted as a licence to practice. For a further elaboration of the differences between these two groups and a comparison of their respective status, see Kenneth PRANDY, *Professional Employees. A Study of Scientists and Engineers* (London, Faber, 1965) and J. E. GERSTL and S. P. HUTTON, *Engineers: Anatomy of a Profession* (London, Routledge, 1966).

12. Louis A. ALLEN, 'Identifying Line and Staff', in Joseph A. LITTERER (ed.), *Organizations: Structure and Behaviour* (New York, Wiley, 1967), pp. 94–104.

13. L. URWICK, *The Elements of Administration* (New York, Harper and Brothers, 1943), p. 41.
14. ALLEN, *op. cit.*, p. 100.
15. See Tom BURNS and G. M. STALKER, *The Management of Innovations* (London, Tavistock Publications, 1961), p. 176.
16. Quoted in Brevet-Major A. R. GODWIN-AUSTIN, *The Staff and the Staff College* (London, Faber, 1927), p. 155.
17. *Report on Training Officers for the Scientific Corps* (London, 1856), p. xxxvii.
18. *Ibid.*, p. 286. Of the 216 officers who graduated from the Army Staff College between 1836 and 1854, only 15 were ever selected for appointments on the Staff. Of the officers appointed to the staff during the three years, 1864–1867, in the ranks of ensign to lieutenant-colonel, 38, the majority of whom were captains, had passed through Staff College, in comparison with the 187 who had not. See *Return of the War Office*, dated 20th March, 1867. Cited in *Parliamentary Reports* (1870), Vol. XXIV, p. clxiii.
19. The characteristics of the *professional interest* are further analysed in Robert MACIVER, 'The Social Significance of Professional Ethics', *The Annals of the American Academy of Political and Social Science*, Vol. 101 (May, 1922), pp. 5–11.
20. See D. KATZ: 'Approaches to Managing Conflict' in R. L. KAHN and E. BOULDING (eds.), *Power and Conflicts in Organizations* (New York, Basic Books, 1964), Chapter VII, pp. 105–114.
21. Eugene LITWAK, 'Models of Bureaucracy which Permit Conflict', *American Journal of Sociology*, Vol. 67 (1961), pp. 177–184. P. R. LAWRENCE and J. W. LORSCH, 'Differentiation and Integration in Complex Organizations', *Administrative Science Quarterly*, Vol. 12, No. 1 (1967), pp. 1–47.

The Changing Military Career in Canada

P. E. COULOMBE

PIERRE COULOMBE is Director of a Special Government Task Force studying the effectiveness of the two official languages programme in the Public Service of Canada. He is the author of a forthcoming book *Military Career and Cultural Dynamics* which he completed as a post-doctoral research fellow in Paris in 1970. Dr. Coulombe who has taught in several universities holds graduate degrees in Business from l'Université Laval, and in Sociology from the University of Minnesota and l'Université de Paris.

The Canadian military organization has undergone profound changes since 1945. Having been reduced to a relatively small scale of forces-in-being with an important mobilization potential immediately after World War II, the armed forces from 1950 to 1964 have expanded and diversified military roles and related weapons systems, thereby requiring an increasingly well-trained and knowledgeable personnel. The activities of the Canadian Forces since 1945 have ranged from nuclear tactical and strategic activities within the commitments of the North Atlantic Treaty Organization (NATO) and the North American Air Defence Command (NORAD), to the relatively sedate U. N. peacekeeping and truce-supervising missions.

As a result of an overall review of foreign and defence policies in 1969, we have seen a reduced NATO role, the phased de-nuclearization of the Canadian NATO force, and an increased emphasis on the protection of Canadian territorial sovereignty, particularly in the far northern regions. Yet one factor has remained constant. Save for two short, ill-favored war-time conscription periods[1], Canada's Forces have been kept on a voluntary basis.

In March 1964 the Government tabled a far-reaching White Paper on Defence that has since been implemented to a large degree. Until it was unified by law, in February 1968[2], the military organization of Canada was composed of the traditional services in order of seniority: Royal Canadian Navy (RCN), Canadian Army, Royal Canadian Air Force (RCAF). The legal unifying of the services occurred after the greater part of the military organization had been integrated at headquarters level, and decentralized into a system of six functional commands, of which a highly mobile and versatile force was to be the basic feature[3]. The present military organization then stands as one structure of ranks and trades under one uniform. The three environments, sea, land and air, are referred to as elements which correspond roughly to the old services.

Although Canada had already adhered to the United Nations Charter and the North Atlantic Treaty Organization by 1950, no significant Canadian military contingent had been posted abroad since World War II. The onset of the Korean War in June 1950 marked a turning point in the evolution of the forces-in-being concept and generated a need for completely new specializations for each of the three services. The total force of 47 200 military personnel in 1950[4] had doubled by 1952, eventually reaching a peak of some 126 500 in 1962. The Defence budget was multiplied five times between 1950 and 1953[5].

169

The Korean effort consisted mainly of fielding a special brigade group, stationing three destroyers and providing some air transport. More far-reaching technical changes were set in motion with the reenforcement of the NATO forces in Europe by Canada's contribution of one infantry brigade group and twelve squadrons of interceptor aircraft. These were eventually equipped with advanced systems which contributed to raising requirements for better trained manpower. In a third area, Canada and the United States agreed as early as 1951 to erect three trans-continental radar networks deployed mainly on Canadian territory. The Royal Canadian Air Force eventually provided part of the personnel that has manned this radar system. NORAD was formally established in 1958. Thereafter, the RCAF deployed nine interceptor squadrons and, after long debate, two squadrons of BOMARC ground to air missiles were established and armed with nuclear heads. The Royal Canadian Navy during this period continued to play its anti-submarine role while concentrated mainly on the Atlantic coast.

The RCAF has known the greatest expansion and increasing diversification of roles during this period of general military expansion. It has developed a rational approach to manpower utilization and organizational effectiveness to the extent that the unified Forces have adopted a large number of air force procedure systems, an example of which is the Rockcliffe Material Command.

The total strength of the Forces at 95 400 in 1952 represents an increase of 47 200 over a two year period. Three fifths of this increase was attributable to the army which had sent a special brigade to Korea. Yet RCAF personnel between 1952 and 1956 was increased by 17 400, while the RCN was increased by only 5 600 and the Canadian Army was decreased by 1 700. The relative importance of each service has remained roughly the same since 1956: 40 to 42 per cent for both the Canadian Army and the RCAF and 17 per cent for the RCN[6]. The total strength of each service increased steadily from 1956 to 1962 when it stood at 126 500[7]. The Government has been reducing total strength steadily since 1962, with the plan level of 82 000 aimed at for 1972[8]. It stands in 1970 at approximately 87 000.

Maintaining a modern, diversified Army without any form of selective service raises important economic and social implications. The military has to recruit new members within a free labour market with ever rising standards in order to meet its growing technological requirements. This voluntary aspect of the military has been animated by the reasoning that military service should be open on an equal opportunity basis to all citizens. Equal opportunity has not worked for all citizens, however,

170

because French-speaking Canadians have not been able to become professional military people in the context of their own language and culture. They have had to learn and to work in English. This is not to say that the military organization has not become aware of this fact. A growing number of organizational measures tend to minimize the numerous problems created by the presence of French-speaking members. The working language of the Canadian Forces, nevertheless, remains substantially English, although the Government's recent bilingualism policy aims at offering better conditions of enfranchisement for the French language in the work environment.

It is both in the light of organizational imperatives stemming from an emerging role as a unified, well equipped and highly mobile 'constabulary force' and in the perspective of rapidly changing social conditions in Canada, that we wish to look at the social recruitment and career attainment of the military.

THE RANK STRUCTURE

The scientific and technical developments in defence systems that have completely transformed military strategy since World War II have had a profound effect on the organization and structure of the armed forces. To operate, maintain and develop equipment, the armed forces have had to recruit, to train and to re-train their personnel, as well as to call upon already trained specialists. Furthermore, the voluntary Canadian military has had to attract and retain skilled personnel and to shape careers in competition with the rest of the Canadian labour market. One might note considerable differences between the relative speeds at which each service has geared itself to technological change, if the unified distribution of ranks is explained by a consideration of the relative importance of each service.

The unified rank distribution of all military personnel presented in figure 1[9] indicates that it departs little from the classic pyramidal form[10]. The pyramid sits on a wide base: 63.9 per cent of personnel are Private, Private 1 and Corporal. The proportion at each rank decreases rapidly as we move from Sergeant to the Warrant Officer ranks. Among officers, who account for one out of six military personnel, the pyramid is somewhat broken by the importance of the rank of Captain which includes twice as many officers as the ranks of Major and Lieutenant.

Since each service has had a different approach to managing its rank structure, it is important to consider how the composite picture of figure 1

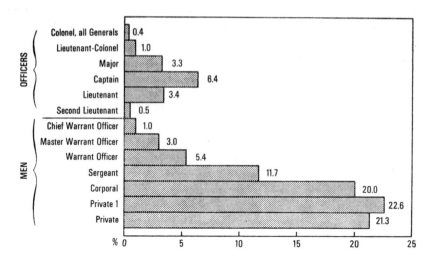

Figure 1

is made up. Total numbers are influenced first by the relative size of each service and secondly, by the importance of each rank within each service[11].

Table 1 shows that the army and the air force are about equal in size, with 41.5 per cent and 41.8 per cent respectively, while the navy with 16.7 per cent is substantially smaller. The similarity between the army and the air force, however, exists only at the aggregate level, for each service has a peculiar distribution of ranks with its respective officer corps differing greatly from one another. The air force has the highest ratio of officers to men, with one out of five an officer compared to one out of six in the navy and one out of seven in the army. Half of all air force officers are Captain and therefore account for 57.5 per cent of all Captains in the Forces.

Relative to its size, the navy has a large proportion of higher ranks both among officers and men. With its small base, its entire rank structure represents the 'thinnest' pyramid among the services. Table 1 indicates that the navy, which includes 16 per cent of the officers, comprises 22.7 per cent of senior officers (stratum A). Non commissioned officers, on the other hand, are relatively more important in the army than in the air force (stratum C).

172

While the composite picture of figure 1 yields a pyramidal contour, table 1 demonstrates that each service has a distinct rank structure and ensuing career lines. Discrepancies in the conditions of rank attainment and career patterns are being corrected gradually with unification. The relations and proportions indicated in figure 1 and table 1, however, must be kept in mind, because they put the relative importance of each group in perspective.

ETHNO-LINGUISTIC BACKGROUND OF MILITARY PERSONNEL

Historically, the three services have played differing roles as manpower employers, each having attracted and tried to retain personnel who not only met with basic requirements but who also adapted to varying traditions. Regional or geographic quotas can be applied only for first entrance into the Forces. Since turn-over is fairly high after the initial term of enrolment, it is more basic to ask who remains in the service.

Voluntary service implies that those most attracted to a military career will form the bulk of senior personnel, while the very nature of organized military life further suggests that its core group will tend to share a number of common characteristics. Since the Forces function with the federal government as employer, can one assume they are representative of the Canadian population? One must account for the fact that the military, more than many other types of human institutions, has maintained itself by adherence to and perpetuation not only of organizational but also of social traditions. Those traditions in the Canadian military are identified and guided by what John Porter in *The Vertical Mosaic* calls Canada's British-origin charter group[12].

A comparison of the ethnic composition[13] of the Canadian population and of the Forces serves to highlight the relative importance of British ethnic groups in the Forces. Table 2 shows that Canadians tracing their ethnic origins to the British Isles account for 43.8 per cent of the total population. This British group includes 64.6 per cent of all Forces' personnel, while it accounts for 58.6 per cent of the entire Federal Public Service[14]. Among officers, it is even more prominent, with 73.2 per cent, army and air force officers being in about the same proportions, 71.2 per cent and 72.5 per cent, respectively. As many as 80 per cent of naval officers trace their ethnic origin to the British Isles[15].

Contrary to the British group, the French and 'other ethnic groups'[16] have smaller proportions in the Forces than in the Canadian population. Contrary to the British group, new Canadians of French and 'other

173

Table 1. Percentage Distribution of Canadian Forces Military Personnel within each Rank and Stratum[a], by Service, 1966

	Army	Air force	Navy	Total
Colonel, all Generals	36.8	41.0	22.2	100.0
Lieutenant-Colonel	35.5	41.6	22.9	100.0
Stratum A	35.9	41.4	22.7	100.0
Major	35.1	43.0	21.9	100.0
Captain	29.6	57.5	12.9	100.0
Lieutenant	36.6	50.8	12.6	100.0
Second Lieutenant	67.2	13.6	19.2	100.0
Stratum B	34.2	50.6	15.2	100.0
Officers	34.3	49.7	16.0	100.0
Chief Warrant Officer	42.5	32.3	25.2	100.0
Master Warrant Officer	41.4	25.7	32.9	100.0
Warrant Officer	33.5	32.7	33.8	100.0
Sergeant	48.2	36.4	15.4	100.0
Stratum C	43.2	33.8	23.0	100.0
Corporal	38.8	47.3	13.9	100.0
Private 1	13.2	67.7	19.1	100.0
Private	77.2	11.6	11.2	100.0
Stratum D	42.6	42.6	14.8	100.0
Men	42.7	40.4	16.9	100.0
All personnel	41.5	41.8	16.7	100.0

a. Stratum A includes the ranks of Lieutenant-Colonel, Colonel and all Generals; stratum B includes the ranks of Second Lieutenant, Lieutenant, Captain and Major; stratum C includes the ranks of Sergeant, Warrant Officer, Master Warrant Officer, Chief Warrant Officer; stratum D includes the ranks of Private, Private 1, and Corporal. The nomenclature used is that established in the Canadian Forces Reorganization Act of May 1967, except that we have distinguished Forces Reorganization Act of May 1967, except that we have distinguished between Private and Private 1 (or Lance-Corporal, Leading Aircraftsman, Able Seaman) while the Act does not do so.

ethnic groups' have not been able to enter military service before receiving full Canadian citizenship, although it is doubtful that many would have come to Canada after World War II to undertake a military career.

Table 2 shows that newer immigrant groups in Canada such as the Italians and the Poles have small proportions in the Forces in relation to their importance in the population. Older groups such as the Ukrainians and more particularly, the Germans have a more equal proportion in the Forces among both officers and men.

Table 2. Ethnic Composition of the Canadian Population, 1961, and of the Officers and Men of the Canadian Forces, 1966 (percentages)

Ethnic Origin	Canadian population		Canadian Forces					
			All personnel		Officers		Men	
British	43.8		64.6ᵃ		73.2		63.1	
French	30.4		19.2		12.5		20.3	
Other	25.8		16.2		14.3		16.6	
German		5.7		5.3		4.2		5.5
Italian		2.7		0.4		0.5		0.4
Polish		1.8		0.8		0.9		0.8
Ukrainian		2.6		1.7		1.7		1.7
Other		13.0		8.0		7.0		8.2
Total	100.0		100.0		100.0		100.0	

Source: Data on Canadian population from Census of Canada, 1961, cited in *Report of the Royal Commission on Bilingualism and Biculturalism*, Book IV, The Cultural Contribution of the Other Ethnic Groups (Ottawa, 1969), p. 32.
a. This group is composed of 34.5 per cent English, 16.6 per cent Scottish, 13.5 per cent Irish.

The French ethnic group is relatively the least represented in the Forces with 19.2 per cent, who are disproportionately concentrated in the men ranks. The army has a larger group of French ethnic origin, 21 per cent, than the air force with 19.8 per cent, although the air force has a larger proportion of 'other ethnic origin,' 17.7 per cent, than the army's 15.4 per cent. The navy has a larger group of 'other ethnic origin' (15 per cent) than of French ethnic origin (12.9 per cent).

Since the notion of ethnic origin relates to the past and does not constitute a standard indicator for all groups, it can be sterile and even misleading taken by itself. Combined with the factor of language of

175

childhood[17], it provides a more valid measure of the degree of cultural continuity or cultural transfer that a group or an individual knows. We found that the great majority of military personnel of 'other ethnic origin' and an important group of French ethnic origin spoke a language in childhood that did not correspond to their ethnic origin. In fact, 78.2 per cent of military personnel recruited in the 'other ethnic origin' segment of the Canadian population were Anglophone in childhood. Among French ethnic origin military personnel, 24.4 per cent were Anglophone in childhood, although only 10 per cent of French origin Canadian population are Anglophone[18]. It is apparent that the Canadian Forces have attracted those who have a better command of the English language in greater proportion than their relative importance in the general population.

Table 3. Ethnic Origin and Language of Childhood of Military Personnel (percentages), 1966

Ethnic origin	Language of childhood				
	English	*English and French*	*French*	*Other language*	*Total*
British	62.2	1.5	0.8	0.1	64.6
French	4.7	3.4	11.1	0.01	19.2
Other	12.7	0.2	0.2	3.1	16.2
Total	79.6	5.1	12.1	3.2	100.0

Table 3 illustrates the strength of presence of the English language in the Canadian Forces. We have seen that the Forces are made up of a larger group of British ethnic origin (64.6 per cent) than is present in the Canadian population (43.8 per cent). Furthermore, the military has recruited a larger proportion of those who spoke English in childhood (79.6 per cent) than there is in the Canadian population (58.5 per cent)[19]. We can see in table 3 that the group of those who spoke English in childhood includes 4.7 per cent of French ethnic origin and 12.7 per cent of 'other ethnic groups'.

Thus it becomes clear that the composition of the Canadian Forces is polarized toward the English language in a substantially larger proportion

176

than in the Canadian population. Among the general population, 41.5 per cent have a mother tongue other than English[20]. The proportion is somewhat lower in the Federal Public Service where 30.6 per cent have a non-English mother tongue[21], while the proportion among the Forces of non-English in childhood is only 15.3 per cent, or roughly half that in the Public Service.

While the composition of the Forces is polarized toward the group of British ethnic origin, it is even more polarized toward the English language shared at different degrees by all ethnic groups in Canada. Since there are a certain number of Francophones in the Canadian Forces, any study of the Forces' socio-cultural composition must consider them as a group because their concentration in lower rather than higher ranks gives them a certain importance. Table 4 shows that while Francophones form 16 per cent of the Forces, they are disproportionately concentrated at 17 per cent among men, while accounting for only 10.3 per cent of the officer corps. Francophone concentration at the lower ends of both the men's and the officers' hierarchies is more pronounced among officers where they comprise only 6.3 per cent of all senior officers (stratum A), two-thirds of these being in the army.

The analysis of ethno-linguistic group differences between Francophones and Anglophones is dealt with extensively elsewhere[22]. One should keep in mind that certain differences that appear in this study are largely attributable at times to the presence of a group of Francophones who come predominantly from the Province of Québec and who represent the most important source of ethno-linguistic and socio-cultural differences in the Canadian Forces[23].

GEOGRAPHIC ORIGINS

A survey of the geographic origins of military personnel gives the truest picture one can have of the Forces' social recruitment. The military has traditionally engaged its personnel by way of regional quotas which differed from service to service when publicity, selection, engagement and training were done by individual services and which have been constantly revised according to openings and training facilities[24].

The proportions given in table 5 represent personnel who stayed in the service to pursue a career rather than reflecting the actual regional intake which cannot indicate the high turnover of personnel in the early stages of the military career. A comparison with the geographic origins

Table 4. Proportion of Francophones and of Anglophones in each Rank, by Service (percentages)[a], 1966

Rank	Canadian Forces			Army			Air force			Navy		
	Franco-phones	Anglo-phones	Total	Franco-phones	Anglo-phones	Total	Franco-phones	Anglo-phones	Total	Franco-phones	Anglo-phones	Total
Colonel, all Generals	6.3	93.7	100.0	12.3	87.7	100.0	2.4	97.6	100.0	3.4	96.6	100.0
Lieutenant-Colonel	6.3	93.7	100.0	11.6	88.4	100.0	3.2	96.8	100.0	3.6	96.4	100.0
Stratum A	6.3	93.7	100.0	11.9	88.1	100.0	2.9	97.1	100.0	3.5	96.5	100.0
Major	7.9	92.1	100.0	16.1	83.9	100.0	4.3	95.7	100.0	1.8	98.2	100.0
Captain	9.9	90.1	100.0	12.4	87.6	100.0	9.1	90.9	100.0	8.0	92.0	100.0
Lieutenant	13.1	86.9	100.0	14.2	85.8	100.0	13.7	86.3	100.0	7.0	93.0	100.0
Second Lieutenant	21.4	78.6	100.0	25.5	74.5	100.0	17.2	82.8	100.0	10.0	90.0	100.0
Stratum B	10.7	89.3	100.0	14.9	85.1	100.0	9.4	90.6	100.0	5.7	94.3	100.0
Officers	10.3	89.7	100.0	14.6	85.4	100.0	8.8	91.2	100.0	5.4	94.6	100.0

Table 4. Proportion of Francophones and of Anglophones in each Rank, by Service (percentages)[a], 1966 (concluded)

Rank	Canadian Forces			Army			Air force			Navy		
	Franco-phones	Anglo-phones	Total	Franco-phones	Anglo-phones	Total	Franco-phones	Anglo-phones	Total	Franco-phones	Anglo-phones	Total
Chief Warrant Officer	5.7	94.3	100.0	9.6	90.4	100.0	1.3	98.7	100.0	4.8	95.2	100.0
Master Warrant Officer	8.0	92.0	100.0	11.2	88.8	100.0	5.4	94.6	100.0	5.8	94.2	100.0
Warrant Officer	9.5	90.5	100.0	10.7	89.3	100.0	11.6	88.4	100.0	6.3	93.7	100.0
Sergeant	14.2	85.8	100.0	14.7	85.3	100.0	14.4	85.6	100.0	12.1	87.9	100.0
Stratum C	11.7	88.3	100.0	13.2	86.8	100.0	12.1	87.9	100.0	8.3	91.7	100.0
Corporal	14.4	85.6	100.0	15.9	84.1	100.0	15.0	85.0	100.0	8.2	91.8	100.0
Private 1	17.1	82.9	100.0	12.3	87.7	100.0	19.7	80.3	100.0	10.9	89.1	100.0
Private	24.6	75.4	100.0	25.3	74.7	100.0	31.8	68.2	100.0	12.3	87.7	100.0
Stratum D	18.7	81.3	100.0	21.2	78.8	100.0	19.2	80.8	100.0	10.5	89.5	100.0
Men	17.0	83.0	100.0	19.2	80.8	100.0	17.7	82.3	100.0	9.7	90.3	100.0
All personnel	16.0	84.0	100.0	18.7	81.3	100.0	16.2	83.8	100.0	9.2	90.8	100.0

a. A Francophone is one who spoke mainly French or French and English about equally in childhood *and* who is of French ethnic origin or who had at least one parent of French mother tongue. Everyone else is classified Anglophone.

of the Canadian population and of the Public Service shows that public servants represent slightly larger proportions of every Canadian geographic region except Québec. The Canadian Forces similarly have a larger proportion of all geographic areas other than Québec, for which the proportion is even lower than for public servants. Foreign-born military also represent a smaller proportion than foreign-born public servants.

The works of the Royal Commission on Bilingualism and Biculturalism have shed some light on the fact of low Québec representation in Federal institutions. From table 5 we can see that Québec accounts for 27 per cent of the Canadian population, 18.3 per cent of the Public Service and 14.4 per cent of the Forces[25]. Table 5 also brings into evidence important differences between the regional origins of officers and men and reflects tendencies for particular services to have regional recruitment patterns.

Officers tend to originate more frequently from Ontario, the Western provinces and foreign countries, while men come in larger proportions from the Atlantic provinces and in a certain measure from Québec. Army officers have a strong Ontario representation, while the air force has the largest group from the Prairies. The navy tends to have a strong Ontario proportion and an equally strong proportion from British Columbia and the British Isles combined. In fact, the navy, which concentrates its activities in the Atlantic region, gets as few as 14.3 per cent of its officers from that region.

The source of men differs from service to service also. Army manpower comes largely from the Atlantic provinces and Québec, air force from the Atlantic provinces, Ontario and the Prairies. The navy draws a smaller proportion of men from the Atlantic provinces than the other services, its largest proportion coming from Ontario followed equally by the Atlantic provinces and the Prairies.

Military personnel in Canada is recruited in all regions, urban and rural, but contrary to Janowitz's findings on American military leaders, its elite is not as rural in origin as that of the United States. Janowitz reports that:

... in 1950 almost 70 per cent of the Army leaders came from rural backgrounds, while, as we expected, the naval percentage had declined to approximately 56 per cent. The Air Force leadership followed the same pattern as the Army, in part, because in 1950 most of the Air Force generals were recruited from the Army[26].

The degree of urbanization[27] of military personnel is generally related to their geographic origin[28]. The Anglophone Canadian military officers of Lieutenant-Colonel rank and above (stratum A)[29] are urban in the proportion of 70.2 per cent, with the army at 75.9 per cent, the air force

Table 5. *Percentage Distribution of the Canadian Population, 1961, and of the Federal Public Service, 1965, by Geographic Origin; Percentage Distribution of Officers and Men, by Geographic Origin and by Service, 1966*

Geographic origin	Canadian population	Public Service	Canadian Forces			Army		Air force		Navy	
			Total	Officers	Men	Officers	Men	Officers	Men	Officers	Men
Atlantic	11.2	15.6	25.0	13.6	27.1	13.0	30.4	13.7	26.7	14.3	20.1
Québec	27.0	18.3	14.4	11.6	14.9	15.4	16.9	9.8	15.0	9.0	9.8
Ontario	25.7	31.4	27.4	30.2	26.9	33.1	27.9	29.4	23.6	26.8	32.0
Prairies	—	—	19.8	24.9	18.9	21.7	14.9	28.8	22.1	19.7	20.9
British Columbia, Yukon and N.W.T.	—	—	7.0	9.6	6.5	9.8	4.0	7.4	7.1	16.3	11.6
Total Western provinces	21.1	26.0	(26.8)	(34.5)	(25.4)	(31.5)	(18.9)	(36.2)	(29.2)	(36.0)	(32.5)
British Isles	—	—	4.3	6.6	3.9	4.1	3.1	6.8	4.3	11.3	4.8
Other countries	—	—	2.1	3.5	1.8	2.9	2.8	4.1	1.2	2.6	0.8
Total foreign countries	15.0	8.7	(6.4)	(10.1)	(5.7)	(7.0)	(5.9)	(10.9)	(5.5)	(13.9)	(5.6)
Total	100.0	100.0	100.0	100.0	100.0	100.0	100.0	100.0	100.0	100.0	100.0

Source: Data on Canadian population and the Federal Public Service from *Report of the Royal Commission on Bilingualism and Biculturalism*, Book III (Ottawa, 1969), p. 387.

at 62.9 per cent and the navy at 74.6 per cent. The same Francophone senior officers of stratum A are urban at 81.2 per cent.

We can see that senior Canadian officers generate their own pattern. Both army and naval Anglophone officers of senior rank are more urban than those in the air force, 21.9 per cent of the latter coming from the rural Prairies. Senior army officers originate largely from urban Ontario (33.1 per cent), British Columbia (17.9 per cent), the Prairies (11.5 per cent) and the British Isles (9.4 per cent). Thus it is apparent that senior Anglophone military officers represent less a single source than many different geographic regions. For the army and the navy, however, they are substantially more urban than all military personnel of whom 61.7 per cent is of urban origin while the Canadian population is urban at 62.7 per cent[30].

A more detailed consideration of rural-urban origin of officers and men (table 6) serves to illustrate some further differences. It is apparent that geographic recruitment from Québec, Ontario, British Columbia, the British Isles and other countries has been predominantly urban in nature. This is equally true for both officers and men. The Prairies, on the other hand, have been the source of rural origin for both officers and men. The Atlantic provinces have a larger proportion of urban officers, but a very slightly larger one of rural origin among men. The rural predominance in the Prairies geographic recruitment for officers is attributable to the air force alone; for men, it is mainly air force with some army recruitment. Air force and navy geographic recruitment of men in the Atlantic provinces is slightly more rural and equally so for the army.

In summary, men are less urban than officers, senior officers being clearly the most urban. These tendencies indicate that the services have had a relatively good pool from which to establish geographic recruiting. A comparison of the geographic origin of public servants and Canadian Forces personnel (table 5) shows that both organizations draw proportions exceeding every regional proportion except for Québec. The Forces in comparison with the Public Service draw a substantially larger proportion of its personnel from the Atlantic provinces, while drawing a smaller proportion in Québec.

SOCIO-ECONOMIC AND RELIGIOUS ORIGINS

The socio-economic origins of both officers and men can be a reliable indicator of inter-generational mobility within the military. Father's

182

Table 6. Percentage Distribution of the Canadian Forces, Officers and Men, by Geographic Origin and by Rural-Urban Origin[a], 1966

Geographic origin	Canadian Forces			Officers			Men		
	Rural	Urban	Total	Rural	Urban	Total	Rural	Urban	Total
Atlantic	12.5	12.5	25.0	5.4	8.2	13.6	13.8	13.3	27.1
Québec	4.5	9.9	14.4	2.8	8.8	11.6	4.8	10.1	14.9
Ontario	7.4	20.0	27.4	7.8	22.4	30.2	7.3	19.6	26.9
Prairies	11.2	8.6	19.8	13.2	11.7	24.9	10.8	8.1	18.9
British Columbia, Yukon and N.W.T.	1.7	5.3	7.0	2.3	7.3	9.6	1.6	4.9	6.5
British Isles	0.5	3.8	4.3	1.0	5.6	6.6	0.4	3.5	3.9
Other Countries	0.5	1.6	2.1	1.1	2.4	3.5	0.4	1.4	1.8
Total	38.3	61.7	100.0	33.6	66.4	100.0	39.1	60.9	100.0

a. A community of 5 000 inhabitants or more is defined as urban, while, conversely, a rural community has 4 999 or fewer inhabitants.

occupation is one of the most accepted single indicators, while religious affiliation, although more relative, can also be useful. We will consider them in turn.

Officers who, professionally, represent middle and higher management are in full ascending mobility in comparison with their fathers' occupations. Army and naval officers have fairly similar socio-economic origins. Army officers have the most military continuity, 11.4 per cent of them having a father of the military profession. Naval officers include the largest group to come from the professional and technical occupations, 16.6 per cent. Officers come from markedly higher socio-economic origins than the male labour force, although air force officers come in substantially greater numbers from agricultural and blue collar milieus.

Men of the Forces come from social origins fairly similar to those of the male labour force, but they count even fewer fathers in managerial, professional and technical occupations. Naval men are less frequently from agricultural backgrounds, and, with army men, have a greater number of military fathers. Table 7 shows that the greater rural origin of air force men is not accompanied by a noticeably larger proportion from the agricultural occupations. It will become apparent later that army men are distinguished from air force men largely by the greater educational attainment of the latter which in turn makes possible greater occupational gains in terms of trade group levels.

Table 8 shows that religious affiliation varies substantially from service to service and between officers and men. These variations can be expected since religious affiliations vary between ethno-linguistic and socio-economic groups in the general Canadian population. They can thus indicate social origins and degree of social mobility[31].

It is quite evident that Catholics are concentrated among men; their proportion is greatest in the army and least in the navy. These proportions are influenced by Francophone personnel who are almost all Catholic (95.5 per cent), and who are concentrated among men. Anglophone Catholics are concentrated in the lower ranks of both the officers' and the men's hierarchies, and are proportionately more numerous among men. The two large Protestant groups, Anglican and United, are more important among officers than men. Anglicans are noticeably more concentrated in the officer ranks. They are even more important among Anglophone senior officers (stratum A), where 41.4 per cent are Anglican and 34.8 per cent, United Church.

The air force differs from the other services in that the United Church is more important than the Anglican, since the former includes 43.6 per cent of anglophone senior officers. This particular United Church

184

Table 7. *Percentage Distribution of the Male Labour Force, by Occupation, 1961; Percentage Distribution of Officers and Men, by Father's Occupation and by Service, 1966*

		Father's occupation					
	Male labour force	Officers			Men		
Occupational structure		Army	Air force	Navy	Army	Air force	Navy
Farmer, farm worker	12.2	7.4	15.4	9.3	14.9	15.5	9.9
Other primary, labourer, production worker, craftsman, transport, communications	46.4	29.6	33.8	25.5	53.1	46.6	52.7
Service, clerical, sales	21.0	11.8	11.9	13.5	11.4	11.8	13.1
Managerial	10.2	24.6	22.0	24.7	6.7	11.2	9.9
Professional, technical	7.6	13.5	10.5	16.6	3.1	5.3	5.9
Military	—	11.4	3.9	7.3	5.3	3.2	5.1
Other[a]	2.6	1.7	2.5	3.1	5.5	6.4	3.4
Total	100.0	100.0	100.0	100.0	100.0	100.0	100.0

Source: Data on the male labour force from Census of Canada, 1961, cited in *Report of the Royal Commission on Bilingualism and Biculturalism*, Book III (Ottawa, 1969), p. 38.

a. This category includes those who 'never had a full-time job' and cases not stated. The question was phrased: 'What was your father's or guardian's main job or occupation when you were 15 years old?'

Table 8. Religious Affiliation of Officers and Men, for the Canadian Forces and by Service (percentages), 1966

Church	Canadian Forces		Army		Air force		Navy	
	Officers	Men	Officers	Men	Officers	Men	Officers	Men
Catholic[a]	24.4	38.7	29.4	43.1	22.8	38.3	18.3	28.9
United	31.5	27.6	25.6	22.5	36.0	30.7	29.8	32.9
Anglican	27.8	18.7	29.7	18.0	23.3	17.9	38.0	22.3
Presbyterian	4.1	3.2	4.6	3.8	3.9	2.8	3.6	3.1
Baptist, Lutheran, Methodist, Unitarian	5.4	7.4	4.8	7.8	6.1	6.9	4.5	7.6
Fundamentalist[b]	0.3	1.0	0.2	1.2	0.5	0.4	0.3	1.5
Other[c]	1.4	1.5	1.5	1.9	1.3	1.5	1.4	0.5
None[d]	5.1	1.9	4.2	1.7	6.1	1.5	4.1	3.2
Total	100.0	100.0	100.0	100.0	100.0	100.0	100.0	100.0

a. Roman Catholic, Ukrainian (Greek) Catholic.
b. Adventist, Christian Scientist, Jehovah's Witness, Mennonite, Mormon, Pentecostal, other Fundamentalist.
c. Greek Orthodox, Jewish, other.
d. Specified: agnostic, atheist, none.

presence reflects the Prairies geographic origins of air force officers in particular, while naval officers, who are more strongly Anglican, reflect their British Columbia and British Isles origins[32].

EDUCATIONAL AND CAREER ATTAINMENT

The military occupation's growing requirements for formal education as a result of important technological development has been well documented for the United States Forces. Kurt Lang says that the increasing trend toward better educational attainment from 1940 to 1960 shows enlisted men running a little ahead of the comparable male civilian group. Harold Wool reaffirms this finding by showing that in 1965, 81.6 per cent of U.S. enlisted men were high school graduates or higher (table 9).

The educational attainment of Canadian military personnel is both substantially lower than that of the United States and is improving less rapidly. We can see in table 9 that in 1966, 52 per cent of Canadian officers had some university training and 35.1 per cent were university graduates. Their American counterparts had a proportion of 85 per cent with some university training and more than half, 57 per cent, were graduates. Among American enlisted men, a noticeable change occurred between 1956 and 1965: the percentage of those with high school graduation or higher increased by 26.4 per cent from 55.2 per cent to 81.6 per cent[33]. This 1965 American proportion (table 9) is much higher than the 30.8 per cent high school graduates for men of the Canadian Forces in 1966.

There is more homogeneity of educational attainment among Canadian officers and men than in the United States because Canadian minimum standards of education for entering the military have been maintained without major changes over many years. The American draft, on the other hand, has brought in personnel at varying educational levels. Canadian educational attainment levels partly reflect substantially lower levels in the male labour force. In terms of university training, Canadian officers are only second to the professional and technical group of the male labour force. Men have much greater high school attainment than blue collar workers. It seems also that there is less inducement for Canadian military personnel than for their American homologues to continue their education while pursuing their military careers.

Median years of schooling for all personnel of the Canadian Forces is 10.5, which is very close to the 10.6 year level of the Federal Public

Table 9. Highest Educational Attainment by level, for the United States Officers, 1960, and Men, 1960, 1965; for the Canadian Military, Officers and Men, 1966; for the Canadian Male Labour Force, White Collars and Blue Collars, 1961 (cumulative percentages)

Occupational group	University graduate	Some university	High school graduate	Some high school or less	Total
U.S. military					
Officers	57.0	85.0	99.0	100.0	100.0
Men, 1960	2.0	14.0	66.0	92.0	100.0
Men, 1965	1.3	19.7	81.6	96.2	100.0
Canadian military					
Officers	35.1	52.0	88.3	100.0	100.0
Men	0.2	3.1	30.8	99.6	100.0
Canadian male labour					
force	4.9	9.2	15.5	55.6	100.0
White collar	14.8	24.5	37.1	81.9	100.0
Professional and technical	44.1	60.0	71.8	95.2	100.0
Blue collar	0.4	2.1	6.0	44.8	100.0

Source: Data on U.S. military, 1960, from Kurt LANG, 'Technology and Career Management in the Military Establishment', in Morris JANOWITZ, ed., *The New Military* (New York: Russell Sage Foundation) 1964, Table 7, p. 55. Data on U.S. enlisted men, 1965, from Harold WOOL, *The Military Specialist, Skilled Manpower for the Armed Forces* (Baltimore: The Johns Hopkins Press, 1968), p. 103. Data on Canadian male labour force from Sylvia OSTRY, *The Occupational Composition of the Canadian Labour Force* (Ottawa, D.B.S., 1967) p. 86c.

Service[34]. The Canadian male labour force is lower with 9.1 years, and white collars are higher with 11.4 years.

An analysis of groups of officers and men dichotomized into strata of senior and junior ranks gives some insight into basic elements of the career profile of each service. Table 10 shows that senior personnel of strata C and A have higher schooling than personnel in strata B and D[35], indicating that higher schooling requirements are being enforced for gaining access to higher ranks. It also means that those who do not have the required schooling must be encouraged and helped to further their studies while pursuing their military careers or they must temper their rank attainment aspirations.

Some important differences in career conditions exist among the

188

Table 10. Median Years of Schooling. Median Years of Age, Median Years of Seniority, for Officers and Men and all Personnel, by Stratum[a] and by Service, 1966

Group	Army			Air force			Navy		
	Schooling	Age	Seniority	Schooling	Age	Seniority	Schooling	Age	Seniority
Officers	13.6	38.1	14.6	12.9	37.0	15.0	13.6	36.8	14.4
Stratum A	14.5	47.3	25.1	13.7	45.7	23.6	13.9	44.1	22.3
Stratum B	13.4	36.3	13.6	12.9	36.2	14.1	13.5	35.2	13.0
Men	9.6	30.5	10.1	10.5	31.2	11.6	10.4	27.5	8.9
Stratum C	9.8	40.8	18.2	10.6	42.8	19.5	10.2	36.0	15.5
Stratum D	9.6	26.2	7.7	10.5	29.0	9.6	10.4	23.6	4.7
All personnel	9.9	31.3	10.6	10.9	32.1	12.0	10.6	28.6	9.6

a. Stratum A includes the ranks of Lieutenant-Colonel, Colonel and all Generals; stratum B includes the ranks of Second Lieutenant, Lieutenant, Captain and Major; stratum C includes the ranks of Sergeant, Warrant Officer, Master Warrant Officer and Chief Warrant Officer; stratum D includes the ranks of Private, Private 1, and Corporal. The nomenclature used is that established in the Canadian Forces Reorganization Act of May 1967, except that we have distinguished between Private and Private 1 (or Lance-Corporal, Leading Aircraftsman, Able Seaman) while the Act does not do so.

services with certain trends running contrary to expectations. We can easily see why air force and naval men have higher levels of schooling than army men. The superior level of schooling of the air force is a reflection of its higher technology and hence of its greater occupational requirements, but a similar superior level of schooling is not reflected in the air force officer ranks. The U.S. Air Force had an important educational deficit as a result of its high war-time personnel intake. While this condition has since been corrected, Lang says on this point:

But officers who failed to acquire additional education and, partly for that reason, were passed over for promotion are being forced out and retired in large numbers as they reach the twenty-year point[36].

It is not clear why more junior air force officers (stratum B, table 10) in Canada are still substantially less educated than navy and army officers of the same stratum. Yet we should note that the greatest difference in schooling between officers and men exists in the army. Army men may be less educated by virtue of their occupation, but it is not clear why senior army officers (stratum A) are the most highly educated Canadian military personnel.

Median age and seniority for each stratum and service (table 10) also show quite divergent trends between services. We can see, for instance, that air force non-commissioned officers (stratum C) have a median age of 42.8 years and hold 19.5 years of service, while the comparable naval stratum has a median age of 36 years and holds 15.5 years of seniority. Such differences have been made apparent in the recent unification of the Forces, but it will undoubtedly take some years to equalize career conditions for all military personnel.

The air force shows the greatest continuity between officers and the men's structure. Table 11 shows that 42.2 per cent of senior officers have been commissioned from the ranks, and that the proportion in junior ranks is maintained at 27.7 per cent. The air force has a small but increasing proportion of Military College graduates. The army has the largest proportion of Military College graduates who, contrary to their distribution in the other services, are most numerous among senior officers. In fact, 23.1 per cent of all Anglophone Colonels and Generals in the army are Military College graduates, while graduates account for only 12.1 per cent among Anglophone army Lieutenant-Colonels. This tendency to favour Military College graduates in higher ranks, however, is less pronounced than in the United States[37].

Career differences for men become apparent when one considers the trade group structure. While men are usually specialists in a given trade or grouping, their proficiency is recognized by a given level of trade

190

Table 11. Type of Commission of Officers, by Service and by Stratum[a] *(percentages), 1966*

Type of Commission	Army		Air force		Navy	
	Stratum A	Stratum B	Stratum A	Stratum B	Stratum A	Stratum B
Military College	14.3	10.0	2.6	4.8	8.7	11.5
ROTP and University	18.1	25.2	18.8	20.3	17.4	14.7
OCTP, Venture	7.0	26.7	4.0	27.0	5.7	24.7
Commissioned from the ranks	20.1	24.8	42.2	27.7	17.4	29.5
Reserve Commission	24.2	6.6	13.2	2.4	18.2	7.7
Other	16.3	6.7	19.2	17.8	32.6	11.9
Total	100.0	100.0	100.0	100.0	100.0	100.0

a. Stratum A includes the ranks of Lieutenant-Colonel, Colonel and all Generals; stratum B includes the ranks of Second Lieutenant, Lieutenant, Captain and Major; stratum C includes the ranks of Sergeant, Warrant Officer, Master Warrant Officer and Chief Warrant Officer; stratum D includes the ranks of Private, Private 1 and Corporal. The nomenclature used is that established in the Canadian Forces Reorganization Act of May 1967, except that we have distinguished between Private and Private I (or Lance-Corporal, Leading Aircraftsman, and Able Seaman) while the Act does not do so.

group (T.G.). Pay increases with higher T.G. level and rank. Table 12 shows that each service has used its trade group structure in a different way.

The navy has a T.G. structure that is bi-polarized. Its low end reflects the youth of many men and the difficulties of retaining personnel. Its high end reflects the presence of a large body of Warrant and Master Warrant Officers in contrast to the other services (table 1). The army trade group structure follows its rank structure, indicating that this service has used its T.G. structure to reinforce its rank structure rather than minimizing it as the air force has done.

By comparing table 12 with table 1 showing the relative rank structure of the three services, we can see that the air force has the highest average T.G., while its men's rank structure forms a flat pyramid with few people in higher ranks. The air force has thus given more emphasis to the trade group structure than the rank structure in professional advancement and

Table 12. Trade Group Structure of Men, by Level and by Service (percentages), 1966

Trade group level	Army		Air force		Navy	
Standard	4.0		4.7		7.2	
1	8.1		9.5		14.8	
2	39.2		9.8		38.8	
Low		51.3		24.0		60.8
3	16.0		14.7		5.6	
3X	12.4		9.8		2.3	
3Y	11.1		8.9		2.2	
Medium		39.5		33.4		10.1
3Z	3.1		27.8		9.6	
4	3.4		6.7		5.3	
4A	2.7		8.1		14.2	
High		9.2		42.6		29.1
Total	100.0	100.0	100.0	100.0	100.0	100.0

recognition of competence and monetary rewards. The air force has a profile of development that resembles the American Air Force, with one major difference. While the Canadian and American air force officers have a fairly similar rank structure, presenting a diamond-shaped profile[38], their rank structures differ substantially for the non-commission officers and men. The bulging of the middle levels in the enlisted men ranks of the American air force is not to be found in the Canadian counterpart which has a traditional pyramidal profile. The phenomenon of the proliferation of skills[39], however, has been the same and it is recognizable in the trade group structure seen in table 12.

THE CHANGING MILITARY CAREER

Apart from the sore conscription periods of the two world wars, the voluntary nature of the Canadian military service has contributed to shading each of the three services with its own distinct regional, socio-economic and cultural patterns. Up to the mid 1960's, each of the services had competed for the acquisition and retention of the personnel best qualified for its own needs and traditions. Basic socio-cultural differences within the unified Canadian Forces of the late 1960's, then, are not so much manifestations of the country's cultural and linguistic diversity as the result of bringing together three separate organizations with manpower self-recruited over the years in the absence of clear Government policies and guidelines.

Rank and trade structures have been the major organizational means used by the military both to create and to maintain effective hierarchies. Yet rank and trade structures by their very nature create new or intensify already existent social and cultural differences. The dynamics of change and adaptation that are necessarily following the amalgamation of the three service organizations can be creative if oriented by managerial decisions made with full knowledge of the composition and function of all military personnel. Until career conditions are equalized for all personnel, however, and social recruitment is fully adjusted to the Canadian social and cultural reality, a truly unified and equalitarian defence force cannot be a fait accompli.

Trends that could emerge as military personnel is reduced to the 1972–1973 objective of 82 000 men and women in uniform[40], are difficult to predict. One might first ask whether new recruits, fewer in number, will be selected according to policies aimed at reducing certain basic disparities in education, geographic origin, official languages, group participation (Francophones and Anglophones), and the like.

The separate evolution of the three services has created different career lines that are being gradually unified under the Canadian Armed Forces. The aggregate military role is gradually being re-oriented toward a more 'canadianised' mode. This emerging constabulary force can become more socially productive while fulfilling its basic role of combat readiness, although even a reduced combat role and increased readiness in support of social needs can have negative aspects if acquired potential reflects and serves the interests of status quo in a country that needs major social-political change. The relevant question to pose then is how to evaluate the probable contribution of a reduced repatriated and unified professional army. Can it be used in support of social change?

1. James EAYRS, *The Art of the Possible*, Toronto: University of Toronto Press, 1961, conscription crisis of 1917, p. 72, conscription crisis of 1944, pp. 90–95.
2. 14–15–16 Elizabeth II., Chap. 96. An Act to amend the National Defence Act and other Acts in consequence thereof, Assented to 8th May, 1967, and coming into force the 1st of February, 1968.
3. This was possible by the passage of a short act, 13 Elizabeth II., Chap. 21, An Act to amend the National Defence Act, Assented to 16th July, 1964.
4. M. C. URGUHART and K. A. H. BUCKLEY, eds., *Historical Statistics of Canada* (Toronto: The Macmillan Company of Canada, 1965) p. 61. Cf., *Report of the Royal Commission on Government Organization*, Book 4 (Ottawa 1963) p. 90.
5. *Report of the Royal Commission on Government Organization, Ibid.*, p. 91.
6. *Ibid.*, p. 90.
7. *Report of the Royal Commission on Government Organization*, Book 4 (French version) p. 94.
8. Press communiqué, Department of National Defence, September 19, 1969.
9. Data on the Canadian Forces presented here come from the Coulombe survey based on a stratified random sample of about 10 per cent of male military personnel conducted in June 1966 for the Royal Commission on Bilingualism and Biculturalism. Much of the survey data is presented and analyzed in *Carrière Militaire et Dynamique Culturelle*, a book prepared by Pierre E. COULOMBE with the collaboration of Lise COURCELLES. Its publication by Information Canada is scheduled for Summer 1971.
10. Morris JANOWITZ, in collaboration with Lt. Col. Roger LITTLE, *Sociology and the Military Establishment* (New York: Russell Sage Foundation, 1965) p. 35.
11. The three services of the armed forces ceased to exist with the coming into force on February 1, 1968, of the Canadian Forces Reorganization Act enacted in May 1967. The traditional roles of the services have continued to be exercised within the sea, land and air environments, mostly by the three corresponding elements within the unified Canadian Forces. Changes are being implemented in a gradual manner. Our survey should be followed up in order to determine the impact reorganization has had and is having on the careers of military personnel.
12. John PORTER, *The Vertical Mosaic* (Toronto: University of Toronto Press, 1965) p. 57.
13. The expression 'ethnic group' is subject to wide interpretation. The Report of the Royal Commission on Bilingualism and Biculturalism has offered some much-needed clarification. See its: *Report of the Royal Commission on Bilingualism and Biculturalism*, General Introduction (Ottawa, 1967) § 4–15, pp. 6–8; and Book IV, The Cultural Contribution of the Other Ethnic Groups (Ottawa, 1969), § 13–19.
14. *Report of the Royal Commission on Bilingualism and Biculturalism*, Book IV (Ottawa, 1969) Table A–29, p. 273.
15. In fact, as we see in table 5 below, 11.3 per cent of naval officers report that they lived in the British Isles during their youth until the age of 15. We can also see in table 5 that only 9 per cent of naval officers lived in Québec until the age of 15. There is clear polarization within this group of naval officers.
16. For a thorough discussion of the 'other ethnic groups' see *Report of the Royal Commission on Bilingualism and Biculturalism*, Book IV, The Cultural Contribution of the Other Ethnic Groups (Ottawa, 1969).

17. We used the criteria 'language of childhood' in our survey after pre-testing and in preference to that of 'mother tongue'. It was felt that it better reflected the true linguistic influence during the socializing years of childhood. It does not refer to the retention of that language in adult life as does the clause 'that you still understand' in the 'mother tongue census question'. The language of childhood question leaves room for those who were raised in an atmosphere where English and French were spoken about equally. The question was phrased as follows: 'During your childhood, did you speak mainly English, mainly French, English and French about equally, or another language?'

18. *Report of the Royal Commission on Bilingualism and Biculturalism*, Book I (Ottawa, 1967) Table 2, p. 23.

19. *Report of the Royal Commission on Bilingualism and Biculturalism*, Book I (Ottawa 1967) Table 4, p. 26.

20. *Report of the Royal Commission on Bilingualism and Biculturalism*, Book III (Ottawa, 1969) Table A–32, p. 387.

21. *Ibid.*

22. In the study *Carrière Militaire et Dynamique Culturelle* (see note 9 above) we defined ethno-linguistic groups of Anglophones and Francophones. We used language of childhood as the main factor in the definition with ethnic origin and parents' mother tongue. For a brief overview of this point, see *Report of the Royal Commission on Bilingualism and Biculturalism*, Book III (Ottawa, 1969) pp. 304–307.

23. *Report of the Royal Commission on Bilingualism and Biculturalism*, Ibid., pp. 293–329.

24. For instance, since it was necessary for a recruit to have a 'working knowledge' of English in the air force, the navy, and the army outside the Royal 22nd Regiment, the language teaching facilities have been set at certain levels, and recruiting of unilingual Francophones from Québec was not to exceed set quotas for a given period.

25. It is worth noting that Francophones of all provinces comprise 28.1 per cent of the Canadian population, 21.1 per cent of the Federal Public Service and 16 per cent of the Canadian Forces. Québec is the province of residence of 83.2 per cent of the Canadian Francophone population. See *Report of the Royal Commission on Bilingualism and Biculturalism*, Book III (Ottawa, 1969); for the Canadian Population and the Public service, Tables A–31, A–32, p. 387; for the Canadian Forces, Table 54, p. 306.

26. Morris JANOWITZ, *The Professional Soldier* (Glencoe: The Free Press, 1960) pp. 86–87.

27. Urban community of origin is defined in our study as an agglomeration of 5 000 inhabitants or more where one has lived longest during his childhood until age of 15. Janowitz's data is based on place of birth, and the urban community starts at a lower limit of 2 500 inhabitants. Morris JANOWITZ, *The Professional Soldier*, p. 86.

28. The Atlantic and Prairie provinces are less urban (40.8 per cent and 49.2 per cent respectively) than Québec (66.1 per cent), Ontario (71.2 per cent) and British Columbia (65.2 per cent). Taken from Census of Canada, 1961, DBS 72–535, Tables 10 and 11, cited in Leroy O. STONE, *Urban Development in Canada* (Ottawa, Dominion Bureau of Statistics, 1967), p. 76.

29. Anglophones form 93.7 per cent of all senior officers of stratum A.

30. Leroy O. STONE, *Urban Development in Canada*, p. 76.

31. Respondents were asked to specify their present religious affiliation. It is likely that some military personnel through marriage and for socio-professional and other reasons have changed affiliation since their youth. This is more apt to have happened within the Protestant churches.

32. The population of British ethnic origin is affiliated with the United Church and the Anglican Church in the following proportions in the Western Provinces:

	United Church	Anglican Church
Manitoba	51.4	25.3
Saskatchewan	55.0	19.1
Alberta	45.3	20.9
British Columbia	38.0	32.3

See: *Report of the Royal Commission on Bilingualism and Biculturalism*, Book IV (Ottawa, 1969) Tables A–91, A–93, A–95, A–97, pp. 308–311.

33. Harold WOOL, *The Military Specialist, Skilled Manpower for the Armed Forces* (Baltimore, The Johns Hopkins Press, 1968), p. 103.

34. *Report of the Royal Commission on Bilingualism and Biculturalism*, Book III (Ottawa, 1969) Table 51, p. 216.

35. Navy men are an exception to this tendency, because of the very 'young' career of stratum D with 4.7 years of seniority which reflects higher levels of schooling of their more recent recruitment.

36. Kurt LANG, 'Technology and Career Management in the Military Establishment,' p. 56.

37. Janowitz is clear on this point: ' Thus while the armed forces display many characteristics of 'civilianisation,' organizational autonomy has been maintained by the device of selecting academy graduates to the highest ranks.' See Morris JANOWITZ, *Sociology of the Military Establishment* (New York: The Russell Sage Foundation, 1963), p. 70. Also, his *The Professional Soldier*, Table 6, p. 106.

38. Morris JANOWITZ, *Sociology of the Military Establishment, Ibid.*, p. 35.

39. *Ibid.*, p. 35. See also Kurt LANG, 'Technology and Career Management in the Military Establishment', p. 69 and 71.

40. Statement by the Minister of National Defence in Minutes of Proceedings and Evidence, Standing Committee on External Affairs and National Defence, No. 16, March 3, 1970, pp. 14–16, 16–27.

Problems of Recruitment and Selection in the Polish People's Armed Forces

J. GRACZYK

JÓZEF GRACZYK is holding the Chair of Sociology in the Military and Political F. Dzierżyński Academy, Warsaw, Poland. He contributed an article on Polish officers to *Military Profession and Military Regimes*, edited by Jacques van Doorn (1969).

In this communication we present some results of research on the recruitment and selection for the officer corps in the Polish People's Armed Forces. The investigation of the history of this problem has already produced certain results regarding the developmental trends within the officer corps.[1]

Quite regardless of the history of the inflow and outflow of the professional army cadre, the results of research on the course of the selection of candidates for officer schools and military academies are also very interesting. Particularly interesting are the results of the research of the forecasting value of entrance examinations.

Problems connected with the evaluation of entrance examinations as an instrument for diagnosing the actual state of knowledge and other predispositions of the candidates for certain directions of studies, and the simultaneous prognosis on this basis of their subsequent achievements during the studies have in recent years attracted the attention of several scientific centres in the Polish People's Armed Forces. Interesting research results have been obtained in this field by the Central Psychological Laboratory of the Polish Armed Forces and several chairs of social sciences of the Military Political F. Dzierżyński Academy.

The research results obtained permit the presentation of certain conclusions concerning entrance examinations as an instrument for the selection of candidates, as entrance examinations have for over a dozen years been of decisive importance for the selection of candidates for officer schools and military academies of the Polish People's Armed Forces. But before presenting certain results of research on the prognostic value of entrance examinations, we shall formulate some remarks of a historical character, which will help better to understand modern criteria of selection.

HISTORICAL CONDITIONING OF ENTRANCE EXAMINATION AS THE BASIC CRITERION OF SELECTION

While building a new officer corps in the Polish People's Armed forces we endeavoured to ensure the leading role of the working class in proportion to non-proletarian elements. The principle of the class selection for the officer corps resulted in that the recruiting commissions giving preference to candidates of working class and peasant origin. Especially during the period of the struggle for power and its consolidation, the criterion of social origin was of fundamental importance. The purpose was really to rebuild the officer corps, as owing to its origin and the political orientation it represented, the old officer corps of the inter-war period could not serve as a foundation for the people's government. Both these factors and the spirit of caste prevailing among these officers, fed and cultivated by the reactionary underground movement, made it imperative to renew the officer corps.[2]

The Polish People's Armed Forces had to be reborn by the removal of class barriers between officers and other ranks, by providing access to the officer corps for representatives of the people's masses and the transformation of armed forces into an instrument serving the interests of the working people. We are, therefore, of the opinion that the recruitment for officer schools of candidates of working class and peasant origin constitutes the basic principle of the formation of an army of a new type. It goes without saying that when the antagonistic class structure is liquidated, the socialist ideology popularized and a new type of intelligentsia is formed, the reservoir of manpower for officer schools will expand, but before these transformations take place, preferred treatment of candidates of working class and peasant origin is of fundamental importance from the point of view of the development of socialist revolution. And this was how the Polish Workers' Party, the creator and organizer of the Polish People's Armed Forces, saw this problem. 'To build a democratic Poland – said Władysław Gomułka in 1944 – means first of all to build a democratic army. The problem is as follows: there can be no democratic Poland without a democratic officer corps'.[3] The above formulation defined the postulate of the formation of the People's Armed Forces and the programme of its rebirth on the foundation of the masses of the people.

The rate of recruitment for officer schools of candidates of working class and peasant origin in the first few years after the recovery of independence may be seen in the proportion of cadet officers in four officer schools in the years 1946-1949.

No.	Name of the school	Proportion of cadets of working class origin			
		1946	1947	1948	1949
1.	Air force officer school	30	33	49	58
2.	Communications officer school	30	43	45	55
3.	Armoured forces officer school	43	50	50	51
4.	Infantry officer school	36	38	47	52

The above table shows that as the result of preferred treatment of candidates of working class origin their proportion was increasing in the first years after the war. This class reconstruction of the officers' corps at the same time democratised relations between the armed forces and the civilian population on the one hand, and between the officer cadre and soldiers doing military service. It is also significant that in the various years of the development of the Polish People's Armed Forces the proportion of officers of working class and peasant origin was not constant, but was always high.[4]

The criteria observed in the recruitment for officer schools in the fifties, particularly in the years 1950-1954, led to a numerical increase of the officer corps. Young people of working class and peasant origin were recruited for the armed forces first of all. Taking into account the fact that as a result of the tense international situation at that time there had taken place a numerical development of the armed forces and the officer corps we had to draw from all sources from which it was possible to recruit candidates for the officer corps, but particular preference was given to candidates of working class origin. Because of this candidates of working class origin constituted over 50% and of peasant origin about 40% of cadet officers in all officer schools, while the remaining 10% were recruited from among progressive intelligentsia.

Trying to satisfy to a maximum the numerical needs, we lowered the requirement with regard to the educational standard of candidates for officer schools. Both to officer schools and to short-term courses we admitted candidates with primary or incomplete secondary education.[5] The admission of candidates with low education to all officer schools created a situation which called for a radical improvement of the existing state of affairs. Therefore, as early as the 1954-1955 school year, the Ministry of National Defence laid a strong emphasis on education. Because of the low educational standard of the officer cadre we organized several dozens of general education schools in which officers acquired additional education. Moreover, we gradually increased the requirements with regard to candidates joining officer schools and gradually extended the training cycle. Finally, a relaxation of tension in the international situation in mid-fifties, as well as the increase of the defence potential of the states of the socialist camp, including also People's Poland, made it possible to adopt some essential measures in the domain of military solutions. These factors caused a reduction of the numerical strength of the army. In the course of three successive reductions (in 1955, 1956, 1957) the recruitment for officer schools was considerably limited, and a large number of officers were transferred to the reserve.[6]

The transformations which took place at that time were aimed at a qualitative strengthening of the officer cadre. Both the selection within the officer corps and stricter criteria in the recruitment for officer schools were aimed at increasing the suitability of officers for military service. The problem was finally solved in 1957, when parliament passed a new law on the military service of officers of Armed Forces of the Polish People's Republic, which legalized and at the same time set out in detail the basic rights and duties of officers. This was the beginning of a new stage in the development of the officer corps. In accordance with the new law, candidates applying for admission to an officer school were required to possess secondary education. Serving officers who did not possess this education were bound by the new law to obtain it. This marked the beginning of a period of intensive additional education for officers. In a short time all officers had filled the gaps in their education.

The increased requirements with regard to the educational standard of the professional officer corps became indispensable because, as the result of the intensive development of the educational system in People's Poland, the Armed Forces were being joined by ever increasing numbers of educated young men. The acquisition of proper education was a must for officers for the execution of their duties. Moreover, the systematically progressing organizational and technical development of the armed forces requires not only an educated cadre, but also its differentiation as regards its professional training. These needs were responsible for the fact that officer schools in the Polish People's Armed Forces were transformed into higher officer schools. To meet the systematically increasing organizational needs of the armed forces we created a separate corps of ensigns as a new part of the hierarchic structure of the Armed Forces (as an intermediate link between the officer corps and the corps of NCO's).[7]

The above remarks of a historical nature permit us to say that in the course of the development of the Polish People's Armed Forces all processes of recruitment or selection of the professional cadre must be examined against the background of much wider conditions and developmental needs of the armed forces, as well as against the background of the transformations which have taken place in the class structure of the population of People's Poland.[8]

FROM RESEARCH INTO THE EFFECTIVENESS OF
THE SELECTION OF CANDIDATES FOR HIGHER STUDIES
IN OFFICER SCHOOLS AND MILITARY ACADEMIES

The results obtained during the examination of candidates applying for admission to higher officer schools and military academies indicate that, apart from the decisive significance of marks obtained during entrance examinations, the admission of a candidate also depended on such factors as: the number of candidates per vacancy, marks contained in the secondary school certificate, and social origin.

The number of candidates per vacancy is a factor affecting the course of the selection, because if the number of candidates is small and the number of vacant places large, the criteria for the classification of the candidates are considerably more lenient than if there are few vacant places and the number of candidates disproportionately larger. The above assertion may be partly illustrated by the number of applications and admissions to higher officer schools in 1957.

Taking into account all candidates who expressed at that time their intention to join a higher officer school, we find that both the proportion of applicants applying for admission to the various types of school and the proportion of admissions differed. We illustrate this by the example of four higher officer schools.

Type of school	No. of applications to the various schools (in proportion to the overall number of candidates)	No. of admissions (in proportion to the overall number of applications in the various schools)
— Higher Officer School of Mechanized Troops	18%	60%
— Higher Officer School of Communications	27%	30%
— Higher Officer School of Motorized Troops	17%	13%
— Higher Officer School of Engineering Troops	16%	30%

If we take into account the fact that the proportion of candidates applying to the four above-mentioned schools amounted to 78% of the overall number of candidates, and the proportion of candidates who applied to the four other schools (Higher Officer School of Armoured Troops,

Higher Officer School of Chemical Troops, Higher Officer School of Anti-Aircraft Defence Troops) amounted to 22%, we note that not all schools have identical conditions of selection. While in some schools the number of applications is much higher than the number of vacant places, the number of applications in other schools oscillates around the number of vacant places. The situation in military academies is similar. The proportions between the number of vacant places and the number of applications are not identical which creates differences in the possibility of the selection of candidates for the military educational system.

An analysis of the selection of candidates during entrance examinations at higher officer schools shows that candidates having good marks on their secondary school certificate had much better chances of passing the entrance examination than candidates with bad marks.

| Candidates | With marks in secondary school certificates | | | |
	very good	good	fair	total
a) pass	0.7%	62.3%	37.0%	100.0%
b) fail	0.3%	13.7%	86.0%	100.0%

If we compare the proportion of passing and failing candidates with the marks in their secondary school certificates, we see at once that the marks constituted a certain indicator of the usefulness of the candidate, but were not decisive. Of decisive importance were the marks obtained during the entrance examination.

Because of the decisive importance of the entrance examination for the qualification of candidates applying for admission to higher officer schools, the Central Psychological Laboratory of the Polish Armed Forces conducted an investigation whose purpose was to determine the value (entrance examination, secondary school certificate, results of psychological examination and social origin) for the progress of further studies. The analysis covered cadet officers for whom there were complete data with regard to the above-mentioned factors, that is the results of the entrance examination, marks in the secondary school certificate, the results of the psychological examination and the evaluation of the environment of the cadet, taking into account the results of the separate years of studies. The groups covered by the investigation numbered: group A – 71 persons, group B – 131 persons, group C – 155 persons. Apart from the determination of the prognostic value, the analysis was aimed at determining whether the entrance examination in its present form is not an instrument of counter-selection with regard to a certain group of candidates. The coefficient of correlation between the various factors and the external criterion in the form of results obtained during the various years of studies are shown in the table below.

Coefficient of correlation with external criterion

Groups	(A) N = 71		(B) N = 131			(C) N = 155
Variable factors	after 1 year	after 2 years	after 3 years	after 1 year	after 2 years	after 1 year
Entrance examination	0.433	0.348	0.203	0.456	0.423	0.407
School certificate	0.551	0.450	0.264	0.457	0.539	0.435
Mental standard	0.284	0.110	0.252	0.158	0.253	−0.096
Environmental questionnaire	−0.244	−0.267	−0.136	−0.313	−0.383	−0.199
Total (multiple correlation)	0.656	0.530	0.394	0.610	0.702	0.553

As may be seen from the table, the highest values are represented by marks from the secondary school certificate. Entrance examination shows a slightly lower but still quite high correlation. The results of psychological examination give the lowest correlation. In the case of environmental questionnaire we obtained negative coefficients, but, as is known, what is essential is the absolute value of the coefficient and the sign has no significance.[9]

It may be seen in the light of the indices obtained that many results obtained during studies differ from those obtained by candidates during the entrance examination. The results of the analysis indicate that the prognostic value of the secondary school certificate deserves slightly more attention during the selection of candidates for higher officer schools.

Similar conclusions are reached on the basis of a comparison of the results of entrance examination and the results obtained by students of the Military Political F. Dzierżyński Academy in the years 1965-1969.

In order to check the prognostic value of results obtained during the entrance examination, an examination was carried out on a group of students. A detailed comparison of the results of the entrance examination with the results obtained during studies permits the assumption that entrance examination is of essential prognostic value for further successes in studies, but does not presuppose the capabilities of the students.

It appears from a comparison of the results of entrance examination with the results obtained during the separate years of studies that the group of officers who passed their entrance examination with a good result shows a much higher degree of correlation than the group of officers who passed their entrance examination with just a fair result.

Officers who had passed their entrance examination with a good result completed the first year of studies in 87.4%, the second year in 77.4%, the third year in 64.5% and the fourth year in 67.7% of cases. This means that their group showed a relatively high degree of correlation between the results of the entrance examination and the results of the subsequent years of studies.

A much lower degree of correlation was found on the other hand in the group of fair results. Officers who had passed their entrance examination with just a fair result completed the first year of studies in 41.4%, the second year in 38.0%, the third year in 24.1% and the fourth year in 7.0% of cases.

It was established on the basis of a detailed analysis that the capabilities of this group of students were considerably greater than would appear from a diagnosis of their entrance examination results. Beginning with the very first year of studies, the majority of these students obtained good results, and during the fourth year almost exclusively good and very good results.

The above conclusions were confirmed by the results obtained during the examination for a master's degree. 33.4% of graduates completed their studies with a very good result, 57.8% with a good result and only 8.8% with a fair result. Thus, the finish proved much better than could be expected on the basis of the entrance examination results.

CONCLUSIONS

In summing up it may be stated that in the early period of the development of the officer corps of the Polish People's Armed Forces, the main criterion decisive for the admission of candidates to officer schools and military academies was their ideological commitment on the side of the people's power and the factor of social origin. What mattered was the preparation of an officer cadre bound by its origin and interests with the working class and the peasantry. This was an indispensable criterion, both in view of the situation inside the country and in view of the international situation.

206

When the people's power became fully stabilized inside the country in the mid-fifties, when fundamental transformations took place in the class structure of the Polish population, objective conditions were created for the adoption of a law concerning the education of the officer cadre. Changes were also introduced in the criteria for the admission to officer schools and military academies.

The fundamental condition permitting application for admission to officer schools and military academies became the possession of a secondary school certificate and the results of entrance examinations. Worth noting is the fact that although officer schools did not receive the status of higher professional schools until 1967, as early as in 1958 officer candidates were required to possess a secondary school certificate, just like candidates for all other higher schools in Poland.

Beginning with 1958 the store of possessed knowledge defined by the marks contained in the secondary school certificate and the results of entrance examinations became the basic factor decisive for admission to officer schools and military academies. This means that the higher military schools introduced the same criteria for the selection of candidates as the civilian higher schools.

The Central Psychological Laboratory of the Polish Armed Forces and the chair of social sciences of the Military Political F. Dzierżyński Academy carried out studies on the prognostic value of entrance examinations, marks in secondary school certificates and the effect of the environmental factor. It appears from these studies that entrance examinations are not always the best method for selecting candidates for higher studies. For among candidates admitted with fair marks, the same officers receive good or very good marks during the senior years of studies. The research results have shown that no classification criterion (entrance examination, secondary school certificate, mental standard examined by psychological tests) taken separately constitutes a satisfactory criterion. It appears that it is necessary to combine numerous criteria into a single whole in order to make a better prognosis as to success in studies.

As may be seen, therefore, from the above arguments, higher military schools in People's Poland must at present solve practically the same problems as civilian higher schools, when it comes to the recruitment and selection of candidates. We have begun in this connection longitudinal five-year investigation in the people's armed forces which is to give answer to the question of what personality factors are of decisive importance for success in studies and the professional work of an officer.

1. Cf. Józef GRACZYK, Social Promotion in the Polish People's Army in: *Military Profession and Military Regimes* (edited by Jacques VAN DOORN), Paris 1969, p. 88.
2. Cf. Janusz ZARNOWSKI, *Struktura społeczna inteligencji w Polsce w latach 1918–1939* (*Social structure of intelligentsia in Poland in the years 1918–1939*), PWN, Warsaw 1964, p. 267.
3. A report of Władysław GOMUŁKA, Zadania partii w zakresie organizacji siły zbrojnej odrodzonej Polski (The Party's tasks in the field of the organization of the armed forces of the reborn Poland). *Z Pola Walki*, No. 2/59.
4. Cf. Józef GRACZYK, *op. cit.*, p. 88.
5. For a better understanding of the sense of the existence of the short-term courses we wish to emphasize that in the years 1950–1954 they played an essential role in the training of officers. If we take for this period all officers as 100% then:
   — 10.3% came after the completion of 2–3 year officer schools,
   — 40.6% came after short-term courses (not exceeding one year),
   — 29.3% were called up from reserve,
   — 19.8% were commissioned straight from the ranks of NCO's.
6. The following numbers of officers were transferred to the reserve during the successive reductions: in 1955 – 11.5%, in 1956 – 6.6%, in 1957 – 20.2%.
7. Up to 1957 the rank of ensign was the first officer's rank in the Polish People's Armed Forces. After the formation of a separate corps of ensigns five new ranks were introduced for this corps (junior ensign, ensign, senior ensign, staff ensign and senior staff ensign).
8. A full set of factors affecting the processes of recruitment and selection are presented by Professor J. SZCZEPAŃSKI in: *Sociologiczne zagadnienia wyższego wykształcenia (Sociological Problems of higher education)*. PWN, Warsaw 1963, pp. 40–52.
9. Kazimierz MIGDAŁ, Zastosowanie równań regresji de przewidywania powodzenia w nauce (Application of regression equations for prognoses of success in studies) in: *Problemy psychodydaktyczne w wojsku (Psycho-didactic problems in the army)*, volume II, Warsaw 1970, pp. 152–161.

Sociology of the Profession of Medical Officer

L. INDISOW

LONGIN INDISOW is Assistant Professor at the Military Medical Academy, Poland and Head of the Chair of Social Science.

The model of the profession of army officer has undergone considerable changes and is now very different from its nineteenth century prototype, which is due to the changes in organization and character of the army. In the last century when mass armies were formed, the fundamental function of the officer was to command groups of men and to teach them various military skills. Nowadays, one can distinguish another, very important function of the officer – having control over complicated techniques. This new function developed out of the technical and scientific metamorphosis of the army, which can be traced back to World War II. The ability to control modern weapons with computers demands highly specialised knowledge. Thus, the task of the army-officer has undergone considerable professionalization, which is characteristic of our epoch in general and of the army in particular. The processes of professionalization are unavoidable and their social sense is based upon the identification of the given group with the given profession, and the drawing together, the integration of the group of professional army-officers. This is especially characteristic of those professional groups whose professional skills are exceptionally useful to society.

'Profession' is an important sociological category, because it assigns the individual practising the given profession to a certain place in society, place of work, local community, social life. One can distinguish here such objective categories as: financial situation, geography of social contacts, possibility of movement, rights and obligations; as well as some subjective ones: such as the ascribed place in the hierarchy of social respect.

We shall deal here with the professional category of army-doctors. Medical functions have a very long tradition in the army. Elementary forms of medical aid were known in the Egyptian and Babylonian armies; the function of doctors was performed by priests.

The same was true of Greece and Rome. Emperor Augustus introduced medical functions into the cohort (medicus cohortis)[1]. The first written sources concerning medical functions in the units of Polish princes date from the XIIth century[2]. Written documents indicate that surgeons were the first doctors in military groups[3]. In general, the function of an army doctor was considered to be important, but secondary.

Various attempts to change the status of doctors who were considered to be clerks and not officers proved futile. In the period when the profession of army-officer came into being (from the end of the XVIIIth century up to the beginning of the XIXth century) doctors in the medical service in the majority of European armies were allowed to wear officer's uniforms and particular medical positions were ascribed particular officer grades (assimilation aux grades de la hiérarchie militaire)[4]. Doctors in the American and Belgian armies were amongst the first to acquire the right to wear officer's distinctions[5]. In European armies officer grades were granted to doctors at the outbreak of World War I (English and Italian armies) and during the war (Polish units). In the French army the question of whether doctors should have the rights of officers and as to whether doctors should be recognized as combatants was discussed, even after World War I.[6]

Under the new conditions created by the modernization and mechanisation of the army, a further delay in recognizing army doctors as officers and not as clerks working for the army was bound to result in the distortion of the hierarchical structure of the army. According to XIXth century military principle, an individual who did not fight with arms could not be called an officer; therefore, neither doctors nor engineers nor economists could be granted officer grades. This situation could have resulted in the changing of the character of the army into a civilian institution.

Granting officer grades to doctors did not always go together with the social acceptance of doctors within the group of professional officers. In the Polish Army (period between 1918–1939) doctors with officer grades as well as other services considered to be 'civil', were treated with reserve, especially by the cavalry officers, who considered themselves to be an elite. This was a natural consequence of feudal traditions in social life. Other units were of middle-class character and the criteria of classification within these units were rational.[7]

We shall now deal with the position, that is the social and professional roles of medical officers in the Polish People's Army. One of the factors determining this position is the hierarchical structure of the army: a set of interdependent posts which guarantee proper functioning of the institution. In the medical service section one can distinguish the following posts: commanding officer of the unit or medical establishment, ward head of the medical section, and army doctor attached to a unit. Other factors determining the position of an army doctor are the place he occupies in the hierarchy and the possibility of mobility. Vertical mobility is closely connected with the dynamics of promotion. The character of the institution and the kind of work one performs within this institution are also important factors; posts held in military units, for example, form a different type of career than those in hospitals and research institutes.

In every social system there exist formal and informal factors, but in the latter case it is more difficult to establish criteria of classification.

The informal factors defining the social and professional position of army doctors are very often more important than the institutional ones. This situation is connected with the ambivalence of the medical profession which has considerable social prestige. In most cases, the officer of the medical service acts as a medical adviser – and not as a representative of authority, which results in the affirmation of his position in society.

The social and professional position imposes a definite form of behaviour upon the subject. Therefore, doctors with officer grades are expected to be equally efficient both in their medical and military performance. They are expected to represent definite attitudes, qualities and knowledge; as well as displaying full identification with the posts they hold. Army doctors should be an integrated, professional group with a fully developed institutional (that is of the army) sense of subordination. One expects, however, that the particular tasks of army doctors within the army should not be entirely limited to this institution, but should be extended over non-institutional circles. The social and professional content of the role of army doctors is determined by the class character of the army, the nature of the professional tasks, and the social content of the work itself.

In the Polish People's Army the idea of the class character of the army (underlying the structure of the 'old' army) was given up. The very fact that the socialist army took part in the foundation of the new state determined the 'people's' character of the officers' staff.

Table 1. Social background of officer doctors according to the type of school they graduated from (1966)

Social Background	Type of School	
	CST, MMF, MMA	*UMD, MA*
Workers	41.2	27.9
Farmers	35.0	14.8
Intelligentsia	21.7	53.5
Craftsmen	1.5	3.5
Other	0.6	0.3
	100.0	100.0

In the later period the percentage of officers with worker's and farmer's backgrounds increased, which was due to the policy of recruiting candi-

213

dates to military schools, and the avoidance of the formal barriers in the grades of promoting officers. It was difficult, however, to apply the same criteria of promotion to the professional group of army doctors. Nevertheless, in the past two decades it has been possible to achieve the desired composition in the group of officers graduating from military schools (table 1). The percentage of graduates with worker's and farmer's backgrounds is 76.2% in military schools, and 42.7% in civil schools.

One can distinguish several stages in the formation of the present officers' staff, taking into consideration the methods of recruitment. It is difficult, however, to separate a particular stage on the basis of the exclusion of the method used, because very often in one stage there were several methods of recruitment. In the period 1943–1945 both army doctors and civilian doctors were mobilized. On 1–5–1945 there were 894 officers in the military medical service (doctors, dentists, pharmaceutists, and hospital attendants)[8], and on 1–5–1943 there were 2522[9].

In the years 1946–1955 civilian doctors were called up and after a period of military training were sent to join the army for an indefinite time. Simultaneously, a group of recruited candidates was schooled in the student company (later on in the battalion) of the University Medical Departments, and since 1949 in the Medical Academy in Łódź. A year later decisions were made and the Military Medical Faculty was founded as a part of the Military Center for Sanitary Training.

In the period 1954–1958 the majority of medical posts in the army were occupied by graduates from military schools and the remaining posts were taken by civilian doctors who had undergone military training at the Medical Academy. These doctors were called up for a period of two years. Since 1958 the medical staff of the army has been schooled at the Military Medical Academy.

At the beginning of 1956 the group of officer doctors consisted of: 33.4% post-war graduates from military schools and 66.6% civilian doctors who graduated from civil schools (including those doctors who graduated from CST – up to the year 1939). Nowadays, the graduates from MMA are in the majority.

The group of professional army doctors is heterogeneous, which is the result of different 'histories of medical education' and, therefore, it is difficult to set forth uniform criteria for the identification of this group with the profession they perform. The very definition of the profession of army doctors with officer grades creates some difficulties, for it should cover two aspects of this profession: military and civilian skills. In our opinion, the claim that 'doctor' should stand for the profession, and 'officer' for the function is false on methodological grounds because it leads towards the negation of professional qualifications (military and medical) of army doctors. This view also negates the exclusiveness of the whole group of professional officers and treats the army as being merely a particular place for the performance of medical services. This conception is incompatible with the very strong tendency within the army towards the integration of the group of professional officers. On the basis of the existing projecting definitions, one can define the profession of the officer-doctor as follows: the essence of the profession is a specific complex of highly specialized medical, medical and military, and general military skills which, due to their integral characters, designate the army as the exclusive place for the professional activity of officer doctors.

To check the degree of identification with the profession it is necessary to take into consideration the subjective factor of motivation. One has to bear in mind, however, that some of the officers decided to choose the medical profession in the army because of their liking for the army, others decided to join the army as doctors by chance, still others remained in the army after the war. A separate group consists of those who were called up to the army for a period of two years and then decided to remain in the army as members of the professional group of officer doctors.

Table 2. Reasons for choosing the profession of the officer doctor

Reasons	Type of school			
	MMA	*MMF*	*UMD*	*MA*
Liking for the army	34.5	33.3	6.0	8.3
Desire to be a doctor	56.3	48.5	10.0	17.6
Financial reasons	3.4	5.1	3.0	6.2
Suggestion of the family	0.8	2.0	—	4.1
Official appointment	—	—	50.0	31.6
By chance	2.5	11.1	20.0	20.8
Other	2.5	—	7.0	5.2
No answer	—	—	4.0	6.2
	100.0	100.0	100.0	100.0

The evaluation of the motivation is very important. The retrospective motivation is, however, determined by the actual success: any professional success increases motivation and any professional failure (even if these are only subjective impressions) results in disappointment.

The motivation towards the medical profession was found to be different among the officers who graduated from military schools and those who graduated from civil schools (table 2). One third of the officers who graduated from military medical schools (33.3%–34.5%) were well motivated and the primary reason for choosing the medical profession in the army was liking for the army. Half of the officers (48.5%–56.3%) wanted to be doctors. Among the officers who had completed their studies before they joined the army the motivation was low and only 6.0%–8.3% chose this new professional role because of liking for the army.

Table 3. The evaluation of the motivation and the motivation for choosing the given profession

Reasons for choosing the profession of the officer doctor	The decision of choosing the profession is considered to be:					
	right	on the whole right	on the whole wrong	defini- tely wrong	do not know	
Liking for the army	71.8	21.2	3.0	3.0	1.0	100.0
Desire to be a doctor	63.2	25.8	4.3	5.5	1.2	100.0
Financial reasons	56.0	32.0	12.0	—	—	100.0
Suggestion of the family	18.2	27.3	45.5	9.0	—	100.0
Official appointment	20.2	25.4	8.8	8.8	36.8	100.0
By chance	33.8	48.6	5.4	8.1	4.1	100.0
Other	42.8	47.6	—	4.8	4.8	100.0
Total	48.0	28.9	6.1	5.9	7.8	*

* These figures do not add up to 100, because 3.3 per cent 'no answer' has been omitted.

The majority of army doctors decided to remain in the army as professional officers (52.4%–70.0%) because of such factors as: professional and family stabilization, possibility of military and scientific promotion, and better retired pay than in the civil medical service.

Table 3 shows that the majority of army doctors (76.9%) entirely accept the decision to serve in the army. Only 5.9% of the army doctors do not consider this decision to be right. 71.8% of army doctors decided to choose the profession of army doctor because of their liking for the army. The second group (63.2%) consists of people who, in the first place, desired to be doctors. The remaining motivations are not so important because of their low correlation with the future attitudes towards the professional group of army officers. We mean here such motivations as inspiration by other people, e.g. family, friends.

Attitudes towards work performed are an important determinant for the identification of individuals with a profession. In our considerations, we have distinguished two aspects of this determinant. Firstly, how the officer doctors evaluate their professional qualifications in the actual performance at the posts they hold, and secondly, to what degree they are satisfied with their professional work. The officer, in his need to maintain a particular position in society, tries to achieve a post which satisfies his ambitions and which creates respect in the environment.

A graduate from a military medical school has a limited possibility of choosing a place of work, that is institution or military unit. Even if this possibility is existent to a limited degree, still most of the graduates follow the advice of their friends and relatives.

The passage from the school to the military unit is a vital moment in the life of a young officer (professional independence). The majority of doctors (81.6%) are of the opinion that their professional qualifications have been used properly (on the whole properly), though they admit that the officer grade and the junior position after graduation are also important. There exists a proportional dependency between the junior position after graduation period and the officer grade, and the number of positive opinions.

The conviction that one's professional qualifications have to be used properly depends upon the character of the work which is connected with the specific type of career; e.g. as an organizer in the health service, a research worker, or clinician. The latter is desired most. That is why the majority of graduates want to work in hospitals and convalescent homes. The career of the organizer is less attractive, in the opinion of graduates. The same is true for other armies[10]. This situation is connected with the lack of traditional characteristics of the health service in the military units; in the place of a hospital or a medical establishment there is a community of, on the whole, healthy people. Thus, the limited possibility of action and the conviction of not 'keeping pace' with colleagues working in hospitals make the career of the organizer of health service in the army less attractive, especially in the case of young people. Later, however, professional successes and life stabilization stimulate positive opinions.

Generally speaking, the attitude towards the work and the satisfaction derived from that work depend on such factors as: past and present experience, the attitude towards the work and understanding the essence of this work, respect created by the very act of performing the given profession, and general human relations. The attitude towards the work and satisfaction are subjective categories, although they are different with individuals in the same situations. The total sum of subjective attitudes is a concrete social fact, and is, therefore, an objective category which must be taken into consideration.

The profession is connected with the characteristic type of behaviour displayed by those who perform this profession. In view of this, the medical profession is generally accepted as useful, though the medical profession of an officer doctor needs additional, necessary qualifications, which must be supplemented in the case of those doctors who graduated from civil medical schools and were then called up to the army. In the relation of military institution to civil institution, one has to do with the commonly accepted usefulness of the medical profession working only in one direction: the army → public health service. This is also true of many other professional specializations which are commonly accepted as useful, so this does not impair the claim that the military medical profession is exclusive, though the bounds of this profession may be

Figure I. Identification (full and partial) according to the year since graduation from school

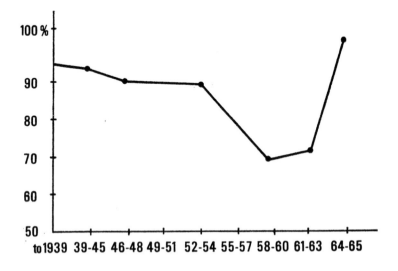

labile in the consciousness of people, which, needless to say, influences identification with the profession. To define the degree of identification we assumed the existence of three possibilities; full identification, partial identification and lack of identification. Those who considered their choice of the profession as 'right' and still wish to work in the army were defined as having possessed full identification with the profession of officer doctor. Those who considered their choice of the profession as 'on the whole right' and those who were called up to the army (or mobilized) – in both cases not having chosen the profession but having accepted a new social and professional role – were defined as having possessed partial identification. Lack of identification was found with those officers who considered the choice of the profession wrong, and did not wish to work in the army.

Figure II. Identification (full and partial) with the profession according to military grade

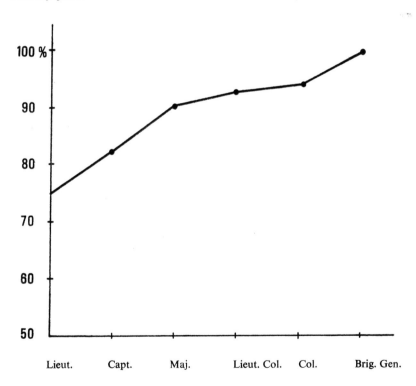

The problems of the identification of individuals with the profession must not be treated statically. The attitude of an individual towards the profession he performs is influenced by such major factors as: interest towards this profession, prestige of this profession, and long-termed success or failure, and by such minor ones as: temporary success or failure, salary, character of the work and personal relations with people. The major factors together with growing professional experience and a stabilized material and social position increase the identification with the profession of the officer doctor. This refers especially to those army doctors who, according to D. E. Supera[11], are in the stage of stabilization (from the 31st to the 44th year of life) and in the stage of preservation of status quo (from the 45th to the 64th year of life). The officers who graduated in the years 1949–1957 are now 33–44 years old. They are living through the period of stabilization during which they create their professional careers and try to secure their position in the military hierarchy.

All those who graduated before 1948 are in the stage of preservation of status quo. Most of them do not wish to change their professional position, which is very often the last stage of their careers before they retire. Other officers graduated in the years 1958–1963 and are now in the primary stage of stabilization. The high percentage, to some extent, of the lack of identification with the profession in this group may be interpreted as a discrepancy between the desired type of career and the real one.

The difference in attitudes towards the profession of officer doctor is the result of the process of mutual influence: that is, the interaction of the institution and the individual who is a part of this institution. This mutual influence is based upon the imposition of particular professional tasks, control and social pressure on the one hand – related to satisfaction derived from the fulfilment of the tasks, on the other. This mutual influence results in the creation of a particular attitude towards one's professional role.

Because of the functions it performs, the army is exceptionally interested in the integration of the group of professional military men, since this is connected with the proper functioning of the institution. It is also important that the officers' staff should be an integrated group of individuals who are prepared to perform the tasks assigned to them. The process of adaptation of officer doctors is slow, because of the wrong interpretation of the professional role they should perform. On the whole, not enough attention is paid to their functions as officers, and the tasks of doctors are sometimes overstressed. This situation does not help to reconcile the medical and military tasks with the individual desires and ambitions.

Difficulties connected with the adaptation of young officers to the new professional role are due to the divergence of this new role with the one which had been assumed.

Military medical schools try to prepare graduates for future work in the process of schooling. Very often, however, the students create their own stereotype image of the future role in the army on the basis of their individual experience. When this image is different from the concrete situation, then what results is a conflict situation.

A conflict situation may be created by the officer himself if his attitude towards the profession and the military service is wrong.

The existence of formal groups within the army, such as party and youth organizations helps to adapt the officers to perform social and professional functions in society. These organizations put much stress upon the patriotic (alongside with the universal) content of education resulting from the definite complex of national and social situation in People's Poland. They also draw attention to the emotional attachment to the army which was formed to defend the security of the motherland. The ideological education which cultivates the socialist content of patriotism and internationalism pays much attention to the political activity of every officer. Particular attention is paid to the moral and ideological attitude of the individual towards the nation and society.

ABBREVIATIONS

MMA   Military Medical Academy (since 1958).
MMF   Military Medical Faculty (1949–1958).
CST   Center for Sanitary Training (1922–1939).
UMD   University Medical Department (– 1950).
MA   Medical Academy (since 1950).

1. L. ZEMBRZUSKI, *Historia wojskowej służby zdrowia*, Warszawa 1927, pp. 3–8.
2. Fr. GIEDROYĆ, Pomoc lekarska w dawnem Wojsku Polskiem, *Przegląd Lekarski*, 1911.
3. Fr. GIEDROYĆ, *Służba zdrowia w dawnem Wojsku Polskiem*, Warszawa 1927 p. 8.
4. O. A. BAJRASZEWSKIJ, *Organizacija sanitarnoj służby w głownych jewropejskich armijach*, S. Petersburg 1910, pp. 26–30.
5. H. H. CUNNINGHAM, *Doctors in Gray*, The Confederate Medical Service, Louisiana State University Press 1960; L. ZEMBRZUSKI, *Historia wojskowej służby zdrowia*, Warszawa 1927, p. 22.
6. W. OSMOLSKI, Stanowisko służbowe lekarza w wojsku francuskim, *Lekarz Wojskowy*, 1921, nr 38, pp. 1215–1216.
7. A. HERTZ, Zagadnienie socjologii wojska i wojny, *Przegląd Socjologiczny*, 1946, vol. VIII, p. 133.
8. W. JURGIELEWICZ, Rozbudowa LWP w drugiej połowie 1944 r., *Wojskowy Przegląd Historyczny*, 1964, nr 3, pp. 49–54.
9. W. JURGIELEWICZ, Stan liczbowy LWP w przeddzień zakończenia II Wojny Światowej, *Wojskowy Przegląd Historyczny*, 1967, nr 2, p. 163.
10. Sbornik védeckych praci, Vojenského Lékařského výzkumného a dośkolovaciho v ustavu Jana Ev. Purkyne, Hradec Králove 1967, 22 = 1, p. 239.
11. J. BUDKIEWICZ, *Psychologiczna problematyka rozwoju zawodowego i stadiów życia zawodowego człowieka*, W: Socjologia zawodów, Warszawa 1965, p. 253–255.

African ex-Servicemen and
Independence Politics in British Africa

K. W. GRUNDY
M. SHANK

MARGARET SHANK is currently on the Faculty of the International School of the University of Ibadan, Nigeria, where she is teaching history. She has done graduate work at the University of Bridgeport, Connecticut and Case Western Reserve University, Cleveland, Ohio.

KENNETH W. GRUNDY is Associate Professor of Political Science at Case Western Reserve University. He was a Visiting Senior Lecturer at Makerere University College, Kampala, Uganda (1967–68). He is a Research Associate of the Center on International Race Relations at the University of Denver. He is the author of *Conflicting Images of the Military in Africa* (1968), *Guerrilla Struggle in Africa* (1971), and is presently finishing a book on International Relations in Southern Africa.

Much of the early literature dealing with African independence movements was produced at a time when African peoples were freeing themselves from colonial political rule. Seldom did the writers have the opportunity for field research into all the areas and subjects covered by an introductory volume. In addition, at that time the continent was not swarming with scholars churning out supportive studies to which the generalists could refer. While this may be understandable and by no means is intended to discredit otherwise useful works, what occasionally happened was that a statement of fact, because it sounded plausible, was advanced and was repeated time and again by subsequent scholars who likewise had not explored that particular subject in depth. Such statements thereby took on an aura of accuracy without ever having been subjected to critical, careful examination.

One such 'truism', if we could call it that, dealt with the ostensibly crucial role of trade unions and trade unionists in the politics of underdeveloped countries. In 1964, Berg and Butler effectively challenged that view when they argued:

in fact, what is most striking about the political role of labor movements in the countries of Tropical Africa is their failure to become politically involved during the colonial period, their limited political impact when they did become involved, and their restricted role after independence.[1]

I. THE IMAGE OF THE POLITICIZED EX-SERVICEMEN

Another, related truism involves ex-servicemen in African independence politics. Stated succinctly, it is argued that Africans who served in the armed forces of the colonial powers and who were posted outside Africa returned to Africa with a new outlook on life and particularly on their colonial condition. By virtue of their new perspectives and the higher status and prestige assigned to them as individuals, they reputedly assumed leadership roles in nationalist movements and as a group exercised an inordinate measure of political influence. 'It is therefore not surprising', writes one authority, 'to find ex-servicemen among the more militant leaders of the nationalist movement [in Nigeria] during the post-war period.'[2] No less a military specialist than Gutteridge expresses this position well:

Individually ex-servicemen came to command a respect which has often given them significant status in subsequent developments. Not only have they had ready access to 'positions of trust', but they have had political influence in many areas. The overseas service of the RWAFF and the KAR in India and Burma from 1943–5 gave them 'a window on the world' at a point where political consciousness was seething at the surface. The exact nature of the contacts with the Indian Congress Party which took place then is not important: the eyes of Africans were opened to political developments in another part of the world while at the same time they were able to observe the sapping of the myth of European invincibility by an Asian power, Japan[3].

The colonial governments themselves, following the same compelling reasoning, were alarmed by the prospects of demobilization. Fearing political ramifications that might be uncontrollable they began, even before war's end, to plan for an orderly and hopefully quiescent process.

It is the purpose of this paper to explore the extent to which ex-servicemen were involved in politics and particularly the independence movements throughout British colonial Africa.[4] We have no desire to claim that World War II was unimportant in these territories – that would be inaccurate. Nor do we wish to say that ex-servicemen did not contribute to the general atmosphere that demanded change and made change possible. We contend, rather, that the political role of ex-servicemen has been grossly inflated, and that their contribution to independence came in forms other than widespread and direct participation in nationalist politics.

Although there are a few dramatic examples of power displayed by ex-servicemen's groups, the number of veterans involved in these incidents was small in proportion to the total number of ex-soldiers. Evidence exists of individuals who rose to political power through the application of service-acquired skills but these were exceptional. Former servicemen who became leaders usually did so because they were members of the educated elite; a wartime service record was merely supplemental to more significant qualifications.

We will be concerned mainly with those Africans who served either in the King's African Rifles (KAR) and who were recruited from eastern and central Africa, or in the Royal West African Frontier Force, recruited in the West African colonies. This involved some 470 000 men. Approximately two-thirds served outside their home territories, and over 100 000 outside of Africa.

To assess the impact of the returning soldier upon his country, one should begin with the man himself. What had he been before he left? What had happened to him during his years away? What hopes – and prejudices – did he acquire? Then, in gauging the potential for nationalist activity, one must examine the communities to which the men were returning. What influences had they been subjected to during the war years? What did his society think of servicemen? What leadership positions could he hope to attain? Were there any differences in post-war

226

conditions in East and West Africa? What specific experiences and incidents help explain the effect of wartime service on the men? In theory, veterans' organizations had the chance to be a great influence; what, in some instances, hindered their effectiveness?

II. THE ATTITUDES WHICH RESULTED FROM WARTIME SERVICE

Before the tremendous manpower demands of World War II had forced a revision of the policy, British military forces in Africa had preferred to recruit men from the putatively 'martial races' of the Northern provinces of Nigeria, the Gold Coast, and Eastern Africa. The earlier recruits had been drawn from the less developed regions of the territory. If they happened to come from a more 'advanced' group, chances were that they were outcasts or misfits who found the army a more comfortable life than that of the unemployed. In any case, they were likely to accept the traditional regimen within the army. The outbreak of hostilities brought an end to the earlier, more casual recruiting practices.

Assigned wisely and approached in a manner which appealed to them, the efficiency of the wartime recruits amazed those who had been conditioned to expect little success from them at tasks that demanded resources other than physical strength. As African soldiers won respect in the eyes of the Europeans, greater means of communication between Europeans and Africans were developed.

This does not mean that attitudes of racial superiority melted in the heat of wartime. But a less formal atmosphere did allow both parties to examine each other more carefully. Europeans developed theories about the future of these men – and indeed, about the future of Africa herself – as the demobilized soldier would resume his place in African society. The African soldier, too, was storing up experiences. It is to an examination of these not always opposing, but frequently misjudged points of view that this section is directed.

Racism existed in the British Army during the war. Many European officers failed to see or hear of dissatisfaction among the Black troops (or saw and heard and did not attempt to improve morale). The following observations by one of the European officers, Major D. H. Barber, illustrate some aspects of the problem:

So far as I know, East Africans were the lowest paid troops
of all the Empire Forces, pay being based not on the jobs they were doing,
nor the cost of living in Egypt, but on their standard of living at home.

The financial position of the African must not be lost sight of ...
of his thirty-two shillings a month, ten are automatically sent home to his wife

or dependents. If he has children in school, he usually will send ten more ...
with boot polish at least four shillings a tin, beer and the civvy cinema at least
one shilling each [living in Egypt is extremely hard for him ...]

Until the African recreation clubs were formed, the African out
of camp had a thin time indeed ... it was a bold African indeed who entered a
[club] meant for British troops. In some cases, he would be welcomed;
in others, cold shouldered ... it is my impression that the individual
common British soldier himself refused to recognize any colour bar [but] in
the army itself, there was strict segregation ... which was necessary to maintain
military discipline ...[5]

Major Barber lists other ways in which the position of an African was inferior to that of the British soldier, seniority and sometimes rank notwithstanding. He concludes that this was merely a recognition of the color bar which existed in the colonies. Growing recognition that the racial relationships of the colonies were not standard elsewhere in the world was to be one of the most significant legacies of Africans' overseas wartime experiences. Some of the more articulate Africans in the forces were beginning to complain about the subjugation of one race by another on the pretext of the need for maintaining 'discipline'.[6] The officer corps, almost an exclusive white preserve, increasingly became a symbol of foreign domination. Though attempts were made after the war to Africanize at least some parts of the RWAFF, lack of funds and officers to train the Africans precluded such activity during the war and immediately thereafter. The perceptions of unequal treatment left a deep feeling of shame and embarrassment which was indelibly etched in their memories.

The wartime soldiers had intensive and extensive contact with ways of life far different from their own. New recruits learned new languages, became accustomed to modern sanitation and health practices, were steadily employed and regularly paid, and cultivated an individual as well as a group consciousness.[7] Moreover, army life provided a means of discussion between groups which had previously had little contact with one another.[8]

European colonial officials were cognizant of these exposures and their reactions to impending African demobilization were diverse. Those in Southern African territories had already indicated their awareness of what the ultimate results of the mobilization of Africans might be when they asked rhetorically: 'Why should we give them weapons?'[9] The British colonial officials that had been forced to draw upon a vast pool of African labor also realized how dangerous had been the influences to which Africans had been exposed during the War. Nearly as soon as they had decided to enlist Africans they began to plan for a speedy and effective demobilization of the troops.

228

In the rise of Japan was to be found a powerful example of what a non-white and underdeveloped people could do in less than one hundred years. Though Europeans writing during this time felt that the African soldier had not learned much from the people in the countries where he had served, evidence would indicate the contrary.[10] For example, Waruhiu Itote, 'General China' of the Mau Mau Movement, tells of his experiences while visiting with some young Indians he had met during his tour of duty there:

... the man told me, 'While you are here in India, you ought to pay attention to what we are doing ... we are fighting for others, but we've received a promise of our freedom when we are finished.' '... you mean when you were told to fight, you just got up and went?' 'You were colonized because you had no education and weapons; now some of you are educated and can get weapons ... is there anything else you have to wait for?'[11]

Aware of the danger of bands of ex-servicemen who had been trained in violence, but not sure of the extent to which they had been influenced by their overseas duty, British colonial governments made their plans to integrate the returnees into civilian society. They arranged for training facilities for servicemen who sought to bring their service-acquired skills up to civilian standards. They made efforts to investigate possible opportunities for self-employment and non-agricultural employment for the veterans. Officials were firmly convinced that the economy could not support large numbers of non-agricultural workers. Their primary solution was to encourage the veterans to return to their local districts as quickly as possible. They attempted to do this in Kenya through measures such as withholding the mustering-out pay of each African and giving him a certificate to collect his pay from his District Commissioner.[12] In other territories, they tried to minimize the impact of service separation payments upon the local economy by depositing the money in Postal Savings Bank Accounts.[13] As there was a three to four months delay in receiving the account books, this was a fairly effective measure, except that it led to further ill-feelings.

Men who before their service training had farmed and lived by the methods and values of their ancestors had acquired new skills, attitudes, and aspirations. These would not easily be discarded. But it was a traditional culture to which they returned. Although that culture had been profoundly modified by the wartime economy, the problems of adjustment were challenging for all concerned.

The situation which greeted the returning soldier is perhaps best illustrated by these excerpts from an editorial published in the *West African Pilot* shortly before the return of the first major contingent of soldiers:

> You are now in a position to learn of the strengths and weaknesses, beauty
> and ugliness, cultural accomplishments and economic efficiencies of people
> of other races and to appreciate them .... Do not expect to return home to find
> the homes which you left ... that is gone with all its narrowness and stupidities
> of tribe, nation, economic injustice, and brutalities .... Nor do we expect to find you
> the same small, petty tribesman you were when you left us.[14]

What had been happening in West Africa during the war? Her location had marked her for a prominent role in the allied war effort. Immediately after hostilities began, she became subject to an influx of men and materials to supply the troops in North Africa. Inflationary forces began to work and the prices of foodstuffs rose enormously. Government price controls and regulations upon the economy were put into operation. Communication with the capitals of Europe and America were strengthened. West Africa was blasted with the full force of the British propaganda machine. Generally, the war had a much greater effect upon the cities than the rural areas of the country.

In some cases the war merely hastened forces which were already in progress. The accelerated demands of the war machine brought workers into the towns. Trade unions enjoyed a rapid growth. Attitudes began to change. Regulating the economy had brought increased prosperity for some people. The quality of African education had improved within those five years and more Africans were able to assume the duties of European civil servants who were no longer available.

While East Africa did not achieve the pace of development of West Africa, the war did affect her territories in several important ways. The need for the services of the British civil servant elsewhere increased the workload of the district offices. The gap between administrative officers and their people increased, leaving much room for misunderstanding. Into this void went the chiefs who functioned under less supervision than usual.[15]

A situation began in East Africa before the war which became even more significant afterwards. As the area developed a cash economy, the money and resultant power did not naturally go to those who had traditionally held authority. The introduction of service money allotments in the reserves and the growth of cash crop production to meet the increased demands of the armed forces further upset this relationship.

The previously mentioned editorial about changes was correct; neither the men nor their homes were the same as they had been. Though both society and the servicemen had changed, conflict arose over exactly how changed men were to be utilized. The tribal and the colonial authorities had conflicting attitudes over the proper place for young men; yet any attempt to return the veterans to the agricultural community from which they had come was looked upon by the servicemen as an attempt to keep them chained to the traditional colonial power structure.

We have already seen that not only the ex-servicemen, but African society itself had been changed in several significant ways by the effects of the War. The roles the former servicemen were permitted to assume were riddled with ambiguities. The result was that ex-servicemen and ex-servicemen's organizations often contributed to nationalist activity but were not significantly instrumental in determining the actual course of events.

Servicemen who returned to areas from which soldiers had been traditionally recruited found themselves in a favorable situation. Among several of the tribes of Northern Uganda, for example, a period of military service was a useful qualification for a man standing for public office.[16] In the Northern regions of Ghana and Nigeria, distinguished members of local communities are often warrant officers or NCO's of good repute who served with the regiment in Burma.[17]

From her first inroads into the African continent, Great Britain established the policy of using locally recruited security forces to subdue the rebellious tribes and protect the lives and property of British citizens. Traditional tribal animosities were exploited to maintain order. The effect of this in certain areas has created a distrust of the military which persists even today.[18]

Since the first recruits into the Royal forces had been illiterate, later recruits were often likewise stereotyped. Even though soldiers who served during World War II had received nearly the equivalent of a grade school education, their training was still not of the caliber of the educated elites who had assumed leadership positions in the nationalist movements.

Soldiers themselves could be blamed for some difficulties they encountered with local populations. 'After both wars, the behaviour of large contingents of troops awaiting demobilization and of unemployed ex-servicemen... was a thorn in the flesh of local populations.'[19] In another case, the abundance of cash which the soldiers possessed created feelings of jealousy within a society that was just then developing a cash economy. Often the general feeling was that the serviceman had had his chance (and made his money) and now should make way for others.[20]

For all of the above reasons (the colonial taint, inadequate education, and the surplus of cash) the ex-servicemen were relegated to minor positions in the nationalist movement. They had first of all to prove their political skill and determination to gain entry into the leadership cadre. Then in some cases, *after* they had received their initial appointment, their service experience proved helpful.

The case of Waruhiu Itote's role in the Kenya nationalist movement is a good example. The Kenya independence struggle was led by the Kikuyu people, a group which had been among the earliest to be educated by the missionaries. 'General China' had served in Burma and India during the war. Mention has already been made of his experiences there; later, as part of a contingent sent to quell a disturbance among the Baganda to the west, he was challenged by an old Muganda who asked why he was serving as a tool of the colonial master, rather than fighting for his own independence.[21] Upon his first mission for the Mau Mau, '… my mind wandered back to my army days in Burma and then jumped to the lessons I had to teach our young recruits.'[22] It can be assumed that the lessons he had to teach were both the ideological lessons he had learned from his conversations with other active nationalists in Asia, and the practical experience that he had picked up in his years with the forces. The fact that he was an embittered Kikuyu had been his first qualification for the position, more so than his previous service experience. If one looks closely at other similar cases, one will usually find that the service experience, while beneficial to the cause, was not the deciding factor in attaining leadership positions.

IV. EX-SERVICEMEN'S ORGANIZATIONS IN POLITICS

In a pamphlet prepared for the use of American soldiers at the conclusion of World War II appears the suggestion that veterans in general, and more specifically, veterans organizations have a tendency to be conservative elements within society.[23] Though this was meant to be a description of American veterans, several of the veterans' groups that organized in Post-World War II Africa followed this same pattern.

In British East and West Africa were found only three cases where unions of ex-servicemen were directly instrumental in the independence struggle. All three were organized shortly after the return of the soldiers. One was directly absorbed into a nationalist group. One never had its moment of prominence until nearly fifteen years after the War's end. The last remained such a threat (at least in the view of the independent

African government) that a special para-military organization was established in an attempt to channel the energies of the ex-servicemen.

1. The *Anake a 40* or *Kiana Kia 40* ('Forty Group') was founded in Kenya in the late 1940's. Although many of the members were ex-KAR, it was not a group exclusively for former soldiers. The organization was very informally managed with its first objective to prevent the required terracing of government lands in the Reserves by African women. The group saw itself as a band of ex-army Kikuyu NCO's against the 'keen, young British Kenya administrators.' The group's only major accomplishment was the Women's Riots in Ft. Hall in 1949. After the Kikuyu unity movement had grown strong enough, the Forty Group dissolved.[24]

2. The Kawonawo Group of Uganda was composed of many of the over 18 000 Baganda who had served in World War II.[25] Uniformly loyal to the traditional king, the Kabaka of Buganda,[26] they appeared during the time of the Kabaka crisis in the 1950's when it was rumored that they were trying to gain control of the British Legion, Uganda Branch. Though only a rumor, the Legion took appropriate measures to block the attempt.[27]

The Kawonawo Group never attracted much attention again until the 1960's when the Buganda government tried to rally support for the continued autonomy of Buganda within an independent Uganda. One of the first attempts to demonstrate its power occurred when the Group tried to build a small but determined settlement of ex-servicemen within territory disputed between the Baganda and Banyoro. The so-called 'lost counties' had been taken from Bunyoro and added to Buganda late in the nineteenth century as a reward for helping the British. An eventual plebescite had been provided for in the independence settlements reached with the British. When it was finally held, in November, 1964, voting was limited to only those whose names had been on the rolls by April, 1962. After the plebescite, the seven or eight thousand Baganda (these are the highest estimates) who had emigrated to the counties found themselves living under Banyoro rule. Some returned to Buganda; those who remained continued to look to the Kabaka as their leader.

Members of the Kawonawo Group served the Kabaka as a personal bodyguard. Between 1965 and 1966 relations between the Kabaka and the Prime Minister worsened; the Kabaka was eventually deposed and, on May 24, 1966, the Army occupied his palace in Mengo and he fled the country. Thus ended the influence of the Kawonawo Group.[28]

233

3. Events in the Gold Coast in February, 1948, provide the most striking example of the role of ex-servicemen in African nationalist movements – the Gold Coast Ex-Servicemen's Riots in which two were killed and others wounded.[29] Rioting broke out at several places within Accra and other key cities. To put these events in proper perspective, one must first look more carefully at the forces at work within the Gold Coast.

Though the *Gold Coast Ex-Servicemen's Union* was organized in 1946 it did not become politically active until 1947. During this year it conducted talk campaigns and agitated for various measures to improve the lot of ex-servicemen. In February, 1948, it made plans to march to Christianborg Palace, the residence of the Governor, and present him a list of grievances.[30] Informed by the Superintendent of Police that such a parade route could not be permitted, the group leaders worked out an alternate march and agreed to present their petition to the Governor at his office.

On February 28, 1948, groups of ex-servicemen began gathering at the old polo grounds. A smaller group was to leave this meeting and proceed to Government House with the petition. Almost immediately the former soldiers were joined by spectators and sympathizers. There was, among these supporters, bands of young men who had recently enforced a boycott on certain trade goods and members of the United Gold Coast Convention. The trade boycott had not produced prices which were as low as the people had expected so some in the crowd were in a belligerent mood. The UGCC had been active in addressing the meetings of the Ex-Servicemen's Union which had been held in the days before the march.

When the whole group began to move out toward the Palace, the guards first ordered them to halt; failing to stop them, the guards fired. Rumors that many ex-servicemen had been killed, and the already restless mood of the crowd, sparked several weeks of disturbances which became known as the Ex-Servicemen's Riots.

Whatever the views of the rank-and-file, it is apparent that the leaders had a close association with the United Gold Coast Convention.[31] The months following the riots were filled with debate between the younger members of the Union who wished to join the United Gold Coast Convention and the older members who felt the purposes of the Ex-Servicemen's Union would be better served by remaining independent of partisan politics. The younger members won. Though some of the older members resigned from the group, many stayed. In June, 1949, the relationship between the two groups was officially recognized when mention was specifically made of them in the statement announcing the establishment of the Convention People's Party.[32] The Ex-Servicemen's

Union was captured by the dominant party and throughout the pre-independence period served as an obedient instrument of the CPP. It provided much of the muscle in the destruction of anti-Party opposition. How instrumental they actually were in Ghanaian independence politics remains contingent upon one's resolution to the question, who is more important to a movement, the leader or the follower?

Kwame Nkrumah realized the potential of the ex-servicemen. Sensing the growing dissatisfaction within the Ex-Servicemen's Union, he organized the Builder's Brigade. Though not strictly for ex-servicemen, it did manage to absorb many of those still unemployed. It is estimated that at one time, 20 to 40 percent of its membership were ex-servicemen.[33]

With the exception of the three groups which have already been discussed, veterans' organizations in British Africa were not politically important. Some, to be sure, were active pressure groups for securing benefits for ex-servicemen; many were sophisticated enough to realize that true progress for the veteran could only occur in the wake of political independence and as part of the improvement of the population in general. An examination of the histories of several of the ex-servicemen's organizations which were in Africa suggests a few reasons for their ineffectual roles despite tremendous potential.

Colonial officials had varying reactions to the appearance of veterans' groups within their territories. The Uganda Protectorate held the following official position:

... in theory, there can be no objection to such societies; but, in practice,
certain undesirable features might appear. ... [T]hey might tend to engage
in political rather than social activities ... encouragement should be given to
ex-soldiers to participate in communal activities and not to exclude themselves in
special institutions. ... [I]f there is a need or wish for ex-soldiers societies,
they will come into being of their own volition. ... [I]n view of the circumstances
we have mentioned, we see no necessity for the government to help
in their establishment by monetary or other assistance. ...[34]

Uganda seemed to have succeeded with her demobilization schemes. Groups which were organized outside of the British Legion (Uganda Chapter) were constituted along ethnic lines. But this equipped them more for internal post-independence power struggles than for anti-colonial action. It is this ethnic distraction as much as any other that underscores their relative ineffectiveness as territory-wide organizations contributing to the nationalist struggle.

In Nigeria there existed an administration-established group, the Nigerian Ex-Servicemen's Welfare Association, whose function was to distribute pensions and care for the disabled.[35] But this group had little money to do much beyond caring for handicapped veterans. There were other ex-servicemen's groups in Nigeria, but their effectiveness was hindered. The political impotence of Nigerian ex-servicemen in nationalist activities was caused mainly by the multiplicity of groups, each claiming to represent all ex-servicemen, and working at cross purposes. This organizational proliferation might be attributed to the following: first, there was a clash of personalities among those striving for leadership; second, Nigeria's vastness and poor means of communication made it difficult for those who might like to work together to get together; finally, tribal politics which was already hampering the nationalist movement in general caused the ex-servicemen's groups to be formed along regional and thus ethnic lines. Instead of devoting full attention to the colonial struggle, they spent their time trying to eliminate one another.[36]

Elsewhere in Africa, notably Central and Southern Africa, the organizations which were formed were controlled by expatriate officials. This meant that little attention was paid to the needs of African ex-servicemen and that the dedication of the organizations to the independence movement was incomplete.

The Sierra Leone Ex-Servicemen's Association (SLESA) was intended to be non-political. It had managed to gain recognition, despite difficulties with the government. To avoid the accusation that SLESA was establishing a pseudo-political body, the group added a clause to its charter: '... making it clear that the association was non-party political, in the context that, much as every member was entitled to his civil rights, the association could not ally itself with any political party.'[37] As a result of this, calm returned to those areas where ex-servicemen had successfully unseated the chiefs (who, as part of the system of indirect rule, were accomplices to the colonial scheme). Later, in the late 1950's, SLESA became captured by the Government Party, receiving annual grants from Government. The Minister of External Affairs served as its President.

Except for the previously mentioned Forty Group, a nationalistic ex-soldier in Kenya was as likely to join a trade union as a veterans organization. In 1946 trade-unionists were militantly nationalistic. Leaders looking for followers often looked to the ex-servicemen as likely supporters who already had a sense of cooperation and unity; if nationalist leaders were unable to achieve immediate results in winning ex-servicemen to their cause, they abandoned them. Thus, the veterans' organizations were often deprived of dynamic leadership that might have helped them use their resources effectively for political purposes.

If one is to give the elaborate demobilization plans of the respective

236

colonial administrations their due, one must say that, at the very least, they provided for a period when the ex-servicemen were occupied by actual projects or promises intensively enough that they lost much of their political motivation. Though there were training camps and scholarships available to the ex-servicemen, the number who actually used them was small in comparison to the total number of men who had been involved in the war effort. Any advantage enjoyed by ex-servicemen upon their return home was directly related to the absence within their communities of others with similar educational qualifications. As an increasing number of Africans acquired more training, the ex-soldiers had to develop further credentials.[38]

For many reasons, ex-servicemen's organizations were not able to achieve what the Europeans had feared – and had worked very hard to prevent. Their careful plans were not so much responsible for the low level of political activity by the African ex-servicemen as were the regard with which the native population held the servicemen and the type of leadership available. The traditional army recruit and the members of the political leadership elites were drawn from different segments of the population; even the more universal conscription of the War did not alter this pattern significantly. Though more was done to educate the servicemen during the war, those servicemen who emerged as post-war leaders were those who had already had extensive training and experience prior to their enlistment. Their demobilization from the service merely meant their return to take up where they had left off.

V. QUALIFICATION OF THE IMAGE OF THE POLITICIZED EX-SERVICEMAN

The *modus operandi* of this paper has been to examine the many elements involved in the relationship of Africans who served in World War II to the nationalist movements in an attempt to support or disprove the view that, 'Wartime experiences prompted ex-soldiers to assume a major role in drives for independence.' It is granted that there were several important incidents in various independence struggles with which the ex-servicemen's organizations were associated. But the numbers involved were only a small part of the total ex-soldier population. When one looks at the careers of the individuals themselves, one sees only a few cases where participation in the war effort specifically prepared men to play a greater role in the movement than they would have had otherwise. In most cases, men who had served in the armed forces and who later became nationalist leaders did so because of other qualifications and interests.[39]

Ex-soldiers played only a minor part in the direct struggle for relief from colonial rule. They did contribute to that indirect battle – the psychological one – which must be won before one can ever hope to defeat an external enemy. Their agitation was not to eliminate the metropolitan power, but to create equal opportunity in the economic segment.

In looking back at the effects of the demobilization plans, colonial administrators almost seemed surprised that the ex-soldier did not assume the crucial role which they had expected. Their haste to return him to his society had caused him to lose much of his identity as an ex-serviceman. The increased money which the war effort had brought to some departments of the government had enabled officials to undertake experiments in the fields of economics and sociology.[40] As the ex-serviceman assumed his new identity as a tradesman or laborer, he accelerated these changes even more.

Granted, education was not uniform throughout the armed services and was rudimentary at best. However, the fact that men who before their enlistments had been illiterate now rushed to obtain copies of newspapers the minute they left troop ships at home indicated that a very important change had occurred.[41] Like all other educated Africans, the men would begin to share the feeling that although they had received a modicum of education, they were still denied the opportunity to earn an adequate salary or to live according to standards they felt they now deserved. For nearly 470 000 Africans who served in the armed forces, the war provided a chance to get their bearings – to learn what it meant to be an individual, yet to work within a cooperative situation. While few African soldiers had been completely socialized, many were eager to accept increased responsibility for more management of their own affairs than had previously been the custom.

The training facilities established according to the demobilization plans were spread throughout the territories so that the ex-serviceman, so the plan envisioned, 'would be absorbed into his community and would not expect any special privileges for himself.' The object was to discourage him from thinking of himself as a soldier, and to encourage him to have a self-image as a farmer, laborer, or mechanic.[42] So it happened that:

The soldiers returned to civilian life without disturbance. Soon, however,
new wants and needs among the people were felt and voiced. More schools
were demanded and more hospitals, more roads, and more permanent buildings,

238

and more water supplies; ... But above all, there was a quickening interest in political matters, a desire to have more control over local affairs.[43]

The ex-serviceman who returned from World War II had been called upon to protect not his own country, but an international cause he did not entirely understand, and which, when he did, he could not comprehend why it did not apply to himself and his people as well. The impact of this was not lost on him, even though he may not have taken direct political action to secure his political aspirations. As he worked to gain what was perceived to be more important to him, economic security, he gradually came to realize that the one was contingent upon the other. He then began to make moves to improve the political environment. But by this time he was working through a trade union, an independence movement, or some other organizations. He was no longer identifiable, nor did he identify himself as an ex-serviceman.

Though Africa might have lost some of her sons during the War, she had gained a tremendous pool of skilled manpower. There were reasons, however, why this potential was never fully realized: first, the many new industries which had grown up during the war had filled positions with the then available workers; secondly, post-war production needs declined and this, combined with an unwillingness upon the part of the industries to bridge the gap between military training and civilian requirement in a particular trade, resulted in less use of this pool than might have been expected. Trouble really began after some colonies began to import European ex-servicemen from the metropole for jobs which might eventually have been filled by Africans.

Transportation and trade were overwhelmingly the favorite post-war occupations of African ex-servicemen. Men in these fields were operating within their original societies, but were, at the same time changing them. For example, the Batoro Ex-Servicemen's Bus Company in western Uganda opened new routes into semi-isolated areas. This resulted in a greater extension of a cash crop economy and increased mobility of the population. This in turn multiplied demands for government services and more involvement with government policies.[44]

Most government demobilization reports recognized the skill gap between army rating and civilian qualifications. Training facilities were established for a limited number; some employment services were furnished to those who would register. While the bureaus complained that there were problems getting the Africans to stay on one job for any length of time,[45] the Africans claimed that the jobs offered them were temporary in nature and offered little security.[46] By and large the transition was not an easy one.[47]

Though industrial jobs might not have been available to Africans, ex-servicemen were encouraged to move into self-employed crafts and trades. 'We think there is almost unlimited scope for the enterprising African to set himself up on his own account as a village craftsman,' said the Uganda report.[48] To this end, efforts were made to release to the ex-servicemen quantities of agricultural and artisan tools which the War made scarce. There was increasing resentment in West Africa over the growing monopoly of certain trades by Syrians;[49] in East Africa, a far worse situation existed with the Asian merchants in control. In imported commodities African merchants were often shut out by the Asian wholesalers. To this problem '... every effort has been made by the Commissioner of Supplies ... to provide some share of the none-too-plentiful merchandise, especially through the African wholesaler.'[50] Africans could also go to Nairobi and purchase surplus army supplies, but the cost of transporting these goods to their homes plus the disadvantage of not being there all the time to pick up the bargains as they came along made this plan unsuccessful.

Greater success came from the practice of reserving for ex-servicemen a monthly quota to purchase second-hand military vehicles. Efforts were made to enable those ex-drivers who wished to obtain civilian licences as a kind of economic insurance to do so.[51]

The attraction of Africans to trade was much greater in East Africa than in the West; West Africa already had many African retail merchants. Trade applications in East Africa increased greatly after 1944. This increase was significant in two ways: one, it resulted in a wider distribution of consumer goods; and two, the native shops provided gathering sites for the discussion of political questions.[52]

Presumably if veterans are going to join organizations for ex-servicemen, they will usually do so either immediately after their discharge or some years later as they think back sentimentally about their time in the corps. In 1961, in Freetown, Sierra Leone, a conference was held by ex-servicemen's representatives from five West African countries. This meeting, some fifteen years after their release from the armed forces, was concerned with working in cooperation with their governments to find ways '... which would encourage ex-servicemen to be self-supporting.'[53]

Fifteen years and many political events later the ex-servicemen were finally beginning to grasp a feeling of what their unified efforts could do. The theme of the conference was basically that:

As a result of the steadily increasing capacities of the member associations, we believe the time is right to engage in a more significant level of activity ... to help ourselves ... lead to the formulation of programs for the common good, not only of ex-servicemen, but of the entire community.[54]

With this examination of the several facets of veteran participation in Africa, what has happened to our truism? Ex-servicemen as such were rarely directly involved in independence struggles. The extensive demobilization plans had worked well; the men had rather rapidly stopped thinking of themselves as ex-soldiers and assumed new identity as farmers, tradesmen, or laborers. What the governments of the colonies involved could not do, however, was erase all service experiences.

These had affected ex-servicemen both positively and negatively: on the one hand, men had been subjected to racism made more illogical than ever by wartime conditions and sacrifices; on the other, the men had gained an education previously unavailable. Men who formerly had seen only hand labor farming now saw tractors used. Men who had been taught that there was an aura around the Superior White Man now saw a world where the myth could not be maintained. Non-white people militarily defeated whites and other non-white people were pressing whites to gain their freedom. Ex-servicemen had come to appreciate the tremendous material wealth and industrial resources of western Europe. They returned determined to share their experiences with their people.

Service experience itself did not prompt great numbers of ex-servicemen to become leaders in the nationalist movements. Those who did so were those who had had previous training and experience. Nor were ex-servicemen numerous among the rank and file of the agitators, though many were active in trade unions that were directly involved in the movements. The economic wants of the ex-servicemen ran into conflict with the monopolies created by the colonial system; the popular unrest that this created grew partly from the hopes that the ex-servicemen had brought back to their societies. The former soldiers contributed to a psychological climate within which the real leaders of the independence movements could work. Ex-soldiers could say they had seen the things which the nationalists were promising, thereby adding an element of credibility to what might have otherwise seemed unreal.

The emphasis in the truism must be shifted from the political to the economic. It was only after frustration occurred in obtaining material wants such as better jobs and homes that the ex-servicemen became involved directly in the nationalist activities. Rather than the ex-servicemen taking the initiatives and supplying the leadership, the predominant pattern was of nationalist politicians using the ex-servicemen and exploiting their grievances to further the independence struggle.

241

1. Elliot J. BERG and Jeffrey BUTLER, 'Trade Unions,' in James S. COLEMAN and Carl G. ROSBERG, Jr. (eds.), *Political Parties and National Integration in Tropical Africa* (Berkeley & Los Angeles: University of California Press, 1964), pp. 340–81.
2. James S. COLEMAN, *Nigeria: Background to Nationalism* (Berkeley & Los Angeles: University of California Press, 1958), p. 254.
3. William GUTTERIDGE, *The Military in African Politics* (London: Methuen & Co., 1969), p. 4. For similar statements see: F. M. BOURRET, *Ghana: The Road to Independence, 1919–1957* (Stanford, Calif.: Stanford University Press, 1960), p. 165; Thomas HODGKIN, *Nationalism in Colonial Africa* (New York: New York University Press, 1957), p. 142; Dennis AUSTIN, *West Africa and the Commonwealth* (London: Penguin, 1957), p. 14; and Ali A. MAZRUI, *Towards a Pax Africana: A Study of Ideology and Ambition* (London: Weidenfeld & Nicolson, 1967), pp. 161–62.
4. The only significant paper directly dealing with the theme of this study arrives at similar findings. See: G. O. OLUSANYA, 'The Role of Ex-Servicemen in Nigerian Politics,' *Journal of Modern African Studies*, VI, No. 2 (August, 1968), pp. 221–32. Related to this is Eugene P. A. SCHLEH, 'The Post-War Careers of Ex-Servicemen in Ghana and Uganda,' in *ibid.*, pp. 203–20.
5. D. H. BARBER, *Africans in Khaki* (London: 1948), pp. 19–20 & 93.
6. See, for example: *West African Pilot* (Lagos), 'Letter to the Editor,' January 14, 1945; and, OLUSANYA, *op. cit.*, p. 221.
7. James S. COLEMAN and BELMONT PRICE, Jr., 'The Role of the Military in Sub-Saharan Africa,' in John J. JOHNSON (ed.), *The Role of the Military in Underdeveloped Countries* (Princeton, N.J.: Princeton University Press, 1962), p. 397.
8. See, for example: BARBER, *op. cit.*, p. 81.
9. As quoted in: Donald S. ROTHCHILD, 'The Effects of Mobilization in British Africa,' *Duquesne Review*, V, No. 1 (Fall, 1959), p. 6.
10. See, for example: *West African Pilot* (Lagos), October 26, 1945.
11. Waruhiu ITOTE (General China), *'Mau Mau' General* (Nairobi: East African Publishing House, 1967), p. 13.
12. Protectorate and Colony of Kenya, *Progress Report on Demobilisation* (Nairobi: 10 February 1944), pp. 4–5.
13. Uganda Protectorate, *Civil Reabsorption: Progress Report* (Entebbe: 1947), pp. 3–4.
14. *West African Pilot* (Lagos), 'The Mission of Our Soldiers,' January 5, 1945.
15. The fact that the chiefs began to exercise more power during this period could have made them even less receptive to the influence of the young returnees.
16. SCHLEH, *op. cit.*, p. 209. Even so, of the 198 candidates for the 1961 Legislative Council elections in Uganda, only twelve were KAR veterans. See: Robert O. BYRD, 'Characteristics of Candidates for Election in a Country Approaching Independence: The Case of Uganda,' *Midwest Journal of Political Science*, VII, No. 1 (February, 1963), p. 12.
17. William GUTTERIDGE, 'The Place of the Armed Forces in Society in African States,' *Race*, IV, No. 1 (November, 1962), p. 27.
18. Kenneth W. GRUNDY, 'The Negative Image of Africa's Military,' *Review of Politics*, XXX, No. 4 (October, 1968), p. 430.
19. GUTTERIDGE, *op. cit.*, p. 26.
20. SCHLEH, *op. cit.*, p. 208.

21. ITOTE, *op. cit.*, pp. 28–29.
22. *Ibid.*, p. 47.
23. American Historical Association, *Why Do Veterans Organize?* (Historical Service Board, 1946), *passim.*
24. ITOTE, *op. cit.*, p. 37.
25. See SCHLEH, *op. cit.*, pp. 212–15, for a fuller description.
26. For example, *Uganda Argus* (Kampala), January 26, 1962: 'A group of Baganda ex-servicemen walked thirty miles to greet the returning Kabaka and mount a guard of honour for him.'
27. SCHLEH, *op. cit.*, p. 213.
28. *Ibid.*, pp. 213–14.
29. A more complete treatment of these events appears in *ibid.*, pp. 210–12.
30. The *Watson Report* lists their grievances as ranging from too harsh prison terms for some men who served abroad to a lack of confidence in the ability of the Secretary of the Gold Coast Legion to represent the men. The Report said the petition had only presented a small part of the true issue. Great Britain, Colonial Office, *Report of the Commission of Enquiry into Disturbances in the Gold Coast, 1948* (Watson Report), Colonial No. 231 (London: 1948), p. 12. Nkrumah's account of these events appears in, *Ghana: The Autobiography of Kwame Nkrumah* (New York: Thomas Nelson & Sons, 1957), pp. 77–78.
31. *Watson Report*, p. 10.
32. NKRUMAH, *op. cit.*, p. 105.
33. SCHLEH, *op. cit.*, pp. 211–12; see note 2, p. 211.
34. Uganda Protectorate, *Report of the Civil Reabsorption and Rehabilitation Committee* (Entebbe: 1945), p. 4.
35. World Veterans Federation, *Reports on the Conference on West African Veterans' Affairs*, WVF Doc. 1055 (Freetown: 1961), p. 2.
36. OLUSANYA, *op. cit.*, p. 229.
37. World Veterans Federation, *op. cit.*, Annex 7, p. 2.
38. SCHLEH, *op. cit.*, p. 209.
39. *Ibid.*, p. 216.
40. Meyer FORTES, 'The Impact of the War on British West Africa,' *International Affairs*, XXI, No. 2 (April, 1945).
41. *West African Pilot* (Lagos), October 26, 1945.
42. *Daily Times* (Lagos), January 16, 1956.
43. J. C. D. LAWRENCE, *The Iteso: Fifty Years of Change in A Nilo-Hamitic Tribe of Uganda* (London: 1957) as quoted in SCHLEH, *op. cit.*, p. 207.
44. SCHLEH, *op. cit.*
45. Protectorate and Colony of Kenya, *Manpower Demobilisation and Reabsorption Report, 1945* (Nairobi: 1945), p. 19.
46. *West African Pilot* (Lagos), June 8, 1945.
47. For example, as late as 1947 in Nigeria, 43 533 ex-soldiers of a total of 100 099 were still unemployed. OLUSANYA, *op. cit.*, p. 227.
48. Uganda Protectorate, *Demobilisation Report, 1945, op. cit.*, p. 4.
49. *Watson Report, op. cit.*, p. 8.
50. Uganda Protectorate, *Civil Reabsorption, 1947, op. cit.*, p. 5.
51. *Ibid.*, p. 6.
52. SCHLEH, *op. cit.*, pp. 207–08.
53. World Veterans Federation, *op. cit.*, Annex 1, p. 11.
54. *Ibid.*, IV, B & C.

United Nations Forces

Structured Strain in a United Nations Constabulary Force

C. C. MOSKOS JR.

CHARLES C. MOSKOS, Jr. is Professor and Chairman of the Department of Sociology, Northwestern University, USA. He was awarded a Ford Foundation Faculty Fellowship (1969–70) to study United Nations Forces in Cyprus. He is the author of *The Sociology of Political Independence* (1967), *The American Enlisted Man* (1970), and editor of *Public Opinion and the Military Establishment* (1971).

On March 4, 1964, the United Nations Security Council unanimously adopted a resolution which recommended the establishment of an international force to keep the peace in Cyprus. The eastern Mediterranean island-republic was in a state of virtual civil war as fighting broke out between its Greek and Turkish communities. The first units of the United Nations Force in Cyprus – UNFICYP – arrived on the island three weeks later. A new episode in the checkered history of international peacekeeping forces was about to begin.

The mission of UNFICYP defined by the 1964 Security Council resolution was '... to use its best efforts to prevent a recurrence of fighting and, as necessary, to contribute to the maintenance and restoration of law and order and a return to normal conditions.' Subsequent semi-annual resolutions passed by the Security Council have kept the United Nations Force in Cyprus in being through the time of this writing (summer, 1970). Although the basic dispute between Greeks and Turks on Cyprus has remained unresolved, UNFICYP has made positive progress in its primary task of pacifying the Cypriot inter-communal war. UNFICYP, moreover, has also made substantial contribution in restoring Cyprus to conditions of normal order and stability. In at least these respects, the United Nations Force in Cyprus contrasted favorably with other U.N. peacekeeping forces in the Congo and Middle East. The Secretary General has thus been able with accuracy to term UNFICYP a 'successful' peacekeeping operation.

THE ORGANIZATION OF UNFICYP

UNFICYP had a total strength in 1970 of approximately 3 700 persons: 3 500 military personnel, and 200 civilian staff. The civilian side consisted of an official staff of about ten persons: the Special Representative to the Secretary General, political and legal advisors, an administrative section, and a public information office. These U.N. civilian officials were serving indeterminate tours in Cyprus. About another 20 or so persons on routine U.N. field service tours acted as secretaries or drivers to the civilian staff. Another civilian component of the U.N. presence in Cyprus were the 175 police officers who made up the United Nations Civilian Police (UNCIVPOL). Drawn in almost equal numbers from Australia, Austria, Denmark, and Sweden, UNCIVPOL performed liaison functions between the police forces of the Greek Cypriot and Turkish Cypriot communities.

It was the military side, however, which was by far and away the numerically dominant component of UNFICYP and which gave the United

Nations presence in Cyprus its distinguishing quality. The bulk of the military personnel were found in six national contingents, each consisting of approximately 500 officers and men. These national contingents were drawn from Canada, Denmark, Finland, Great Britain, Ireland, and Sweden: respectively referred to as Cancon, Dancon, Fincon, Britcon, Ircon, and Swedcon. Each of the national contingents was charged with responsibility for a specific region of Cyprus. Depending on the locale of their deployment, the national contingents performed duties such as: guarding 'Green Lines' (i.e. *de facto* borders between Greek and Turkish communities within cities); manning outposts – 'o.p.'s' – on the edge of Turkish enclaves in the countryside; patroling both Greek and Turkish Cypriot areas to monitor military movements and buildups, and supervising daily automobile convoys of Greek civilians through Turkish-controlled areas.

Each of the six national contingents were all similar in their being organized along the lines of reduced infantry battalions. They also shared in common a six-month tour of duty in Cyprus. There were, however, major differences between the national contingents in their recruitment and formation. Britcon and Cancon were ongoing integral military units composed entirely of regular career soldiers. Such units as the 'Pompadours' of Great Britain and the 'Black Watch' of Canada were made up of men who had soldiered together before coming to Cyprus and would presumably continue to do so afterwards. Dancon, Fincon, and Swedcon, on the other hand, were formed specifically for UNFICYP duty and were demobilized after their tour (to be replaced by another *ad hoc* unit). Moreover, the Scandinavian contingents consisted – except for senior officers – of reservists who had taken a temporary break in their civilian pursuits to volunteer for UNFICYP duty. The Irish contingent followed yet another pattern. Like the other English-speaking contingents, Ircon consisted of career regular soldiers, but like the Scandinavian contingents, it was an *ad hoc* volunteer unit formed specifically for a six-month tour in Cyprus.

A seventh national force, though not of contingent size, was the Austrian Field Hospital (AFH). The AFH was a 50-man military unit, including nine erstwhile civilian medical doctors and dentists fulfilling their Austrian military obligations. The AFH had the responsibility of treating UNFICYP soldiers whose ailments (or wounds in the event of combat) could not be handled by national contingent medical officers. The AFH also offered free dental care, a service of which great advantage was taken by UNFICYP personnel. Like the national contingents, the AFH personnel also served a six-month tour of duty in Cyprus.

250

In addition to the nationally homogeneous six contingents and Austrian Field Hospital, there were two multi-national military units in UNFICYP. One was the small 60-man Military Police Company consisting of soldiers drawn from each of the six national contingents. 'M.P. Coy' had jurisdiction over UNFICYP soldiers outside the camps of their respective national contingents. The UNFICYP Military Police, however, had no powers of punishment; violators were returned to their national contingents for disciplinary action.

With the exception of the Military Police Company, only Headquarters UNFICYP existed as a multi-national unit. With its approximately 500-man complement (about 50 officers and 450 other ranks), Headquarters was composed of representatives from each of the seven nations contributing to the United Nations military force in Cyprus. Both at the Headquarters offices and the Headquarters Officers Mess there was a genuine intermingling of disparate nationalities. Even at Headquarters, however, the multi-national representation was largely limited to staff officers; all seconded to UNFICYP from their home military establishments to serve minimum one-year tours in Cyprus. The supporting infrastructure and lower ranks of Headquarters UNFICYP was almost entirely a British affair. UNFICYP's logistics, ordnance, workshops, air support, reconnaissance squadron, and transportation corps were closely allied with the British Sovereign Base Areas. These 'SBA's' were themselves a vast complex of preexisting British military installations on Cyprus.

COLLECTION OF DATA

From October 1969 to May 1970, I was in Cyprus doing full time research on UNFICYP. Owing to my credentials as an accredited correspondent and the cooperation of the U.N. Press Office, I was granted the status of 'temporary official assignment' with UNFICYP. This allowed for my virtual complete access to all levels and ranks of UNFICYP military personnel. During the time of the field research, extended periods were spent with each of the national contingents, the Field Hospital, the Military Police Company, and Headquarters. In addition to formal interviews with 100 military officers (close to one-third of the entire UNFICYP officer complement), my findings are based on participant-observations in a variety of contexts: tactical situations, formal social affairs, informal gatherings, and perusal of UNFICYP documents and records. The openness of UNFICYP to the probings of a visitor allowed for a wide ranging opportunity to examine the social organization of a peacekeeping force. Perhaps, in some

251

ways, this researcher was able to get a more complete picture of the social dynamics of UNFICYP than many of its formal members.

SOURCES OF CONFLICT

The variety of theoretical schemes available to the analyst of formal organizations are legion. Yet when all is said and done, there are probably only two major conceptual approaches to the examination of concrete social organizations. One approach is to ascertain what are the stated goals of the organization and then examine how much success or failure the organization has had in achieving these goals. The second perspective is to ascertain what are the kinds of differentiation within an organization and then examine the amount and types of conflict deriving from these internal cleavages. In this paper I have adopted the latter frame of reference.

There is the premise that the conflict approach can serve as an especially appropriate analytical framework to describe *all* social organizations. It does not imply that UNFICYP was a notably conflict ridden organization, but it does mean that UNFICYP like any social organization had its own internal and external sources of social strain. It is by this elemental comprehension of the inherent conflict in a social structure that researchers can begin to determine the essential sociological makeup of the organization under analysis. What follows then is in no sense an *exposé* of UNFICYP, but rather the application of a general form of social analyses to one particular formal organization.

Conflict between UNFICYP *and the United Nations Organization.* Strain between the UNFICYP organization in Cyprus and the United Nations Organization (UNO) in New York was apparent on several counts. One major source of dissatisfaction with UNO revolved around the lack of funds appropriated to UNFICYP military expenditures.

A Headquarters staff officer: 'This is the biggest penny pinching outfit you can imagine. The U.N. wastes millions on foolishness, and we can't even buy a wide-angle camera. Can you imagine! For a few pennies they will jeopardize the success of the whole operation.'

Another source of contention with UNO was the restrictions placed on the UNFICYP military in the performances of its mission.

A Canadian officer: 'We're sent here with our hands tied behind our backs. We're like traffic cops, we can only wave our hands. The politicians won't let us have any authority. If we could use a little muscle, this whole mess would be over in two weeks.'

252

Conflict between UNFICYP *and the home military establishments of contributing nations.* Because of the nature of the recruiting system – men seconded and units temporarily assigned to Cyprus from their home armies – UNFICYP often found itself at odds with the military establishments of contributing nations. Most of this strain centered around assignment of military personnel to the Headquarters UNFICYP staff. Whether or not an officer's tour would be extended depended ultimately on decisions made back in his home country's defence ministry.

There was also the general question as to what effect assignment to Cyprus had on the military careers of UNFICYP's serving officers. On this issue there were mixed views. Some believed U.N. duty offered an opportunity to demonstrate personal capabilities in an operational force, while others felt that absence from the mainstream of military advancement at home was detrimental to their military futures. The latter possibility, of course, could be a serious source of organizational strain. In either event, the elemental fact was that UNFICYP was an anomalous military structure: an officer served in a centrally commanded international force, but the power of permanent assignment and promotion rested in his home military organization. This meant that no matter what an officer's personal commitment toward a U.N. peacekeeping force might be, he knew that in both the short and long run his career advancement depended entirely on how he was evaluated within his own national army.

Conflict between Headquarters UNFICYP *and national contingents.* Much of the conflict between Headquarters UNFICYP and the national contingents was similar to that usually found between headquarters and line units in any military organization. There were criticisms by the national contingents that Headquarters was over-staffed and overly bureaucratic, or that it failed to take the contingents into account when policies were changed. For example, when the national contingents were redeployed in the spring of 1970 (in anticipation of a forthcoming reduction in UNFICYP strength), there was contingent resentment at the need to move out of established areas and be relocated in new surroundings.

A Danish officer: 'It will be disastrous to move the contingents around. It takes years to get to know the local situation and who is who in both Greek and Turk sides. If Headquarters is thinking about cutting back, the first place to start should be at Headquarters. The men in the contingents are working full-time seven days a week, at Headquarters they work half-days five days a week.'

Another vantage point illustrates a different kind of conflict between a Headquarters unit and the national contingents.

An officer in the Military Police Company: 'We have a hell of a problem trying to get cooperation from the contingents. The Irish and the British try to keep control over their own M.P.'s even though they are assigned to M.P. Coy. Another case. Just after I arrived, I had to send a Finn M.P. back to Fincon because he couldn't do the job. I mean he was lazy, mean, and dumb. To make matters worse he couldn't even say hello in English. Six months later Fincon is supposed to send us another man. They send back the same guy, only this time he's a sergeant. Now we're stuck with an absolute fuck-all who outranks my good men.'

Conflict between national contingents within UNFICYP. One would expect differences between the national contingents would be a major source of conflict within UNFICYP. In fact there was such conflict, but the bulk of the inter-contingent strain derived from organizational features peculiar to UNFICYP rather than hostilities between nationalities *per se*. One such organizational tension was over the division of labor within UNFICYP.

A Swedish officer: 'We can pull our maintenance on our vehicles, but we must send them to Dhekelia [in the SBA's]. This means the work is done slower and not as well as we could do it. But, of course, this is to give the Brits at Dhekelia a job. They have to find something for them to do. The Brits are using the U.N. for their own purposes.'

An Austrian officer: 'The report [of the 1969 Economic Committee on UNFICYP] was unfair in the way it computed costs. This made the Field Hospital look bad compared to the British base hospitals. The report did not mention the work the Field Hospital is doing on dental treatment, outpatient care, and taking care of UNCIVPOL. The Chief Medical Officer at Headquarters was a Brit and he fixed the report to make us look bad and the SBA's good. The Brits are trying to get UNFICYP to use the British hospitals and close down the Field Hospital.'

Another organizational strain centered on the quite real differences in the pay scales of the various contingents. On this score the British in particular had cause for resentment. Alone of the national contingents, Britcon received no special U.N. pay allowances. Although most pronounced in Britcon, the differential in U.N. allowances was a source of resentment for other nationalities as well. These allowances – paid for from United Nations funds were in addition to base salaries paid for by home military establishments – were highest for the Swedes and Danes: approximately $330 U.S. monthly for officers, and $100 U.S. monthly for other ranks.

A British officer: 'How do you think my men feel? A British soldier makes £10 a week and a Swede two miles down the road makes £30 a week for doing exactly the same thing. How do I explain to my men about making the world safe for peacekeeping? They want to know why they're not getting paid what that Swede is getting paid. And I don't know what to tell him myself.'

A British officer: 'We had a British captain at Headquarters who found that his Danish driver was earning twice as much as he was. We feel like poor relations here. Even when we go to Cancon they do the treating because they know we don't have any money.'

Although often in a humorous vein, there was also some inter-contingent

254

asperity of a more chauvinistic nature reflected in negative stereotypes acquired in Cyprus.

An Irish sergeant: 'Sure we can speak English with the Canadians, but my god, they're a rowdy bunch. Nobody likes a drink and a good time more than an Irishman, but those Canadians are something else again. They get loud too early, if you get what I mean.'

A Danish officer: 'When we took over Xeros from the Irish, you couldn't believe the filth there was. These Irish aren't civilized. The first thing we did was kill millions of cockroaches. Millions and millions of them. We made mountains out of them and burned them. They even spoke Irish. The Irish were with those cockroaches for four years and lived together like one big family.'

Genuine hostility between nationalities, however, was rare. And in those cases where it was present, the animosity had origins long preceding UNFICYP assignment; most notably, that of many Irish toward the British, and a few British toward the Austrians.

An Irish officer: 'We just don't talk politics with the English. It's better that way, because a lot of us couldn't control ourselves once we start talking and thinking about the old days and what's going on up North right now.
It's a miracle there hasn't been a good punch-up between us yet.'

A British officer: 'Don't forget all the top Austrian officers were Nazis. They run the Field Hospital just like a stalag. One of their officers can get damn obnoxious once he gets a few drinks in him. That's when he starts complaining "why can't I wear my [German] medals. I won them in honor." It's hard enough to forget the War without him always reminding us.'

By far, however, the most frequent point of disputation between the national contingents involved invidious comparisons of their respective military prowess and organizational effectiveness.

A Danish officer: 'The British have an army to solve their unemployment problem. The Black Watch aren't soldiers, they're lumberjacks and timbermen from Canada. These are men who can't make a living at home and bring their troubles into the Army.'

A Swedish officer: 'Our men are not collected from the slums of their countries. They are volunteers who have been carefully picked. They are the cream of the crop and a much higher grade of men than you would find in a regular group of soldiers. Just compare their intelligence and manners with the Brits and the Irish and the Canadians.'

A Canadian officer: 'The Canadians and British are the only real soldiers here. The Irish are a sloppy army. The Danes and Finns are really civilians in uniform here for a vacation in the sun. The Swedes with their beards and necklaces are a hippy army.'

A British officer: 'How can you seriously compare a unit like the Pompadours with the others except the Black Watch. We and the Canadians are an army. The others are a mixed batch of civilian tourists, half-soldiers, and a few professionals who never fought a war'.

Conflict between different components within the same nationalities. In some ways conflict within the national groups represented in UNFICYP was more noticeable than that between nationalities. Common to all contingents was a tension point introduced by the shortness of the six-month rotation cycle. Due to the brevity of a contingent's tour, there was a tendency to let matters – especially housekeeping and maintenance standards – slide. Advance detachments of about-to-arrive contingents were thus often placed in the position of having to receipt property which was not always fully accounted for or in proper condition. The conflict between departing and newly arriving units was manifest in the latter's complaint that little had been done previously to beautify the compound area or establish adequate standard operating procedures. Each unit tended to see itself as 'really the first to get things in shape.' There were repeated remarks in all contingents along the lines of: 'You can't imagine how bad things were here before we came over.'

Another source of intra-contingent tension was applicable only to the Scandinavian units. The contingents from Denmark, Finland, and Sweden had officer complements consisting of both reservists and career professionals. The reservists on temporary active duty were on 'contract' for a specific UNFICYP tour. There pay was equal to that of career officers of the same rank. Many of the professional officers viewed their reservist counterparts as being in Cyprus sheerly for a paid vacation. For their part, the reservists often saw the career officers as overly concerned with military formality and picayune discipline.

A Danish career officer: 'The reserve officer comes here on contract to make some easy money and have a good time. He cares nothing about making the army run a little better because he is not part of it. You tell me what kind of army pays its amateurs more than professionals.'

A Swedish reserve officer: 'You can write a whole book on what's wrong with the Swedish Army. It is rigid and authoritarian. Men who would be failures in civilian life are on the top. It is only the reserve officer who brings initiative and common sense into a fossil system.'

Three of the nations contributing military units to UNFICYP – Austria, Denmark, Sweden – also contributed civilian policemen to UNCIVPOL. The relationships between the UNCIVPOL policemen with their fellow nationals on the military side of UNFICYP was a curious blend of cordiality and calculation. Natural ties of common nationality in a foreign society were sometimes strained by questions of seniority. On more than one occasion seemingly petty issues of protocol and precedence could lead to uncomfortable social situations.

The special situation of the British with their large military bases on Cyprus made for another kind of resentment. Although relations between British serving in UNFICYP and the British military in the SBA's was not one of conflict, the Britcon soldier was hard pressed not to contrast his position unfavorably with that of British servicemen in the SBA's. The latter enjoyed more lenient pass privileges, more modern living accommodations, and a much greater array of post facilities. Thus the Britcon soldier suffered a sense of relative deprivation not only in comparison to his higher-paid UNFICYP counterparts but as well to his more privileged fellow nationals serving in Cyprus outside the United Nations.

A British sergeant: 'Kitchener lived in this very camp in the 1880's. And it hasn't changed since, except that it's more run down. Yet a few miles down the road are the most comfortable British barracks in the whole road [in the SBA's]. Britcon is neither fish nor fowl. The British government cuts us off because we are part of UNFICYP. The United Nations cuts us off because we are part of the British Army in Cyprus.'

Conflict between military personnel and civilian staff within UNFICYP. Without doubt, the most structured conflict in UNFICYP was not between or within its constituent national forces, nor between different levels in the military hierarchy. Rather, the most evident strain was between UNFICYP military officers and the U.N. civilian staff in Cyprus. In one sense this was a restatement of the prevalent belief on the part of UNFICYP officers that the civilian staff – in Cyprus along with UNO in New York – was letting erroneous political considerations stand in the way of military effectiveness.

A Danish officer: 'In 1967 the Dancon commander went down to an O.P. on the Green Line where a Danish soldier had been disarmed by some Turkish fighters. He went down there with an automatic weapon and waved it at the Turks. He threatened to shoot the whole bunch right there on the spot. It worked. But it got the commander into a lot of trouble with the civilians back at Headquarters. They were out of their minds. But that is the kind of officer I would want to serve under. An officer's first responsibility is to look after the safety of his men. How can you bring peace if your men don't respect you? This is what the civilian mind will never understand.'

An Irish officer: 'A little while back there was a Finn soldier who was shot at from a Greek village. The Finns drove up their armored cars and threatened to shoot the whole village right then and there if there was another shooting. This was the only correct thing to do. Otherwise the Cyps think you're free game. You have to protect your men above all else. But the Fincon commander was in serious trouble after that. The Headquarters civilians really took after him. "No, no, no. You can't touch a hair on a Cypriot." But I'd do the same thing.'

But beyond the almost *pro forma* complaints of the inadequacy of the civilian support given military commanders, there were numerous other tensions between military personnel and civilian staff within UNFICYP. These tensions derived from differences in social background, organizational authority, and socio-political attitudes. Indeed, the differentiation between the two groups made UNFICYP a kind of microcosm of the civil-military conflict long noted in independent state systems. Perhaps most apparent was the pervasive resentment of the UNFICYP officer corps toward the privileges and life styles of the U.N. civilian staff.

A Finnish officer: 'The civilian staff are the aristocrats of Cyprus.
They live like diplomats while soldiers do all the dirty work and live in old buildings and tents. I used to believe in the United Nations and give donations to it.
But not after coming here. They should give money to those soldiers on the Green Line and the O.P.'s who deserve it. Not to the high living U.N. civilians.'

Compounding the military's displeasure with the particular life styles of the civilian staff in Cyprus, there was a generalized resentment of what was thought to be a deepseated civilian arrogance and condescension toward military personnel. On the part of some UNFICYP serving officers, there was even an ultimate questioning of the very morality of the civilian staff in their peacekeeping role.

A Swedish officer: 'Ralph Bunche – we call him "bunk" – detests soldiers.
This is true of almost all U.N. administrative staff including that in Cyprus.
It starts from the very top. We soldiers are a different breed to them.
The big problem in the U.N. is racism. Not the usual kind, but civilian racism against the military. But we soldiers are like women. The U.N. can't live with us, but can't do without us.'

A Canadian officer: 'You must remember that while we change every six months, the civilians stay on and on and on. This gives them a chance to dig in.
They have their lives invested in this operation. If peace comes what would they do? You know the U.N. types, good at languages and not much anything else. Smooth and glib, but with no place to go home to. Men between countries. They live like ambassadors. The easiest way to save money for the U.N. is to take away the limousines and big apartments of the U.N. officials here. What's keeping us here is the civilians wanting to keep this thing going and milk it for all its worth.'

The underlying resentment of many UNFICYP military officers toward the U.N. civilian staff took one notable form in the rather frequent, and always favorable, mentions of Major General Carl von Horn. A Swedish career officer, von Horn had an impressive background in various peacekeeping activities, including command of the U.N. forces in the Congo. Von Horn had subsequently written a book scathingly critical of the U.N. civilian leadership. By a coincidental circumstance von Horn was living in retirement in Cyprus at the time of my field research. Although he was *persona non grata* in U.N. official circles – in and out of Cyprus – there were circumspect, if not subterraneous, informal contacts between von Horn and some UNFICYP military officers. But the comments given below were typical of many UNFICYP officers who had never personally met von Horn.

A Finnish officer: 'Soldiers are always looked upon by the civilian staff as an inevitable evil. The military is something dirty for U.N. officials.
This is what von Horn told so well in his book. If you see him, tell him he has many secret admirers in UNFICYP. He knows how soldiers are made to feel like

258

second-class citizens by U.N. officials. We have three enemies in Cyprus, you know: the Greeks, the Turks, and the U.N. civilians.'

A British officer: 'Von Horn wrote what a lot of us feel. Only we can't so publically. But somebody had to blow the whistle on what these U.N. civilians are doing to the military. Von Horn is a sort of underground hero to a lot of officers who've been in the U.N.'

ORGANIZATIONAL CONFLICT:
U.N. PEACEKEEPING VIS-À-VIS NATIONAL MILITARY FORCES

A more complete assessment of the sources of conflict found in UNFICYP requires that they be evaluated in terms of whether they are unique to United Nations peacekeeping forces (as typified by UNFICYP), or whether they are general to military organizations in the main (as represented by mono-national military establishments). This is done in the comparisons given in Chart 1. The structured strains noted in UNFICYP – both civil military and intra-military – are categorized as to whether they are: (a) applicable to most or all military organizations, (b) characteristic of most or all military organizations, but especially evident in U.N. peacekeeping forces, and (c) characteristically found only in U.N. peacekeeping forces.

One set of conflicts was that seemingly generic to military organization, inclusive of UNFICYP. Thus in civil-military relationships there was the dissatisfaction of UNFICYP military personnel with the amount of funds and kinds of facilities allotted for military purposes by civilian authorities. On this score certainly, neither its multi-national membership nor its peacekeeping mission excluded UNFICYP from one endemic source of complaint on the part of armed forces establishments.

Within the military organization of UNFICYP itself, there were the tensions between staff and line units, between reserve officers and career officers, and between officers and lower ranks. Again these kinds of UNFICYP strains were organizationally akin to virtually all national armies.

On a second level, there were the conflicts characteristic of all or most military organizations, but especially evident in UNFICYP. The political restrictions placed by civilian authorities on field commanders in their use of force have often been a source of contention in civil-military relationships. However, the novel nature of the peacekeeping mission – the very *raison d'être* of UNFICYP – placed especially heavy strains on the traditionally trained United Nations military personnel in Cyprus. Similarly, civil-military relations in national military establishments are often characterized by the military's resentment of the higher living standards of

259

civilian officials. Such resentment is aggravated by the military's perception of civilian arrogance and condescension toward military personnel.
These frequent sore points in standard civil-military relationships were
exasperated in UNFICYP due to the smallness of the force and the resultant
close interaction and observation between its military officers and civilian
staff. Moreover, in most cases, the living and working conditions (but *not*

*Chart 1. Levels of Conflict in military organizations: comparisons of U.N.
peacekeeping with national military forces*

Generality of Conflict	Source of Conflict	
	Civil-Military Relations	Intra-Military Factors
characteristic of most or all military organizations, whether national or U.N. peacekeeping forces	military resentment of lack of funds appropriated for its use	staff vs. line reserve vs. career personnel officers vs. lower ranks
characteristic of most or all military organizations, but more evident in U.N. peacekeeping forces	political restrictions on military's use of force military's perception of life styles of associated civilian officials military's perception of arrogance and condescension of associated civilian officials	division of labor invidious comparisons of military prowess by constituent units
characteristically found only in U.N. peacekeeping forces		power of assignment/ promotion residing in other than operational unit official language other than that of some units pay differences between national units negative stereotypes between national units

pay) of UNFICYP military personnel were of a lower order than was the case in their home countries.

On the same level of conflicts prevalent in most military organizations but more notable in UNFICYP were certain intra-military factors. A prime quality of much of the UNFICYP subculture centered in the invidious comparisons made between the UNFICYP contingents as to their respective military prowess, recruitment policies, and organizational merits. Although these comparisons were in fact based on real differences within UNFICYP, similar parallels can be found within mono-national armed forces; namely, conflict between services and between elite forces and regular units. The division-of-labor squabbles between certain UNFICYP units and the British bases were in one sense unique to the Cyprus operation. But in another manner these were again similar to inter-service jurisdictional rivalries within single national military establishments.

On a third level was the set of conflicts normally absent in national militaries but characteristic of U.N. peacekeeping operations as typified by UNFICYP. None of the observed civil-military conflicts fell into this category. Rather, the strains peculiar to UNFICYP lay in its internal military organization. There was the apparently unavoidable difficulties resulting from the official use of a language which placed about half of the UNFICYP military personnel at varying degrees of disadvantage. That some negative stereotypes of other national units existed – whether preexistent or acquired in Cyprus – seemed likewise unavoidable. More serious, however, than either linguistic hurdles or unfavorable national images were the pay discrepancies between constituent national components. Whether due to initially higher base salaries received from home military establishments or the system of U.N. allowances for Cyprus duty, the resentment of the lower toward the higher remunerated was a pervasive source of tension within UNFICYP.

Another conflict unique to U.N. peacekeeping forces was found in the relationship between UNFICYP and its contributing national military establishments. This was the structured strain resulting from the organizational separation of the power of assignment and promotion from the operational unit in which an officer served (i.e. between the officer's national army and UNFICYP). In other words, unlike service in the standard armed forces where duty and promotion/assignment are under the same chain of command, service in UNFICYP offered no permanent assignment nor any sort of advancement through United Nations channels.

As is probably apparent, the organizational conflicts unique to U.N. peacekeeping forces do not necessarily derive from their peacekeeping mission *per se*. The strains resulting from differences in language, inter-

261

unit national stereotyping, discrepant pay scales, and the intermesh of career paths alternating between international and home military assignments are also those similarly inherent in other multi-national commands. At the same time, the distinctive tensions emanating from the multi-national aspects of UNFICYP overlay other more basic conflicts typically found in mono-national military organizations. Thus, UNFICYP, along with its being the first major 'success' in U.N. peacekeeping operations, displayed organizational qualities with ample precedent in conventional military structures.

We conclude then by reiterating a cardinal point made earlier in this essay. The use of a conflict framework as an interpretive variable does not stigmatize UNFICYP as especially rent by strife. Indeed, the emphasis on conflict given in the description of UNFICYP has purposefully distorted reality by obscuring the countervailing tendencies toward consensus also existing in UNFICYP. But it is to say that like all organizations UNFICYP was no exception in possessing external and internal sources of conflict; and it is in the comprehension of these conflicts that much of the underlying structure of UNFICYP is revealed. Moreover, the conflicts of UNFICYP were in the main common to all military organizations with the added strains peculiar to multi-national forces. Finally, and perhaps most important, if and when the United Nations is employed as a peacekeeping force in other locales and crises, the sources of organizational conflict found in the UNFICYP case will almost certainly be recapitulated.

Appendix 1. ORGANIZATION CHART OF UNFICYP

Key:

MPIO: Mil. Public Info. Officer
COO: Chief Operations Officer
CSO: Chief Signals Officer
CPO: Chief Personnel Officer
CMO: Chief Medical Officer
FE: Force Engineer
CLO: Chief Logistics Officer
EME: Electrical Mech. Engineers
UNCIVPOL: United Nations Civilian Police

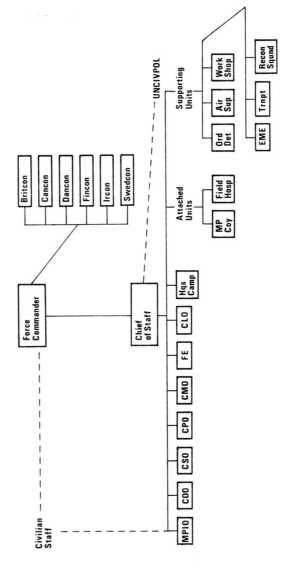

Index

270

Contents Part I
(On Military Intervention)

271

MIDDLE EASTERN AND ASIAN PATTERNS

M. Janowitz/The Comparative Analysis of Middle Eastern
Military Institutions
A. Al-Qazzaz/The Changing Patterns of the Politics of the Iraqi
Army
C. I. Eugene Kim/The Military in the Politics of South Korea:
Creating Political Order
C. H. Lande/The Philippine Military in Government and Politics

LATIN AMERICAN EXPERIENCES

M. Kossok/Changes in the Political and Social Functions of the
Armed Forces in the Developing Countries: The Case of
Latin America
Ph. C. Schmitter/Military Intervention, Political Competitiveness
and Public Policy in Latin America: 1950–1967

JANOWITZ   DOORN eds . On military
ideology.

WITHDRAWN

300096038T